PENGUIN BOOKS

LONDON OVERGROUND

'Sinclair [is a] peerless London literary wanderer and street-level cultural archaeologist . . . delirious, often hilarious urban palimpsest where pin-sharp observation, cultural hauntings and offbeat memoir fuse in sentences that catch your breath like a lurid toxic sunset over Hackney Marshes . . . Sinclair the prophetic scourge of London's hype-addicted developers has always had a gift for celebration. "A book is a city," he proclaims. And a city is a book that, for as long as Sinclair writes, no bulldozer will ever close' *Independent*

'A rapt noirish vision. There is the urban-pastoral, the phantasmagorical and the urbanely satirical . . . *Overground* is bound to have something to delight any bookish Londoner. Long may the man's legs hold out' Steven Poole, *Guardian*

'Sometimes dark, sometimes wry . . . for the aficionado, *London Overground* will deliver all the delights of Sinclair's edgy and hard-edged prose; for those who do not know his work it is an accessible starting point for one of the most rewarding oeuvres in twenty-first-century literature' *Scotsman*

'Utterly sincere [and] highly personal . . . Iain Sinclair has identified the new flavour of the present upheavals . . . his own London memories are woven into a celebration of "an imagined city"' *Times Literary Supplement*

'Sinclair's ongoing mission to breathe proper eccentric human life into [London] is necessary and triumphant . . . ever alert to signs and wonders, there is a lifetime of observation in each purposeful stride' Tim Adams, *Guardian*

ABOUT THE AUTHOR

Iain Sinclair was born in Cardiff in 1943. He is the author of numerous works of fiction, poetry and non-fiction, including *Lud Heat*; *White Chappell, Scarlet Tracings*; *Downriver*; *Radon Daughters*; *Lights Out for the Territory*; *Rodinsky's Room*, with Rachel Lichtenstein; *Landor's Tower*; *London Orbital*; *Dining On Stones*; *Hackney, That Rose-Red Empire*; *Ghost Milk*; *American Smoke*; and *London Overground*. *Downriver* won the James Tait Black Memorial Prize and the Encore Award. Iain Sinclair lives in Hackney, east London.

London Overground

A Day's Walk around the Ginger Line

IAIN SINCLAIR

PENGUIN BOOKS

PENGUIN BOOKS

UK | USA | Canada | Ireland | Australia
India | New Zealand | South Africa

Penguin Books is part of the Penguin Random House group of companies
whose addresses can be found at global.penguinrandomhouse.com.

Penguin
Random House
UK

First published by Hamish Hamilton 2015
Published in Penguin Books 2016
001

Set in 11.28/13.96 pt Dante MT Std
Typeset by Jouve (UK), Milton Keynes
Printed in Great Britain by Clays Ltd, St Ives plc

A CIP catalogue record for this book is available from the British Library

ISBN: 978-0-241-97149-9

www.greenpenguin.co.uk

MIX
Paper from
responsible sources
FSC® C018179

Penguin Random House is committed to a
sustainable future for our business, our readers
and our planet. This book is made from Forest
Stewardship Council® certified paper.

For Paul & Susan. Gareth. Slim.
And Stanley (whoever and wherever he is).
Torchbearers at the dark frontier.

Railways do open up the territory, don't they? They give you space and they give you light and they give you movement.

   – Leon Kossoff

They embody a state
which our still encircled world
looks toward from the past

   – Edward Dorn

Contents

Contents

Goat Mask Replica

A puddle of exposed meat and blooded feathers. A first-light pigeon catastrophe at the crown of a frosted road. The small head was already gone and a pair of glistening crows, as if shaking themselves from an ink bath, disputed strips of pink flesh. This roadkill feast was still warm and gave off wisps of steam, as the large black birds tore and gouged.

The chain of causality ran back to a lonely woman who emerged from the flats, crossed to the park, invisible to post-code gangs who were still in bed, invisible to entitled cyclists and charitable joggers. From a black bag, she shook out a carpet of crusts stiff as linoleum samples. Every morning, at the same hour, the feral pigeon cloud descended like a minor plague.

I noticed, as I made my circuit, that she wasn't there. The crows, mob-handed, strutting and bouncing across the ground with a skunk-smoke swagger, were not bothered. They were glutted on the residue of boozy barbecues, the earth-scorching scars of the party people of new Hackney. The birds gorged, as on a battlefield, on everything – chicken wings, sauce sachets, pizza rinds, saturated card packaging – apart from the bent brown stubs of cigarettes, trodden into the dirt like a midwinter spring. And the grey torpedo tubes of pressurized gas known as 'whippets'. The kind they use to fire up fancy lighters or put fizz into simulated cream. The small cylinders were the only evidence left of cackle and blah: the shrieks of weekend balloon babies, festival chasers. Grey bone fingers of a defeated robot army. And shreds of coloured rubber like the sad aftermath of joke condoms. Metallic traces of the carnival of laughing-gas sniffers defy the early-morning hygiene crews and the recycling police. Nitrous oxide hobbyists party for a twenty-second buzz. A dissociative anaesthetic snort against the nuisance of city life and the dull pull of the old world bringing them down with its responsibilities. Criminal mortgages. And the price of Anya Hindmarch handbags in Chatham Place.

But the balloon babies of London Fields are not to be denied. They are the present occupiers, supporting a trickledown substratum of Turkish minimarts, secular Muslims working impossible hours to supply wine, beer, vodka, firelighters, charcoal, barbecue trays, fresh fruit, table-tennis bats. The woozy cocktails sniffed from an inflated cartoon bubble also contribute, as an incidental by-product, to the paranoid miasma of greenhouse gases. The fear of the thing is as real as the thing itself. Euphoric 'hippy crack' blends with a drench of pesticide perfume from the imported strip of 'wildflower meadow' that has replaced the former red-top football pitch kicked to dust by no-limits communal collisions in the last century: unsponsored Sunday-morning games that ran, more or less, from the 1966 World Cup black-and-white TV triumph to semi-final exit in Italia '90.

Along with distressing the dignity of ancient, gnarled London plane trees by wrapping them in purple skirts that attempt to take credit for (and impose control over) what was now a de facto party zone, the council razzle-dazzled the red dirt with a drop-in, industrial carpet of showy wildflowers, sprayed with the pesticide glyphosate. This was a highly selective wildness, applicable only to approved flora, and merciless to bugs. The kill product is marketed by biotech giant Monsanto. Meadow strips such as this, laid out like those psychedelic bandages across the bleeding edge of the Olympic Park, look great in photographs. But they are meadows only in the sense that a sewage outfall pipe is now a Green Way. The designer Katharine Hamnett, waging T-shirt war (ACT LOCAL THINK GLOBAL), declared that glyphosate usage has proven links to infertility and birth defects. 'In planting a wildflower meadow,' Hamnett said, 'they have planted a deathtrap. Sitting on the grass, eating with your hands near an area that has been sprayed with herbicide is the shortest route to ingesting it, bar drinking it straight from the bottle.' Kim Wright, corporate director of health and community services for Hackney, a woman charged with 'improving the quality of life for all', pronounced: 'This product has been declared safe and environmentally friendly by government and is used by councils everywhere across the country for weed control.'

Official disapproval of unauthorized pigeon caterers, and persons who stock their suddenly desirable, million-pound property wrecks with damaged hawks and buzzards, had consequences. The bag lady vanished. A deprived pigeon ventured on to asphalt to investigate a pizza box dropped from a speeding motorcycle and was splattered. Very soon, a chain reaction created a meat island that threatened to become a continent. One of the crows pecking at the ex-pigeon was tyre-tracked into oblivion. Brothers, hypersensitive to the fresh smell of death, fluttered down to feast. The carnage spread. Birds eating birds, in promiscuous same-species and victim-species abandon, were culled by motorists busy getting a hit of smoke into the lungs, while ranting into agitated fist-phones. A horrible skidpan of mashed avians, pecking, dying, grew from the first discarded tomato crust to a bloody road-hogging stain that promised to become a symbol of something much worse than itself.

It was a morning to move on. To explore territory in which I could cut free from a sense that narrative, like our managed landscape, was a fix. Reading matter, however exotic the source, no longer did it for me. The story was the same everywhere. Thomas Pynchon, riffing on another time and another place, seemed to be describing the trivial annoyances of my immediate locality: 'zapping loudmouths on cellular phones, morally self-elevating bicycle riders, moms wheeling twins old enough to walk lounging in twin strollers'.

This old-man sourness is addictive. Period pains from the inability to accommodate change. When nature pricks and the heart engages, people long to go on pilgrimages. Atavistic instinct draws us to the sacred spike of the Shard and a long, lustful tramp down Old Kent Road in the general direction of Canterbury. I have spent many years postponing that walk as too obvious. Today was the day.

You never cross water without some psychic toll. Careful citizens secrete a coin about their person, to pay the ferryman. Coming down through the permitted gulch of the City, between roadblocks and roadworks, Crossrail dumper trucks and vanity tower quarrying, I overtook several buses decanting irate commuters some way short of their promised destination. Tourists for the dungeons of the black museum were dumped on the wrong side of the Thames. And swept aside by the human surge agitating over London Bridge in a wasp-storm of electronic interference.

The exhilaration for me, above and beyond movement, the glimpse of sedimentary thickness in the river, was the lack of agenda. Nothing to be recorded. Nothing to be written. No maps. No timetable. No rucksack. Nothing ahead, beyond the random impulse of that morning: to start a new season seeking stranger strands, without the Chaucerian requirement to deliver a tale. I thought as ever of John Clare in the madhouse at Lippitts Hill in Epping Forest, and how, after four years of benevolent incarceration, he seized the day, took off, marching vigorously in the wrong direction, before setting his mark on an English road, and hurrying towards the indifferent dead: his inspiration, lost anima, innocence. A journey to shred illusions, burn off the cobwebs of the past. A clean sheet: alienation, severance from family ties, suspension of inherited duty. Writer as writer: a clattering skull on a stick of bone. 'I am here in the land of Sodom where all the peoples brains are turned the wrong way,' he reports in a letter to his wife, Patty. 'I think it is about two years since I was first sent up to this Hell.'

Southwark Cathedral, where pilgrims might have prayed before setting out, if they were not too well lodged in the pub, is dwarfed by overweening structures that don't quite fit together: all sheen, no substance. Giant shadow-makers. Premature ghosts. If architects were involved they had blundered, but nobody could afford to admit it. There was a satisfying level of activity on Borough High Street; people of all shapes, sizes and persuasions, in work, are coffee-transporting, cell-yapping, queuing for buses, queuing for cigarettes, queuing for top-ups. For misleading information, bacon rolls, chewing gum, haircuts.

I noted David Bomberg House. Good to see the undervalued painter's name referenced on a block of residential properties for postgraduate students. Bomberg, in his partial eclipse, taught

5

at Borough Polytechnic Institute. He grew up on the other side of the river, in Spitalfields, and never let himself be inconvenienced by false modesty: 'Giotto stands to Cézanne as Cézanne will stand to posterity; and I who am of the line and inherit the blood stream should not be treated as a stranger in my Father's house.'

After exhibiting with the Vorticists in 1915, while standing apart from their manifestos and stunts, Bomberg's strength came from his isolation, the unbroken conviction that he was a spurned man, an outsider. He engaged with London in war, but the great city, its building sites, railways, warehouses, was not really his subject, in the way that such motifs would obsess his two most distinguished pupils, Frank Auerbach and Leon Kossoff.

Noticing the nameplate, David Bomberg House, was as far as I wanted to take it. That a man who regarded those years of instruction, imposing his strict doctrine on students and amateurs taking evening classes, as a banishment from the light, a necessary drudgery, should now be a permanent aspect of the street: without the residents having any idea who he was or without the students looking closely at any of his works. Bomberg's methods live through Auerbach and Kossoff, the intense scrutiny they bring to place; the practice of drawing, over and over, until the moment arrives for the physical assault, the statement painting.

The proportions of the tight street, with its courtyard pubs, its access to a major rail hub, open out into a road that is also a destination: Great Dover Street. Generous pavements almost as wide as the road itself are planted with London planes that break up pavings, splitting asphalt into interestingly fissured mounds. And then, after negotiating a notorious roundabout, I find myself on a route fitted for all categories of urban pilgrimage, however debased: Old Kent Road. Fragments of Georgian and early-Victorian terrace coexist with opportunist detritus, metal-shuttered premises and secure booths where visibly wired penitents hop from foot to foot trying to remember the five-digit number that will give them a crack at an extension of a payday loan.

THE DUN COW SURGERY IS A REGISTERED YELLOW FEVER CENTRE. I remember talking to an old Haggerston villain banished to this part of town when he came out of prison on licence. The idea being to keep recidivists away from former associates, familiar drinking dens where they would be lured back into crime. A futile proposition: the senior contractor for the disposing of inconvenient East London stiffs operated out of a small boozer on Borough High Street. But that three-mile move was too horrible for my man. He died within six months, his best Friday-night suit still in hock. The shame of it: to be found slumped in a plastic recliner in a pair of elasticated tracksuit bottoms and a Billy Bonds T-shirt.

Lebanese fast-food war-zone escape hatches. Bike-snatched phones unblocked. Money transferred to Nigeria. HUNGRY BEAR HALAL BURGERS. HOTEL ELEPHANT. LA CABANA with its flyers exhorting voters to register for Bolivian elections. Self-medicators in condemned railway terraces without the stamina to crawl out for their yellow-fever injections. Windblown shuttered piazzas marooned from earlier eras. 'Looks better by night,' says a passing disability Hummer, snowploughing me off the pavement.

The valid action is all in the road. A few walkers, of varying ethnicities, went about their business; quietly, discreetly, with none of the powerwalk entitlement of my side of the river. Ankles were safe from bankers on roller blades, balloon-sniffing Twitter analysts on customized skateboards. And Boris Johnson dressed as a fireman.

The sharpest youths of the current generation, those who

respect the past by stealing some of the hippest style fetishes, navigate by way of infinite layers of spoiled pixilation, pink-dyed negatives, seltzer-fizz surfaces strobing and seething. They muddy perception with pictorial degradation, looped sound, weird fragments that reverberate like operating-theatre chit-chat as you go under. Ordinary working streets, if they encounter them, seem perversely undercooked. Techniques of recording have a bias towards banality. The world is all noise and discriminations of headache.

But Old Kent Road was a powerful antidote. Much of the swirling cloud of cannibalized imagery, pictures of pictures that could be sustained only by tapping on a tablet, was left in Shoreditch, buried with the utility cables and the accidentally excavated Mithraic artefacts in the Crossrail quarrying of the City. It fell to modest incomers to rescue the old pilgrim route.

I settled to a quality coffee that really was coffee, by smell, look, taste, in *le panier a brioche*, a lower-case patisserie managed by Mr F. Rafik. It catered to solitary males of a dignified Somali appearance who sat with their phones on saucers, empty cups in hand, waiting for messages that never came. From time to time, a woman in a hijab would step inside, and stand waiting at the counter, studying all the possibilities. On being served, the successful client would leave immediately, nursing her purchases against dark folds of enveloping robes.

I admired the racks of colourful fruit and vegetables on display outside a minimart on the far side of the road. And I wondered about how much lead and heavy metal the skins of those peaches and apricots had absorbed, how much carcinogenic dust from the zone around London Bridge Station, how much road dirt lifted by the remorseless passage of traffic.

Yellow-green ambulances. Fire engines. Unmarked squad cars with sirens screaming. A conviction that road accidents, birth pangs, outpatient axe attacks in betting shops, were being attended to so efficiently warmed the heart. Those exhausted professionals are under constant threat from a system and a philosophy that can no longer afford them.

I had not walked more than twenty minutes towards Canterbury when Old Kent Road began to promote out-of-town ambitions: a giant green free-standing ASDA sign, the triumphalist yellow arch of MCDONALD'S, the pale blue office block of NEW COVENANT CHURCH. A 78 bus shuttled a quorum of the undead towards the cemetery park of NUNHEAD, a destination that once signified a safe distance from the city. The kerbs, I noticed, were thick with red paint, double lines spilling over drains and obstacles like tyre tracks after a gruesome fatality.

At the junction where Rotherhithe New Road swings away towards Deptford and Greenwich Reach, there was a disaster exhibit framed by blue-and-white tape and guarded by two solid community-support officers, while the real cops, windows down, sat in their car checking registration details and scrolling porn sites. The van driver was smoking beside his dented vehicle, explaining himself to a potential witness, while a policewoman took down his details. A lot of blood was trickling into a storm drain, which was embossed with raised letters: NIAGARA 5760 METRO. On the black-grey boards of the barrier separating the road from a small retail park where a low shed hawked BUILDING PLASTICS, TIMBER, INSULATION, ROOFING, I noted the spectral remains of a promotion poster: E SKULL.

Now came the necessary confirmation that I was still on the right road. On the side of a building offering FREE WALK IN CONFIDENTIAL MEDICAL ADVICE: BLOOD SUGAR TEST, URINE TEST, PREGNANCY TEST was a set of ceramic tiles depicting various London journeys, including the Canterbury pilgrimage. I thought of Chaucer's doctor and his Natural Magic, grounded in astronomy, his understanding of the bodily humours. A man 'rather close as to expenses', the quack held gold tight to his heart as a natural stimulant.

AND OFF WE RODE AT SLIGH-
TLY FASTER PACE THAN
WALKING TO ST THOMAS'
WATERING–PLACE; AND
THERE OUR HOST DREW
UP, BEGAN TO EASE HIS
HORSE, AND SAID 'NOW
LISTEN IF YOU PLEASE –

Chaucer is depicted, riding with his fictional pilgrims. Like Alejandro Jodorowsky taking the lead in his own midnight movie, *El Topo*. Religion, the road, stories within stories.

The pilgrims left behind a city dominated by what looks like a premature vision of the Shard, a weathervane cock on its summit. Jack Cade's peasant army from 1450 are marching in rebellion to London on the next panel. Men of Kent driven to protest government corruption and the crippling drain of foreign wars. They are met by armed citizens ready to defend London Bridge. The last panel is a feathery coop of Pearly Kings and Queens, grim-faced under a black sky in which a red airliner is about to collide with a red helicopter, before the debris smashes into a tower block.

After this potted history lesson, the next stretch of the road was notable for George Livesey House, a former library, former museum, now under discussion as a potential venue for yoga classes. The charitable Livesey (1834–1908) was the owner of the South Metropolitan Gas Company and 'one of Southwark's greatest industrialists'. A man in a beard stood at the door, explaining that there was no longer a museum, no funding for

that, no books, but that an empty shell with legacy *was* a
museum of another sort: a museum of memory. Another
house of refuge, its grey windows masked with slatted blinds,
declared itself: HOLY GHOST ZONE.

The man in the goat mask and the girl in gypsy skirts and
flounces were hanging out, waiting for something better,
beside the London Overground station at New Cross Gate. A
whiteface voodoo drummer in top hat swayed from side to
side, accosting random commuters who looked as if they were
hurrying to or from hospital appointments, juvenile courts,
drinking dens. Or slouching, reluctantly, towards an art school.
That is what I assumed: kids from Goldsmiths in fancy dress, as
performance or concept or video demonstration. Another girl,
waving, in full theatrical slap, long funeral coat and not much
else, slalomed through honking traffic. After hugs and kisses
and cigarettes, others joined the group: a short man in a rubber owl mask with sharp beak and huge yellow eyes, and a
scowling girl of Slavic inclination with a prison-cropped head.

I bought the goat a coffee. There was something compulsive
in the radiant bone-whiteness of that mask. Ridged plastic
with rudimentary horns and stiff ears became a mirror, the
death cast of some reforgotten poet. The shape of the mask
contrived an elegantly contoured triangle willing me to contemplate pedestrian adventures far wilder and less predictable
than my suburban trudge towards Canterbury. The albino
goat, coming out of nowhere, saying little, was a whole new
story.

If this boho rabble could be persuaded to walk a little way
down the road to Shooter's Hill, drumming and bird-whistling
and frolicking with Afghan hounds, it would enforce my sense
of pilgrimage. And I would treat them all to pints in a pub I
knew, the Bull Inn, in exchange for their unmediated anecdotes.

They had other affiliations. They belonged to the Ginger Line, as they called the recently completed circuit of the London Overground railway. They met to party, mystery locations revealed at the last moment, by text, somewhere along the line: it might be Peckham Rye, Imperial Wharf, Kensal Rise. Today it was Shoreditch, the white goat said.

I was reminded of the microclimate cooked up by the launching of the M25 orbital motorway in 1986, and how the simultaneous arrival of bathtub-cooked ecstasy and mobile phones turned the tarmac tourniquet into a floating fiesta. Locations for raves, in barns or abandoned airfields, were announced to initiates as the start of an era of instant, compulsive communication. Everything, back then, tended to Essex: the rise of security on the door as figures of cultural significance. Steroid gyms. RIBs skidding across to Holland. Butchery with power tools in new estates perched above chalk quarries. Range Rover assassinations.

The New Cross goats and rubber owls had responded by morphic resonance to their motorway predecessors. They texted and tweeted and ear-wormed their way around the novelty of this railway circuit of London. The Ginger Liners met at previously unknown stations for balloon parties, gossip, the taking of selfies. The traditional antisocial, mute, infolded, hate clusters of the Underground now became a means of Internet partnering. And the investigation of territories where accommodation might not be so ruinously expensive. It was sad to see that much of their conversation was about money, competitive levels of debt.

'My friend, he gets a one-bed flat and develops it into a two-bed. Lives out west, Willesden or wherever? With the Overground, no problem. He can buy in . . . Clapham, Shadwell? You're looking at two hundred for a one-bed. Living space is *tiny*. Like, "legal" means nothing. He rents to the council. Guaranteed return. This guy's clearing seventeen grand a year. Like, guaranteed.'

The gypsy, the drummer, the futurist girl with the shaven head are unimpressed.

'He uses his brother's income. He takes the train. Like, he jumps off anywhere, Forest Hill? Finds another property. I've got two jobs now: property and charity. Charity's just great for contacts. Councils love charity.'

By now the double red stripes at the edge of the road are trumped by the lurid orange coveralls of railway maintenance staff preparing for chemical warfare. The Overground, linking everywhere with everywhere, had spawned dining clubs for young marrieds bored in Denmark Hill. And changed the lives of lecturers living in Walthamstow and teaching in New Cross. There were also, so the rubber owl told me, orgies in Peckham Rye, partner exchanges in Kensal Rise: no guilt, no chance of running into your rug date on the school run. Late trains were reliable and patronized by a democracy of nightworkers.

Once again I aborted my Canterbury walk without reaching Bexleyheath. I followed the Ginger Liners down to the platform and took a train home to Haggerston.

At Rotherhithe, two sets of twins, male and female, faces painted the Lucozade-orange of sunbeds, joined the New Cross coven, whooping, helium-high, and synch-spitting their 'likes' and 'omygods' and sweet little nothings in Mickey Mouse cheeps and trills. A late goth, a phone-slate in each hand, came aboard in Whitechapel. There was an intriguing and affectionate communality at work. It took me a couple of stops to appreciate that none of these people knew each other. They had never met, but the train made them, instantly, brothers and sisters of the night. When they spilled out into Shoreditch, I realized that I had blundered once again into a version of London about which I knew nothing. And which I would have to find some way to investigate. As he passed my window, the goat held up a finger to his lips. A warning I was foolish enough to ignore.

Fish Magic

For several days, I sleepwalked through streets so familiar they felt like sinister fakes, replicas of themselves occupied by new tribes. Tribes who had arrived yesterday and would be gone tomorrow. The canal was still there (even if it was closed for unexplained excavations). Packs of charged banker-cyclists, swerving through sluggish traffic, competing for pavement space, kept pedestrians on their toes. I hugged the Overground railway, head in a bag, listening to the siren song of the metal tracks, and watching for signs.

And then I found the cave.

Hidden under one of the deeply recessed archways, a small miracle of fish. Lustrous. Comic in their doll's-house dignity. Cartoon yellow. Or pink as a razoring of live meat waiting for transplant. A long, chill, smooth-bricked cavern dimly illuminated by golden candle-points beamed upwards to mimic a baronial torture chamber. Autopsy tanks of violet-blue light. Anorexic screens replete with some mysterious liquid, purer and brighter than water, in which tiny but perfectly formed tropical inbreeds flicker like vanishing quotations.

CHARTERHOUSE AQUATICS. You can see right through creatures intended as stress filters, Zen blobs of non-being, barely materialized wafers of cosmic drift matter.

In my 'moment of conscience', as the poet Vernon Watkins called it, my New Year pilgrimage of disaffection, I followed the railway line like the stripped spine of a beached monster I had no hope of recognizing. The weirdness of the fish cave drew me in for a tour of inspection. I smelled possibilities for a future routine, an essay, a surrealist catalogue of the most unlikely enterprises to be found beneath an elevated railway.

I thought of Paul Klee's 1925 painting *Fish Magic*. And of the provocative notion in one of André Breton's automatic texts: *Poisson soluble.* Fish dissolving like complimentary bars of hotel soap. A liquid medium that was part water and part fish, with no sense of one element having precedence over the other. Humanoid doodles, trapped within the rectangle of Klee's composition, can breathe freely, floating among flowers, fish and stars. Between 1924 and 1926, Klee painted the series of piscine works that must have inspired – although they don't know it or acknowledge it – the designers of CHARTERHOUSE AQUATICS. It took a poet-painter of his tough delicacy to foresee how the shape of the canvas or panel anticipated the laptop screen as a cinema-aquarium. That balanced equation of elements. Colours of earth and heaven in which our failure to understand is suspended. The flatness is both the flatness of the world as we once understood it and a tapestry of disconnected symbols. The anthropomorphic figure at the bottom of *Fish Magic* is waving goodbye. His head faces both directions at once, like a person who has just witnessed a fast train, carrying away a relative or lover, leaving the station.

Ducking under the curve of old brick, beneath the neurotic weight of the London Overground railway, with the constant arrival and departure of trains confirmed by the voice of a never-seen oracle, is to risk immediate dissolution inside a whirlpool anomaly within the space–time continuum. Walk that tight chasm, between blocks of new-build flats and the railway, and you risk becoming one of the city's soluble fish. The particle accelerator of our snail-rail version of the Large Hadron Collider spins seated humans (with all their electronic slates and earplugs) both ways around the orbit of London.

Sexualized moans and whistles challenge undercroft tranquillity, the expensive dharma of those designer fish. *Fish ownership as a lifestyle*.

Fish previously encountered in this ward, about to be plunged in a bath of sizzling fat, or hooked gasping from the canal, were slippery and scaly. And thick. The Klee offprints exhibited in the drowned-TV aquaria, on offer for upwards of four figures, have to be viewed side-on, with all their intricate workings on show. They are flat as silk bookmarks. Colourful ghosts of a better way.

The inappropriate screech of trains overhead. Like the secret groans of celebrity predators. And the price-exclusive tranquillity of the fish cave. They slide against one another. Taking this casual Hackney drop-in pedestrian out of his comfort zone. Into the challenge of how to respond to a high-concept space which is not quite an art installation, not quite a start-up Silicon Roundabout operation. Not quite a Chinese supermarket in Silvertown in which you are invited to choose your lunch from a bubbling tank. I think of the way fish have become a code for money. As well as slang for a prostitute, a vagina, a gambling chip, a pound note, the new inmate of a prison. Heron Tower, a recent cloud-scrape development in Broadgate, sells itself in a skirt of soothing fish motifs – without appreciating the special relationship between sharp-beaked herons and their watery breakfast.

Sunday-afternoon attendees at CHARTERHOUSE AQUATICS are subdued, museum-disciplined. Hushed kids straining at the leash. Adults in discriminations of black. Techno-geeks in sloganed T-shirts, tapping at keyboards, tweaking lights, invite you *not* to make an approach. The background thrump and drip of computer muzak is just loud enough to phase out overhead train rattle: serial heartbeats setting a mood, which would otherwise be too melancholy to solicit credit-card action.

Plinths dressed with flat screens. A sympathetic design concept bleeding into mute fish action. Slow-mo promotional trailers for meditation packages that come with the sound switched off. 'Made from acrylic, not glass ... Acrylic has a transparency rate of 93%, making it the clearest material known.' Zero green tint. The whitecoats at the University of Veterinary Medicine in Hamburg ran tests on oxygen concentrations, to prove that you don't need a large surface area of water to produce an optimum oxygenation exchange. In other words, those antique Chinese-restaurant tanks, and the goldfish bowls favoured by expelled council-flat-dwellers relocated to Loughton, are now as redundant as primitive personal computers, the size and weight of the safes of Bethnal Green moneylenders. So redundant, in fact, that they'll soon be back in the retro boutiques of Broadway Market, and the pits of neo-junk dealers returning to the arches under the railway alongside London Fields, in anticipation of dross-sentimentality on the part of incomers with slender bicycles on the narrow balconies of their dropped-in flats. Schoolroom maps with an excess of red. Dysfunctional portable typewriters. Rusty scythes of a discontinued peasantry. All the beachcomber detritus of vanished worlds. Everything CHARTERHOUSE AQUATICS disavows.

The London Overground arches between Haggerston and Shoreditch have been colonized by German and Japanese enterprises primed to exploit the frontier aspect of the undefined post-Olympic legacy moment. Flagrantly localized car-repair businesses have gone. Or transferred to the street as all-weather, roofless improvisations, shuttles around wardens, neighbourhood watchers and civic improvers. The former railway caves were heroically polluted, corpse-clammy, and shuddered with perpetual radio noise to set the nerves on edge. Room would be found for a warm glass cabinet in which sat an impressive woman with scarlet talons and a smoker's cough, leafing through brochures for the next winter cruise to the Caribbean, and relishing a good gossip before handing over the bill (no credit cards, please). The hollow-chested mechanic would present you with some apparently damaged part, in a pool of oil, as evidence of work undertaken. I miss all this theatre, the people. The new economy of the arches is not covert, subterranean. No longer a chain of survivalist troglodytes in dingy pits, but a brick mall, a linked street of *calculated* economic and subcultural decisions.

Shadow the Overground in the direction of the canal, once an attractively illegitimate gulch, a slice of oily-handed marginalists and crumpled drug wraps (outside the range of surveillance cameras), and New Hackney stands revealed. Before the winter sun rises, freshly installed flat-dwellers are hefting weights. Tight young women in black leotards, down on their backs, raising wagon-wheel discs. Number crunchers grunting at resistance machines. The arched tunnel behind a curtain made from overlapping fronds of translucent plastic looks like a high-security-prison gym; masochism and narcissism striving for improved body image and the cult of infinitely sustainable youth.

There is always an artisan bakery 'promoting well-being and recovery from mental ill health' by endorsing traditional methods (of flour-grinding, not health care). Hot-spiced loaves drip a trail of authentic grain from brown paper bags.

Then, beyond CHARTERHOUSE AQUATICS, in symbiotic connection, a stylish Japanese restaurant: TONKOTSU EAST. Slanting roof across yard. Long bar. Raw fish-meats arranged in poetic portions on white plates.

These interconnected enterprises, nudging one into the next, mimic the sleepers of the railway overhead. An endless tunnel – food, fitness, money-art, van hire, storage – looping, cave after cave, around the span of London. Parasitical on blocks of secure flats selling themselves on the spectacle of those twinned pseudo rivers, the Regent's Canal and the elevated railway. Balconies jut over the cobbles to within a few yards of the Haggerston platform. Station announcements, every two minutes, punctuate sleep. Dream destinations: Clapham Junction, New Cross, Crystal Palace, West Croydon, Dalston Junction, Highbury & Islington.

The new line, with its new bridges, artisan bakeries, blue-bike racks and coffee shops, was opened by Boris Johnson, Mayor of London, on 27 April 2010. The first train left Dalston Junction at five minutes after midday. And I was on it. I liked the experience so much, the wide carriages, the views, the orgasmic hiss of the brakes, the absence of pioneer clients, that I stayed with the shuttle: to Surrey Quays on the wrong side of the river. And back.

I might have settled permanently in the time capsule, this cynosure of a transport system that actually worked, if it hadn't been for the din from a couple of profoundly deaf mutes. One of them had cropped silver hair, ear attachments that hummed, and a bellicose thrust of chin. The other, serene to the point of dead stop, was Japanese. They debated, discussed, translated, revised at Morse-code velocity, across the carriage's generous aisle. Threatening silences were broken by strangulated yelps from the white man – who I took, on no hard evidence, for Northside Dublin. Wanting to come closer, to feel the projectile impact of unspoken words, their excitement at something beyond the journey they were presently undertaking, they relocated. Repeatedly. The Irishman thumped down next to me and waved his friend to the vacant slot on the other side, leaving me caught in the middle like a referee with no idea of the rules of the game.

My head was ringing. The more the Japanese man displayed his beatific smile and pre-chemical calm in the face of the onslaught of dumb-show dialectic, the more his study partner insisted. The tensed hush of the other widely dispersed travellers was absolute, clenched: trainspotters, railway buffs entering details in notebooks, a great transport occasion. They remembered all too vividly that this novel fairground railway, Boris-puffed, freighted with boasts and predictions, surfeited on statistics, was a very old railway revamped.

In 1853, in that remote boom-industrial age, the East & West India Docks & Birmingham Junction Railway changed its name to the North London Railway. The original line ventured from Camden Town to Poplar, linking arbitrary destinations in a way that opened new connections, fresh ways of reading the territory. In just the fashion that, in our own day, in my first years in London, the accident of the North London Line sweeping from the brown riverside at North Woolwich, by way of Camden Road (and Compendium Bookshop), to Kew Gardens, set the agenda for so many expeditions and family outings.

In 1865 it was decided, the City and its money machines hungry as ever, and requiring a rapid infusion of clerks and functionaries, to pleach a branch line from Dalston Junction to Broad Street, a satellite of the Liverpool Street terminus. The new station thrived, expanding to nine platforms. Think of this status, in terms of short-haul colonialism, as being equivalent to the grander transactions of that launch pad of Empire, Tilbury Riverside: its cavernous baggage hall designed by Sir Edwin Cooper, its numerous platforms offering rapid transit to the heart of the metropolis. Think of the regiment of hopeful immigrants.

The Dalston Junction to Broad Street espalier, away from the main line, thrived and remained in use – I was happy to take it – until 1986, that fateful year. Margaret Thatcher, who believed that anybody over the age of twenty riding on a bus, or enduring public transport, was a self-confessed loser, pariah, potential socialist, closed the link: with the claim that it was unpopular, no longer paying its way. She tore down Broad Street and got on with the real business of making a chunk of the City into a pastiched New York: ice rink, status art, golf equipment, James Bond car raffles, wine bars that looked like tomato sheds. We lost stations and gained hubs: the slower the service, the more time marooned on concourses, the better the shopping opportunities. So take to your cars: as our modest commute to the City was terminated, the M25 orbital motorway was opened, the ribbon cut on 29 October 1986.

For the next twenty-four years, up to the point where the Olympic imperative demanded a major linking hub (never brought into play) at Dalston Junction, the stretch of elevated railway running down to Shoreditch remained in limbo. The old Dalston Junction Station was reduced to rubble. And, in time, the Victorian theatre alongside it would follow. I thought of a charming remark by Elizabeth, the late Queen Mother, after she had failed some minor academic challenge in the neighbourhood: 'Gott strafe Dalston Junction.' Hackney Council, like the bloody knights sent galloping to Canterbury by Henry II, took her literally.

Almost as soon as access was forbidden, invasion began: schoolkids looking for adventure, muggers and street-feeding Apache opportunists scanning twilight pedestrians from a perch above the Middleton Road bridge, drug providers and their twitchy clients, rough sleepers. And the usual drift of psychogeographers auditioning an evolving wilderness.

And so, yet again, the non-space, the zone that is unmentioned, no part of any official development package, becomes the *only* space, covert, returned to nature, half wilderness, forbidden. It was difficult back then, and near impossible now, to find a secret way, truly green, free of cars, and outside time. Saplings grew into small woods, railside forest screens. Wildlife and lowlife multiplied. Contraband was dumped overnight. You could pick through the trash of a new morning and recover your emptied handbag, books or papers not worth burning.

It would have been a great thing if the elevated track had been allowed to complete a circuit of London, without trains, and with the sort of edgeland fecundity that Richard Mabey celebrates: mind-food for free, a walk in parallel, and above, the traffic of the working city.

After close to a quarter of a century of fruitful neglect, development caught up: Legoland ziggurats, light-stealing towers, investment silos. And the launch of London Overground. The direct connection to Liverpool Street and the City was no longer possible, lost to Broadgate Circus. Now City workers and Hackney folk wanting to make the connection with the Underground service at Liverpool Street were decanted at Shoreditch and invited to make a detour through Spitalfields. Every rail halt, every Tesco Metro, every petrol station, every cash machine had its resident beggar with dog and cup.

If I could no longer walk above the city – I left those adventures to a new breed of infiltrators, risk-takers – I could plod beneath the full circuit of London Overground, with the 'final link' being completed on 9 December 2012. It was easy to imagine this necklace of garages, fish farms, bakeries, convenience cafés, cycle-repair shops, *Minder* lock-ups, stretching right around London. If the M25 was the significant geography for the Thatcher era, a landscape of decommissioned hospitals converted into upmarket compounds with no history, then the new railway, which was not new at all, but a device for boosting property values, looked like the right walk for our present doleful period.

On the day that I took the Overground train back to Haggerston from New Cross Gate, after my aborted Canterbury pilgrimage, I had a glimmering of what my next project should involve. A walk around the circuit of the elevated railway, that accidental re-mapping of London, in a single day. That's what it had to be. If it could be managed. And if Andrew Kötting, the film-maker and performer, could be persuaded to join me. As foil, informant, partner in absurdity. A shamanic bear in unconvincing human disguise recently returned from his mountain hut in the Pyrenees.

Haggerston to Wapping

The diagrammatic outline of the London Overground is a flaccid rugby ball that some large person around Caledonian Road has sat on, very firmly, squeezing a nipple-bud out beyond Willesden Junction. Thirty-three stations and thirty-five miles to tramp. With inevitable and unforeseen detours and false steps. Would we make it in a single day, if I failed to get Kötting on the hoof before ten o'clock? He was camped in the suburban obscurity of Forest Hill and would be cruising across town on his large motorbike. If he wasn't sleeping in a ditch, a forest, on a beach, he didn't spring from his chrysalis pouch at first light. On the *Swandown* film, when we pedalled a plastic swan from Hastings to Hackney, I fretted, watching drifts of autumnal mist burn off across river meadows, that lovely alchemical redness dissipating, while the boys in the camper van argued over burnt bacon and rancid socks.

Andrew has been staying with his favoured photographer, Nick Gordon Smith, the man who shot *Swandown* and the delirious and eccentric round-Britain adventure of *Gallivant*. *Gallivant* was my initial experience of Kötting and I was captured from the bizarre opening sequence, which was clearly designed to boot audience expectations out of the window. A bearded black weatherman in a stiff suit signs and deaf-mutters against contradictory subtitles, sending up all sorts of politically correct conventions, while at the same time summarizing the theme, the plot and the subversive poetry of the voyage we are about to undertake, in the company of a feisty grandmother and an astonishingly present child: Eden. Andrew's daughter rises above her Joubert's syndrome disadvantages with miraculous bird-throated whistlings. Even as a babe Eden had been wired so that brain anomalies could be mapped, malfunctions scanned and plotted. Now she embarked, coming and going from the *Gallivant* shoot around the ragged fringes of our island, on her accidental odyssey.

Most of Kötting's work exploited this model: identify the journey, press-gang the necessary characters, *get them moving* (dragging swan lures or inflatable fathers). Arrange collisions, raid archives and reverse engineer meaning. These were great films to experience, at least once, with your eyes closed. Soundscapes were layered and crafted against the jumps and gestures and neurotic kineticism of the visuals. With the director swinging in and out of frame, plunging from rocks into a wild sea, licking the lens.

They say of Samuel Beckett, one of Kötting's touchstones, that he was loveable: despite the terrifying silences, the burning eyes, the drink. Trembling actors were brought to breakdown by failure to satisfy Sam's demands, his refusal to answer questions of interpretation. Sam the inimitable. He would drift away on one of his walks, exiting Sloane Square in the general direction of World's End. Where he recalled the worst of London days: poverty, skull-splitting pressure, an ugly and indifferent city. Kötting's troop felt much the same: bring it on, captain. All the mud, the madness. 'Beckett wasn't a saint at all,' said the theatre designer Jocelyn Herbert. 'And thank God he wasn't.'

A day tracking a railway through London barely merited an entry in the Kötting catalogue of absurdity, but Andrew appreciated my notion of spillage; how one project leaks incontinently – and immediately – into the next. I have a prophetic disc known as 'Lull's Device'. Three wheels held in place by a central pin. 'Traditionally used to stimulate discussions among circles of friends gathered together for spiritual and self-improvement. It is not a toy. It should not be done more than once a day.' I agitated the discs to cast our railway walk: IGNORANCE, LAUGHTER, REMORSE. That sounded about right.

In our part of London, when floor-camping with another of his faithful and tested collaborators, the Russian-bearded audio designer Philippe Ciompi, Andrew liked to swim punishing lengths of London Fields Lido, pushing against the morning cabal of skullcapped and begoggled water cyclists. Ploughing chlorine furrows, before the day's duties, was a welcome penance, a contemporary substitute for beating the bounds and other border-affirming rituals of place. Dawn athletes do it in controlled spaces for which you must pay an entrance fee – and accept, as collateral damage, the patronage of councils and health professionals who boast of their benevolence (quietly forgetting the padlocked shells of former pools, the ghost cathedrals of inconvenient survivors). Andrew told me that by choice at this season of the year he would take himself off to his shed, his recovered shelter in the Pyrenees. And he would go alone, with a sleeping bag, deep into the forest. Where he would howl. *Howl.* In mortal anguish. Howl like a wolf. Howl for the world. For his awareness of the melting human candle. In the dead hours of the night. Under brilliant and heartless stars. *Howl for it.* Eternity. The Abyss. 'But I'm always in tune,' he said. 'And the wolves reply.'

Andrew's entrance that February morning, bursting on set, crashing through the door, motorcycle helmet under arm, canvas straps across broad chest like Jack Palance as a Mexican bandit, was marred by picking the wrong house. The man has difficulties with numbers. Our neighbours, terrified, denied all knowledge of my existence, and backed away behind the sofa. Boots on, fretting to go, I heard the disturbance and went outside, to find myself clamped in a bear hug of scratchy overnight beard and steaming cloth. The marathon-swimming film-maker had his suits built, not tailored, by his gifted wife, lover, collaborator, the long-suffering Leila. The orbital outfit was project-appropriate for an H. G. Wells time-travelling romp, an Everest assault from the good old days. The jacket was sculpted from thick asbestos cloth, bullet-buttoned. Tubular trousers were thornproofed for barging through hedges. After a day's sweaty tramp the suit would be freestanding, an auxiliary tent. The look was rounded off with dark glasses and the sort of red cravat favoured by Oxbridge ramblers and the heartier breed of *plein air* sketcher. Decorative paisley cuffs were folded around the sleeves to make a single all-embracing garment. When the cloth stiffened as it dried, Andrew's arms would set like plaster of Paris. I'd have to cut up his meat and feed him when we stopped for breakfast.

It was late, but we were camera-loaded and ready for that big beast, the city. The living metropolitan organism panted as we patted the flank of a stone serpent in a strip of permitted park, and paused for a moment to experience the new Haggerston Station, which modelled itself, with a modicum of tact, on the retrospectively acknowledged achievement of blocky modernism in such Underground halts as Park Royal. The square chimney elevation of Haggerston in an understated taupe-grey nudged us, quite gently, in the direction of Felix Lander's 1936 Park Royal ventilation tower. With the implication that our swallowed Hackney village was now a born-again suburb, twinned with Acton (but lacking the brewery, allotments, prison). The London Transport designer Frank Pick, on the presentation of the Gold Medal of the Royal Institute of British Architects in 1936, described the new stations as 'punctuating the suburbs'. Pick, it is said, haunted London by day and night. An obsessive. Another of those figures seduced by the mysteries lying behind almost-familiar places. David Lawrence in *Bright Underground Spaces*, his 2008 book on the station architecture of Charles Holden, wrote about how Pick 'immersed himself in local peculiarities'.

Local peculiarities in Haggerston have been taken care of by the commission of a tile mural, flanked by lifts, in the open concourse of the station. This conceit by Tod Hanson is called 'The Elliptical Switchback', and is a downloaded homage to the astronomer Edmond Halley, a Haggerston boy. And also, in its schematic obligation to soft modernism, a nod to 1951's Festival of Britain. Halley's comet loops around a futurist lodestone against a multi-spotted, Hirst-poxed backdrop. Halley's distant traces, like his Haggerston manor house, have been reduced to dust. His comet, visiting us with the frequency of ministers capable of carrying forward reform without basking in a rictus of self-congratulation, has given its name to a local nursery school. Hanson's elliptical hula hoop, looking like radio waves circling the transmitter in that old BBC ident, are here translated into bands of other-worldly light making haloes around the pencil of the mosque at the end of Whiston Road.

'Tod Hanson is interested in a world over-amplified and speeding up,' his website asserts. 'The telescoping of industrialised environment, the consumer spectacle, celebration, delirium, waste and war through time.'

The far wall, beyond the mural, is loud with consumer spectacle, popular books and theatre events attractive to the passing throng: a blitz of posters above a rack of bikes.

The floor has a magic carpet advertising the City Mills development that has replaced the long-established neighbourhood estate. BRAND NEW 1, 2, 3 BEDROOM HOMES. REGISTER YOUR INTEREST FOR THE NEXT RELEASE. Colourful panels flag up a promised street-market-browsing, art-snacking lifestyle that comes with the purchase. This station, the promotional floor implies, is nothing but an atrium to the better life at City Mills. Which is not in the City and was never a mill.

We begin among winter ruins. The sentence of death on a community provokes a final spasm of image-making: banners, meetings, questions that are not questions but broken statements of grievance. The fates are unkind. Who can be blamed? Kötting, in a publication produced to accompany a show of his daughter's paintings, said: 'After quarter of an hour, no one can observe another's despair without impatience. So we invent things to do and move on.' How often do we find ourselves at the back of a public meeting, drumming our heels and barely listening to torrents of statistics, specifics of corruption and neglect, illegal or immoral imprisonment, laws subverted, families unhoused. We yawn. 'Darkness of old times around them,' Blake wrote in *The French Revolution*, 'utters loud despair.'

The wall art on the condemned Haggerston estate, condemned for being too close to the canal, too convenient for the railway, is outside because there is no inside left. A silent oasis with a few stubborn souls holding out. Crystal icicles barring empty window frames. A handwritten boast in black crayon on whitewashed bricks in the empty shell of an abandoned flat: CCTV IN OPERATION 24 HR.

The drawings are of red-eyed vampires grinning and swaying in a death dance, figures in a subversive tapestry of eviction: sunflowers, chickens, three-clawed shark-head deformities. Drunk on apocalypse. Paper tatters peeling and windblown are stripped away, exulting in impermanence. Unsponsored, unapproved, unapologetic. If the lives of the flat-dwellers had been undisturbed, I wouldn't be here. I'd be walking briskly south, heading towards Shoreditch, too much the aesthete of blight.

Striding alongside Kötting, and aware that the clock was

ticking, we invaded one of the abandoned buildings, simply because we could, because there was no one to stop us. The last holdouts were barricaded in crannies and alcoves, behind chipboard, without a chink of light. The developers cut water and electricity as a first move.

On the first floor, with access to a balcony bricked off by a temporary wall, we find a space occupied by squatters: empty bottles of E&J Brandy beside plastic flagons of Olympic-branded Coca-Cola: the twilight cocktail of choice. Window panels have been washed over in aquamarine and muddy ochre and brought to a painterly finish. A couple of young builders engage with Kötting in harmless banter and then we move on.

The road to Hoxton, our second station, is a confusion of recycled container stacks, new-build flats, and converted warehouses with spectral trade signs for veneering operations long since vanished. Rail zone is still settling into its identity as a generator for investment, a Viagra overload for property prices. The high railway under its pergola of wires. The compulsory blue-bicycle rack. Rescued cobbles. The heady waft of proper coffee. If you move a little to the west, the traffic stutter of Kingsland Road, that old London narrative, is still present, but revised by the remorseless *swoosh* of elevated torpedo trains. On many of the tributary roads, white bicycles have been hooked to railings: a procession of memorials to the madness of colliding forms of transport. An outfit repairing computers has rebranded itself to pick up on the buzz of the emerging railway corridor: APPLE REPAIR STATION. The sign mimics the red circle and blue band of London Overground.

The railway feels like a set of ladders laid on water, as our ancestors once arranged precarious walkways across the fens. Hangars of naked brick, low lit and plain-tabled: so many canteens for City foot soldiers.

We stop to examine a flat-topped plinth decorated with a grey laurel wreath, a vegetable version of the Overground logo in relief. Railways and cycles of disaster: derailments, fires, failed signals, exhausted or fugue-susceptible drivers. IN MEMORY OF NORTH LONDON RAILWAYMEN WHO FELL IN THE GREAT WAR, 1914–1919. Does this mean that the war went on a year more for railwaymen? Or did they die when it was over, being returned to a different uniform, a different set of trenches and earthworks? Revised and improved stations like King's Cross are embarrassed about their duty to remember, the truly terminal aspect of a transport hub; they downgrade or hide away the lists of the war dead.

Art is more knowing in the Hoxton/Shoreditch quadrant. An audience is required. The presence of the railway stimulates the compulsion to leave your mark, to address passive travellers – who will, most of them, be heads down, swimming in the shallow digital puddle. In earlier, braver times, the hit was to deface the actual trains, aping New York City, junk for art's sake; the visceral thrill of beating the goons, night-raiding, signing your guilt in eyeball-affronting capital letters. Now railside infiltrators are out of it, high, drunk, fleeing the police in incidents like the death of promising young cricketer Tom Maynard; on the tracks near Wimbledon Park Station, electrocuted, hit by a train. Or some unfortunate caught under helicopter beams and running towards disaster. Or white-van pirates stripping overhead wires and electrical cables for their scrap value. And bringing about more rail delays and suspensions.

A standard post-Banksy piece has taken up residence near Hoxton Station – which is not really Hoxton at all. True Hoxton is a street market, illegitimate, pisshead, traditional (but under revision, café-bar for grease caff). True Hoxton is the birthplace of the Kray twins (with all the slipstreaming myths of bare-knuckle hardmen, spivs, deserters). It belongs on the west side of Kingsland Road, cluster-flats in which to vanish among legends of world-class shoplifters like Shirley Pitts, and old-school villains emerging from wartime rubble to an afterlife of ghosted memoirs, the rosy glow of self-aggrandizing fictions dictated to bored scribes. But Overground stations make as free with geography as the namers of new educational establishments. Want Brighton University? Try Hastings. And don't expect to find a cruise liner moored at Surrey Quays.

But we can console ourselves that politicians are beginning to take an interest in this blighted zone. Richard Benyon, reputed to be 'Britain's richest MP', acquired a stake in the consortium buying the New Era housing estate in Hoxton. He delivered the warning that tenants can now expect to join the Big Society by paying a proper 'market rent'. A hike of three times the present amount. Mr Benyon, whose constituency is Newbury in Berkshire, served as Environment Minister in the Coalition until October 2013. When public outrage became loud and visible to the media, attracting Russell Brand and others to the Hoxton barricades, the Benyon family company decided to sell its stake. Mr Benyon's own modest estate includes a stately home surrounded by 3,500 acres of woodland.

Ironies multiply to the point where they cancel each other out in a drizzle of white noise. Competitive Hoxton graffiti is the acceptable face of vandalism. Where a tolerated station beggar should sit against the wall, we find the stencilled cartoon version: wool cap, accusing eyes, slumped, supporting a handmade placard. NEED MONEY FOR BEER & WEED.

The sad coin collector on the street outside the pub on Columbia Road, the one I noticed on another Christmas walk, when unsold trees were being grabbed by customers who kept their nerve to the very last moment, was too smashed to rescue his tipped beaker. Pound coins had run away. The sentiment of this tableau, and the knowledge that the pub was a recruiting place for vagrant children, like Sarah Wise's *The Italian Boy*, who would be drugged with a mix of porter and laudanum, before being stripped and drowned in a well, had me digging into my pockets. It doesn't make much sense to support those who are already gone, while stepping around the professionals on their railway pitches. But I couldn't bring myself to pension the Bishopsgate pavement artist, with the healthy dog on his lap, when I heard him rattling away on his mobile phone, fixing an evening meet in a Shoreditch bar.

On the brick stack to which an iron gate has been hooked to protect the entrance to a set of Shoreditch railway arches, there is a spray piece, communally achieved, one artist working over the residue of the last. A stripped black boxer, harsh light polishing his raised gloves, anchors the composition. He is superimposed on the present queen.

At the point where the Overground sweeps west like a suddenly broad river over Kingsland Road, there is a special island, a triangle formed by Shoreditch High Street, Great Eastern Street, Old Street. A hidden zone-within-a-zone. A Gulliver landfall waiting for its Swift. The railway makes this corral into a spectacle of permitted gazing: decommissioned Underground carriages on flat roofs, self-consciously cinematic figures moving behind the frames of naked windows, monster murals of fabulous beasts, secret yards with romantic smokers at wet tables. Spectators on the Overground have only a few moments, before the train recrosses the road for the Shoreditch station. With that soothing recorded voice prompting you to rise from your seat, ready for the flickering red button that must be pressed for release into the world of pedestrians. By way of concourse-haunting charity muggers, flower sellers, generic coffee empowerment. And hawkers of black-wrapped cosmetic packs with smiles they can't switch off.

Sometimes, as with so many elements of this precious rail service, the recorded voice goes out of synch. So that, sliding in above the pop-up shops of Shoreditch, we will be warned to prepare ourselves for Whitechapel. Then, vanishing into a tunnel, the Whitechapel approach is flagged as Shadwell. The tentative reality of London dissolves; without official confirmation, anywhere is everywhere. There are no uniformed humans onboard, no reassuring presences on the platform. TfL employees cluster at the automatic ticket barriers, ready to challenge defaulters or to open gates for bona fide travellers refused by the filtering machinery of the ticket-swallowing exit.

The covert Shoreditch zone, when we followed it on the day of the Kötting walk, felt quite distinct and divorced from everything else on that run between Haggerston and the plunge beneath the Thames at Wapping. On Rivington Street, in 1968, the anti-psychiatrists around R. D. Laing and David Cooper, along with the usual suspects of that time, established their anti-university, a cultural black hole far more powerful than it appeared to be at the time, drawing so many strands into this railway-shadowed margin of the City. Without acknowledging the relationship, they honoured the first Elizabethan theatres, the Hoxton asylums, a shifting borderland. The premises at 49 Rivington Street were being occupied at the very moment I arrived in Hackney.

It was an endgame as much as a beginning, a consequence of the gathering at the Roundhouse in Camden in 1967, the Congress on the Dialectics of Liberation (for the Demystification of Violence). Potential students paid £8 to sign up, with a further ten shillings (50p) for individual courses. No diplomas or degrees were on offer. There might or might not be talks by Yoko Ono, Alex Trocchi, C. L. R. James, Robin Blackburn,

Jeff Nuttall, Bob Cobbing. John Latham, sculptor-philosopher, book-burning heretic, was a numinous presence. David Cooper spoke about radically changing the 'rules of the game', breaking the nuclear family out of its cage. The nominated building was bleak, unwanted. The aura was soot-stained, nicotine-choked, passive aggressive. Guardedly articulate Vietnam War refuseniks delivered most of the TV interviews. They met documentary interrogators with a modulated drone of theoretical resistance. Tieless in uniform black shirts and drab corduroy.

Black Mountain College, London Free School, Kingsley Hall, Situationism, Black Power, Sigma, *International Times*, Arts Lab, psychogeography: all the current arrows of influence thudded into this peeling Shoreditch door. They predicted the coming shift, a mass migration to the east. The anti-university, flaring for a season and fading from sight, was the first intimation of that exodus from Notting Hill. Even before histories of the period were adequately researched and composed, ephemeral documents from this countercultural flare would be offered for sale in the galleries and retro boutiques of Hoxton.

The Shoreditch look on the day of the Kötting walk was original Rivington Street grunge given the kiss of life by smart, genre-promiscuous entrepreneurs: odd chairs and random tables, heaps of books as set-dressing. Skinny trousers. No socks. Bright shoes. Pavement roll-ups. English as a second language. Stapled magazines as style, not content. Unthreatening urban vamps, booted and leather-jacketed, and bloodless youths with fringe-beard manifestos, skittering between endlessly revised appointments, yelping into invisible phones, swept effortlessly past us, as we puffed and panted up the tragic dunes of age and alienation.

The transformation of the Shoreditch/Hoxton reservation had been gradual, barely perceptible; it took time for developers to work their way north from the old Truman's Brewery on Brick Lane to Bethnal Green Road. The railway was part of it, the functional elegance of Victorian arches and catacomb tunnels became a symbol of vulnerability; a battleground between antiquarians, lovers of the fabric of place, and thrusting futurists. The argument resolved in an interim colony of inessential shops and five-a-side football pitches for group bonding by City traders.

Unrequired corners of once-active meat or vegetable markets are ceded to small-timers for a show of handbags, costume jewellery, vinyl LPs, heritage postcards, grainy bread and brownie briquettes. Neighbourhood bars are constructed around vintage photographs of bohemianism. Georgian properties are restored by name artists to a pitch of authenticity that was never part of the original settlement. Conceptual wealth is made visible, investment silos for the privileged gulag of the City: jagged skyline like a fever graph made manifest in glass and proud steel. Dirty money was never so bright, so blatant. So protected by the politics of know-nothing quiescence. Disgraced bankers are shamed with bonuses, then redeployed like sacked football managers. The bigger the scandal the heftier the premium. Being sentenced by a court – rarely, rarely – is a miraculous cure for cancer, senility, Alzheimer's, dead hearts.

Shoreditch/Hoxton, by the mid-1990s, was black-windowed, clubland ecstatic, sweat-burrowed with gay saunas, leather bars. The railway arches were adaptable, many exploited their current emptiness and offered secure parking for nightbirds. Right alongside the brick gatepost with the glistening portrait of the stripped and rippling black boxer was a cave. The kind of retreat, or private space, at an oblique angle to the traffic of mundane London, in which the footballer Justin Fashanu hanged himself in May 1998. His life was complicated and increasingly messy, his moment in the sun was over. He had been cruising in the male-on-male Hoxton bars. He faced an alleged sexual-assault charge in Maryland. A warrant had been issued for his arrest. Brian Clough, his former manager at Nottingham Forest, shipped him out when Fashanu declared himself to be homosexual. There were fabricated tabloid affairs with Tory MPs. His brother, John, the Wimbledon bruiser, had broken off communication. The body was discovered on a dim Saturday afternoon, between markets, between parties.

They have a swimming pool on the roof of Shoreditch House, the private members' club now occupying a couple of floors of what was once a tea warehouse. Part of the remit, in terms of sophisticated entertainment, is to promote events that touch on local history and heritage.

I gave a talk in a bamboo bar where the gins kept coming on silver trays and the Ditchers were alert and responsive to alternative myths of place. One heavy presence, tieless in a loose designer suit that gave off sparks as he moved, blocked a doorway, swilling pints of fruit-topped cocktail and grousing. When the time for questions arrived, he grabbed the microphone and fisted it towards his broken cosmetic snarl like a liquorice toothpick. History, he said, was pigs' bollocks dipped in sherbet. But if you want to listen to . . . Arthur Morrison, *A Child of the Jago*, *Tales of Mean Streets*, Arnold Circus, Charles Dickens, furniture sweatshops, bagels and . . . blah-blah-blah: OK, fine. Each to his own. But these are *not*, my friend, the realities of the moment. You know *fuck all* about that. About the rewrite of territory, the rescue of the old shitheaps, for which he was responsible: a player, an investor. He put his money where his mouth was. And his tongue was blistered with diamonds.

At first, the bright young women running the gig didn't know how to play him. He swayed and staggered in a spray of expensive eau de toilette and class contempt. When the liberal mutters started, he cranked up the volume, the obscenities, and looked for someone to hit. They manoeuvred him out. He got his hands around the organizer's throat. The consensus was: kick him senseless and drop him in the pool.

From the rooftop oasis, new Shoreditch was a jackpot of honeyed light: roof parties, showroom windows behind which products were being launched, deals celebrated, fortunate lives lived. Railway margins. Discontinued lines. More walls to deface. The modest dead, keeping their own counsel, crouched in pissy doorways, out of reach. The violence we used to encounter, of rubbled wastelots, subsistence prostitution, faded away, subsumed in more complex interactions behind concierged desks.

When V. S. Pritchett introduced a new edition of Arthur Morrison's *The Hole in the Wall* in 1956, he identified the riddle exercising the drunk Shoreditch House property developer. Morrison's tale of Ratcliffe Highway and the riverside reaches grew from the ground we were now headed towards on our walk. Do the wounds of the past heal? How deeply are we implicated in historic crimes? 'There was a London like this,' Pritchett wrote, 'seedy. Clumsy and hungry, murderous and sentimental. Those shrieks were heard. There were those even more disturbing silences in the night. Docklands, where the police used to go in threes, has its authentic commemoration.' A book is a city. Pritchett echoing Morrison echoes Thomas De Quincey. A never-ending chain that pragmatists, schemers, improvers, grabbers will always try to snap.

I'm told they call this section of the line the 'Hipster Roller-coaster'. Shoreditch High Street Station is a retail concession buried under a wobble of temporary boutiques. This was once a smart notion, the metroflash equivalent of filling the gaps in dying high streets (made redundant by out-of-town supermalls) with charity shops. Until it became a charity to step through the door: that smell of posthumous bed linen, the lab-rat plastic of empty DVD cases, lumpy, book-sized VHS tapes waiting to come back into fashion (it's happening). Pop-up shops are no longer Tracey Emin and Sarah Lucas flashing attitude in 1993. Tracey has moved on to Emin International, an outlet managed by her aunt, and trading in exclusive artist-branded product.

The current Shoreditch stack, a profoundly dispiriting gantry calling itself, with no sense of absurdity, a 'Pop-Up Mall', features outlets for Calvin Klein, Farah (Vintage), NikeiD, Puma, Levi's: columns of names like the backdrop for an aftermatch interview with Wayne Rooney. You have to push through a thick fly-curtain made from strips of yellow plastic, offering the potential for interestingly distorted colour photographs. Kötting as a blood-red psychopath. He stares across the road at the excesses of Shoreditch House. At the relief model of a white swan, S-necked on a high panel, a memorial slab for a brewery and for so many demolished public houses.

Descending to the station entrance, we are blown against a mesh fence jangling with padlocks, a brazen orchard customized with loving messages. MY HENRY. The fence establishes the point at which the railway zone refuses access to inappropriate pedestrians. It is under option, awaiting the next tranche of finance. Blank grey walls lift from a tolerated field of cinders.

Wall art intensifies, punkish, playful, or hoping to be invited inside. Queen Elizabeth II, with her postage-stamp face, is ripped to naked brick. Flowered Mexican skulls. A plaster cast with a gaping bandaged mouth: the death mask of William Blake. NEVER FORGET. And then, on one empty lot, a troop of hushed, camera-lofting urbanists, fake-fur'd, leopard-printed, stalled beneath an endwall, messianic portrait of Usain Bolt. They are being lectured, authoritatively, by a spray-paint scholar. Bolt is realistically rendered, speared by a psychedelic shower of heavenly beams: as if a high sun were blazing through a stained-glass window on a new prophet. The lecturer's critique compared and contrasted lesser pieces, gryphons and scaly apocalyptic beasts, with the religiose virtuosity of the Olympic demigod. Mere tags were not tolerated. Amateur daubs were scorned or patronized. The tour moved on through the constantly replenished open-air gallery of Shoreditch and Brick Lane. Every demolition was a fresh opportunity. Every enclosure. Every corrugated-iron fence. The orbital railway, without fuss or expenditure, had become the patron of London's most active display of walls, recorded and evaluated, but as yet beyond the reach of the next Saatchi. Although Saatchi, his hands around the throat of Nigella Lawson, does feature on this great shifting Doom mural. Pixels of newsprint converted into something like a smudged frame from Derek Jarman's *Caravaggio*.

My spirits revive at Hare Marsh, on the railway crossing opposite the old villains' pub, the Carpenters Arms. This high-sided bridge has been a territorial marker for so many years. Emanuel Litvinoff in his memoir, *Journey through a Small Planet*, describes the bridge as a rite of passage, out of adolescence towards self-knowledge, another country. The author photograph on the back of the dustwrapper has the dapper Litvinoff posing, in two-button check suit, cravat, with hooded eyes, narrow sideburns, on the Cheshire Street steps of the bridge, heading south towards Whitechapel.

The spread of the railway – all those tracks out of Liverpool Street, before they divide – is exhilarating. Anti-vandal devices, a rim of spinning fish hooks, confirm the impression of a border post, one of the more obscure entries to East Berlin. Litvinoff often spoke about how his family, his neighbours in the Fuller Street tenement, held to the sense of existing in a village, with Bethnal Green Road and Whitechapel Road as neighbouring townships, and the West End, Soho, Bloomsbury, more alien and remote than Warsaw, Kishinev, Kiev, Kharkov, Odessa.

Fording the great riverine span of the tracks, down that narrow metal passage with the cacophony of sprayed tags and obscenities, was to experience one of London's great viewing points. Nobody has made a monumental painting of the type Leon Kossoff delivered from his railway bridge at Willesden Junction. The tidal rush of curving tracks and the stumpy towers of the City against a darkening sky. The spinning hooks of the anti-vandal barrier were a tracery of thorns frozen into steel. Most of the new bridges on the Overground circuit are constructed to abort vision, deny ocular trespass. You'd need to be Usain Bolt or a seven-foot basketball player to get a glimpse of the restored line running from Dalston Junction to Haggerston. Where there is the ghost of a chance of craning on tiptoe to catch a glimpse of a train, they'll add another course of bricks, dress the wall with a pelmet of blue board. Railways have to be heard, felt in the disturbed air.

Which is why Kossoff's paintings are so heart-rending: ordinary life transformed into a reality as absolute as Turner. The domestic narratives delineated by Litvinoff, and by the novelist Alexander Baron in *King Dido*, the sexual initiations, ritualistic fist fights, petty crimes, market trades, cruel poverty, are swallowed in the rectangular frame of a high-angle vision of the great west-flowing railway.

*

Our zigzagging descent takes us into liminal land, disputed, ruined, recovering: with the virtue of escaping surveillance, slipping away from official heritage promotion. *It isn't happening yet.* Railway arches are breeze-blocked, developers have mesh-fenced unredeemed earth mounds: with warnings from 'professionals in security' about 'advanced forensic marketing'. Strict corners of nowhere are schizophrenically divided between the next urban improvement and tired green space with horses and play-farm trappings.

The guerrilla artist specializing in snake-necked, sharp-beaked, black-and-white emus has worked some *trompe l'oeil* trickery to present his hairy creature as emerging from a hole in the railway embankment, above a stack of black rubber tyres. We are at the point where our track goes underground. To stay with the orbital circuit we'll have to dowse. I know that Whitechapel is the next station. And I can see the silhouette of the enlarged Royal London Hospital. What happens after we are excluded from the sight and sound of the railway is guesswork. We won't experience, as I did on my attempt to walk around the M25, acoustic footprints, the hum of the road carrying back over winter fields.

A WIZARD SHOULD KNOW BETTER. Here was a graffito worth recording. Kötting is fired by what he sees as the Tarkovsky aspect of this stretch: *Stalker.* He has to have a number of projects cooking at any one time to keep the black dog at bay. It helps if the new venture is more difficult, more absurd and improbable than the last. If he has swum with his brothers across the English Channel, he'll go it alone from Hastings to Land's End. The darkness inside is a form of tremendous energy; stray humans encountered on our walk are buffeted, pitched against fences, left breathless in his wake. The scheme he's chewing at is set underground, the deserted caverns and brick arches of the railway inspire him to sketch a little of what

43

he wants to attempt. A procession of mummers, Jack in the Green folklorists, morris dancers, straw bears, bikers, pirates, holy fools, will climb through a French forest to a cave. In heretic country. Near Mont-Ségur. Tortured history. Kötting will enter the cave and, if possible, remain there for forty days and forty nights (according to biblical precedent). Beyond this, a measure of Tarkovsky crawling and dragging through flooded cellars, carcinogenic wasteland, is advocated. I therefore position the film-maker against the grey fence. Another parallel-world tag: THE CAVE MAN. Our shattered narrative beginning to fit like a fun-house mirror: his *Underland* and my *Overground*. The elevated railway circuit is also a tunnel.

I told Andrew about the poet Douglas Oliver's book: *In the Cave of Suicession*. Like Kötting, Doug was using darkness to exorcize darkness. He climbs into the abandoned Peak District lead mine known as 'Suicide Cave', a worm edging towards his elective oracle, with impossible questions to be asked if not answered. 'The inquirer carried into the main entrance a torch, two fat candles, typewriter and paper, bottle of beer, bag of crisps, boat oar, length of rope, pair of binoculars, and a "sacrificial cake" bought at a Derby bakers' a few hours previously.' Rattling away at the typewriter, in lightless confinement, mistakes in transcription were made. And retained. As part of the texture of the experiment. 'I have no more ambition for this text. I renounce it,' the supplicant says. 'Now we are beginning,' the oracle replies.

Andrew will never read this book. And I know that he won't read it. But it needs to be referenced. I need to borrow some of the luminescence of Doug's poem and some of the difficulty. Kötting's cave squat will be both a performance, an endurance test, a way of provoking the shadows on the wall into a form of primitive cinema – and a ritual for not being at home, trapped within his entombing body, the way it ages and endures. The son of his father and the father of the reverberating voices in his head.

A NEW WORLD CLASS, AFFORDABLE RAILWAY. A boast painted down the side of the only way left to cross the tracks and gain access to Whitechapel Station. Here is a hub brought to prominence by the Overground link and the tunnelling required for the epic and unnecessary Crossrail project. A project that has already claimed its sacrificial victims: cyclists crushed by earth-moving trucks. Where are they taking all that gouged earth, that bone-rich clay? The old station with its labyrinthine layers, romanced in Jock McFadyen's paintings, has nothing as advanced as a lift service. Which is an inconvenience for the halt and the lame, the incapacitated, and the heavily pregnant women making for the Royal London Hospital. If your injury is traumatic enough, you will land on the roof, collected by a red helicopter. But the station remains trapped between eras: regular Overground shuttles, links to a hobbled District Line service, antiquated stairs, exposed sky, rags and tatters blowing in strange hollows of exposed pipes, with ferns, cobwebs, pyjama jackets and sparking wires.

Somehow it was possible, darting across Whitechapel Road, through the hospital car park, beyond the bleak Safestore facility where my cans of degrading 16mm film are hoarded in an expensive tin box, to believe that we are directly above the Overground tracks. An M. C. Escher paradox. Keep walking, stay on the move without reference to maps, and the throbbing train travels with you, communicates. But there are no railway arches, no caves to commerce. Safestore, selling its services as 'self storage', is a booming business operating out of a posthumous yard, a secure parking lot with a few broken-wheeled trolleys and a set of inefficient industrial lifts. The self I was storing was my memory-bank, home movies going back to childhood, student films, visual diaries of our early life in Hackney.

I liked the geographic coincidence of the relation of my Safe-store archive to the Royal London Hospital, with its library of locality, its early X-ray mementoes, its cast of the Elephant Man's deformities. The Whitechapel triptych was completed by the minatory Tower House, Jack London's 'Monster Doss House' from *The People of the Abyss*. The history of poverty within this gaunt, twin-towered building, from the lodging of respectable migrants to squatting addicts and squalor, achieved its inevitable outcome in its present revision to a set of private pods with a pastiched art deco doorway. A nudging invocation of the wrong mood and the wrong period.

On Sidney Square we found a white ghost bike, a memorial to an accident victim, a dead man called Andrew.

Shadwell is the point where the Overground connects with the DLR, the unmanned fairground ride to Docklands, the City Airport, the ExCel Centre and Beckton. Navigating towards Wapping and the river, we operated on instinct. The traffic flow was all west–east, roads and railways. It was a perversion to carve south from Whitechapel through Shadwell to Wapping, collecting our Overground-station snapshots like Boy Scout badges. But we were on the right track, the vibrations in the ground compensated for the absence of railway arches, visible cradles of electrified wire.

I began to notice a series of circular brochs, like brick remnants of some remote industrial era breaking through paving slabs and phantom clusters of public housing. The Shadwell brochs were not survivors of an Iron Age Orkneyian cult brought in on the Thames, but they had the same kind of essential beauty: sophistication as the simplest solution. If we strain our ears, we can pick up an oracular whisper of trains, or ancestors, or primal winds, in the open-topped funnel of brick. Ventilation shafts, I guessed, for the buried Overground. Broch by broch, we closed on Wapping and the first big decision of the day. How to cross the Thames?

The unseen railway was working its magic. Walking through the sprawl and spread of London without losing hope, or the lineaments of personal identity, requires a framing narrative. A thread. A device on which to hang anecdotes and observations. There is a contagious urban neurosis: to collect decommissioned Tube stations, or to climb to the roof of secure towers, thereby acknowledging the potency of this novel architecture of cruelty. A fractured alphabet of gigantism dominating views that can only be achieved from protected penthouses. The Overground, even when it is lost from sight, is a ladder of initiation. If we could get inside one of the circular brochs, we would become part of another script. We would be making a premature start on Kötting's *Underland* project. Morlock-world was within easy reach, if we heaved ourselves over the lip of a ventilation shaft.

Not today, not now. Our separate madnesses cancelled each other out, bringing us to a truce of sanity: *keep walking*. Major detours had to be set aside if we were to complete the thirty-five-mile circuit in a single day. If we were to achieve whatever answer the oracle of foot-foundered determination would gift us.

My notion of pushing downriver to the Rotherhithe Tunnel is set aside. The morning is running away from us. We'll ride beneath the Thames, taking the Overground for one stop from Wapping. After that, it is a trail between the little known and the unknown. And a return for Andrew to home turf, the first years with Leila, the weekend market stall, the gym, the Millwall mob at the Den.

'*Top of the Pops*, a pickled egg, Beckett before bed,' he said.

After days scrap-hunting in a Transit van. Now, as he paces the narrow station platform, a landing stage for our linking voyage, he quotes Gilles Ivain: 'All cities are geological; you cannot take three steps without encountering ghosts bearing all the prestige of their legends. We move within a *closed* landscape whose landmarks constantly draw us towards the past.'

Rotherhithe to Peckham Rye

*There's real estate and unreal estate . . . He tells them look how nice, a
tree, a shrub, see how it makes up for the noise and monstrousness of
tearing down an old building and putting up a new building. That's
the whole secret of corporate structures, my friend. Tell the enemy
you'll plant some trees.*

– Don DeLillo

Accepting defeat, another day, more of the same, I have
attached that time bracelet: my Swiss Railway Watch. Hours
big and black enough to register. The date window is a little
eccentric, after 31 it runs on to 32, 33, trying to stretch the dying
month. To wear a watch is to accept a form of tagging. There
are appointments, duties, places to be at certain hours, the
exercise walk, the coffee hit, ten minutes with DeLillo, back to
work. Watchstraps don't last, they sweat through, lose their
teeth, but that gives me an excuse to return to a cave of electrical goods on Bethnal Green Road. A new strap is a new
beginning. Another stretch on the elective Swiss railway.

Walking all day, and especially when walking with Andrew
Kötting, I never look at the watch. Mean time is suspended, we
calculate by degrees of hunger. Andrew's form of relentless
energy requires regular fuel intakes, cheek-stretching buns,
chocolate bars, blue tins to suck. 'Anyone got a spare Scotch
egg?' The convenient aspect of location filming is that if there
is any kind of budget, you get a runner. A pleasant young

woman, with a backstory and private interests of her own, capable of withstanding the banter. And a person who can be sent out into the countryside, swamp or desert, moor or mountain, to return every couple of hours with a tray of hot food, marked coffee containers with correctly recorded doses of milk and sugar.

The white moon of the Swiss Railway Watch with its schematic black sleepers, its red conductor's baton, is a relief tattoo. The external symbol of a beating heart. A modest design possession like a small portable Mondrian. *Mondaine.* Even the name sounds like that spontaneous purchase you carry home from Tate Modern in lieu of a stolen Richter.

We turn left out of Rotherhithe. After I've photographed Kötting and noted the understated symmetry of the station, the windows in satisfying proportions, Moorish eyebrow-curves that seem to reference both wavelets on the Thames and the best kind of railway arch, we double back to the river. I remember what it felt like to look across the water from the other side, the north shore, when I was trying to write about the early Narrow Street developer who chained himself to the slimy wall and waited for the tide to swallow him.

'Rotherhithe was not a place to which he had previously given much consideration. It looked foreign, and somewhat estranged from itself. The significance of this apparently random assembly of buildings awed him. He became aware of patterns, meanings, distributions of unexpended energy. His sense of colour was overwhelmingly *personal*. It hurt. It hurt his blood.'

Andrew could never get on with *Downriver*. At the time he was assembling his short Thames comedy, *Jaunt*, friends told him that he should try my book. He might be able to steal a few lines. He tried. He hated it. Kötting was a voracious reader, he carried books on trains and boats and planes. Sometimes he opened them. A paragraph at a time, a sentence. A word: *confabulation*. That's why he loved Beckett: the white spaces. But the essential flaw in *Downriver* is that he didn't appear in it. Early on, I'd called that novel 'a grimoire of rivers and railways'. And I've never really advanced from there. Rivers and railways as a system of divination, invocations of supernatural entities, angels, spirits, demons.

The Thames bounced light. On the diminishing Rotherhithe beach, fathers encouraged their sons to dig for Roman pottery, pilgrims' tokens, broken stems of clay pipes. To die here, out with the tide, as my *Downriver* character did, was to solicit a special blessing. The river does take us beyond ourselves. An hour witnessing the interplay of water and sunlight is remission from whatever follows. Bury the watch in the claggy slop or tramp a teasing narrative out of the false river of the Overground.

My compass bearings are shot. The Thames floats us, lifts our lumbering feet. We navigate territory that is straining for some way to salute a maritime past: deepwater docks, the cargoes of the world, sailors' pubs, dockworkers' terraces. The promoters want a way to crane that picturesque version of the past into a CGI landscape of shopping centres, libraries unencumbered by books, community arts.

As a lad, Andrew came down here to deliver messages. Posing at Canada Water for his station photograph, he shoves his fingers into his ears. A spontaneous but effective gesture: the noise of this hub, buses, cars, vans. A wanton accumulation of effects with no processing mind, no editor. In his thick Black Forest suit, Kötting stands transfixed, acting and becoming Werner Herzog's Kaspar Hauser, the changeling, the holy innocent from the 1974 film *The Enigma of Kaspar Hauser*. Kaspar arrives in the Karlsruhe of 1812 as if hearing the traffic of

Canada Water, a stowaway out of Hamburg trapped in the wrong century with no Swiss Railway Watch. Andrew, like Hauser, might have been hidden for years in a cellar, and now exposed to a place he dreamed as a youth in the wide-eyed innocence of his first job. He can't move or blink or pull his fingers from his ears.

Like Michael Moorcock, the other great memory-man from this side of the river, Andrew began with that most Dickensian of occupations, boy messenger. The city favours these apprenticeships, testing the best by offering them the freedom of the morning, close to the smell of the docks, where they are tasked with searching out mysterious buildings, eccentric clerks, minor Circumlocution Office hirelings barricaded behind dusty ledgers.

'I came down this road. There was a big fire. That building is still there. It wasn't me.'

Norway Dock. Greenland Dock. Rebranded, in alliance with the Overground Railway, as Canada Water. A retail hub from an earlier generation than Westfield, Palaeozoic to Mesozoic. We cross a bridge to enter the shopping zone, as we crossed the railway in Cheshire Street. Kötting is upbeat about the development; he has come here, in former times, to buy sports kit, budget trainers. The whole deal is cheerfully budget, South London vernacular, easy in security. Canada Water has a heritage name, an aspirational connection with the money-laundering private fiefdoms on the north bank: Cross Harbour, South Quay, Heron Quays, Canary Wharf. Canada Water trades on the confusion of strangers, simpletons who go underground on the Overground, only to emerge in Rotherhithe, thinking they have made it to the *Bladerunner* set of Thatcher's Docklands. There is a social gulf between the unmanned DLR carriages on their Expo rides through icy bankers' towers and the Overground cargo haulers trundling towards New Cross or Queens Road Peckham. Rotherhithe is a tumour, a non-malignant nodule, a hump cut off by the red strip of the railway, infiltrated by docks given over to retail parks and leisure boats.

At Surrey Quays, no true quayside but a significant branching point on the Overground, Kötting is coming closer to his beloved Deptford. He can smell it. He can smell bacon in the pan. Gastric residues bubble and fizz, intestinal anticipation leaks in warm detonations of sage and honey, filtered through wet tweed. He shakes his thornproof trousers to disperse gaseous damage. Time for breakfast.

The station is post-architectural, a glass-fronted bus shelter with an upgrade. Rotherhithe was a proper station, a considered brick construction, a railway mosque respecting the dignity of travel. Surrey Quays is all function. A borehole for the retail island of Canada Water.

If we hadn't been stalking the Overground, we would have sampled Southwark Park. The park is the best kind of green blot, it enhances the experience of passing through, drifting, slowing down, taking a clean, resinous breath before the next slam of diesel, nicotine and fox-licked jerk chicken. This oasis for the unaligned urban wanderer, a South London equivalent of Louis Aragon's Buttes-Chaumont from *Paris Peasant*, or one of Arthur Machen's lost paradise gardens, is a resource for the neighbourhood, all ages, all temperaments. Long-dead cricket heroes are remembered. Henry Poole's draped caryatides, rescued from Rotherhithe Town Hall, have found refuge among the shrubs. Late-rising urban athletes and sabbatical drug dealers work out on free equipment. Swans dress a small lake. There is a café with few pretensions. And two art galleries. One of them, Dilston Grove, is a former chapel where Kötting has been given space to present performances, evidence of projects, pinhole portraits, doctored maps, vitrines of scavenged feathers, tide-smoothed bricks, defaced books.

The unfussy tranquillity of Southwark Park, a park that does not waste energy bigging itself up, keeps the surrounding terrain in balance. Andrew recalls patting the hot saddle of his motorbike. And sitting at an outside table to wait for friends. He does not howl. He grins. Aragon caught the atmosphere: 'I ask myself what is dead within me and what is still effectual.' A quick snort of nature under the sails of the trees, along the sightlines of branching paths, around the lake, makes the pain manageable. But when he has to return to the street, the French poet 'acts the dog and bawls for the dead'.

The imaginary lines of influence these walkers leave behind, their neurotic sensitivity to sights and smells, become a set of mental rails linking parks, cemeteries, deserted pubs, rooms where forgotten writers once lodged. Hidden allotments, yards of distressed garden statuary. When Aragon quit his park, he inscribed evidence of the real, in order to re-anchor himself in a particular place at a particular time: RAILWAYS. OUTER-CIRCLE LINES. STATIONS: BELLEVILLE-VILLETTE. PONT-DE-FLANDRE.

You know where you are when you know where to eat. Kötting has our breakfast lined up in an old haunt called La Cigale in Lower Road, Surrey Quays. A good choice. In a street of interest, undisturbed by the Canada Water mall or urgent traffic heading for Evelyn Street (memories of the seventeenth-century diarist), and the pull towards Greenwich and the east.

In 1661 John Evelyn published *Fumifugium or The Inconvenience of the Air and Smoke or London Dissipated*. Outside La Cigale, London is dissipated. Lost in fumes. Inside, settled in the window slot, Andrew demands another oxymoron: *very strong* cappuccino. The proprietor, barely awake, fiddling to get the machines functioning, insists that all his cappuccinos are of a uniform strength and flavour. His reputation depends on it. And how would the overheated signor like to take his panini? 'With gherkin. Mayo. Brown sauce. Both mustards: French, English. Horseradish. Onions. The lot.' Mr K mops his dripping brow with a bookie's spotted handkerchief.

We have tuned in to conflicting radio beacons. But we are receiving Deptford loud and clear, channelling another diarist: Sam Pepys. Bence House, Pepys Estate, is the council flat where Andrew brought Leila at the start of their joint venture. When Margaret Thatcher offered the chance to buy (and later sell), Andrew took it, despite Leila's sound socialist objections. It was the only way, so he asserted, to achieve living/working space: move out, move on, to St Leonards-on-Sea. Before the Hackney mob colonized it.

While we made our fourteen-hour walk around the circuit of the Overground Railway, Kötting composed fourteen 'ponderings'. Songs of place. Trampish meditations.

Carry me home you old sea spray
Drag me back to a life with Deptford.
We were young in old Deptford.
When the wind blows east and the ferryman pulls away from the pier
He might carry me home to old Deptford.

It floods back, the romance: after a spell as a lumberjack in Sweden, it was lovely, loud, river-smelling Deptford. The view from the balcony. 'South London, paradise . . . GEORGE DAVIS IS INNOCENT . . . D&C Metals and Salter's Paper to the Dog and Bell and selling wicker furniture with Jack Sharp in Deptford Market . . . Evelyn Street in the rush hour. The city of lookback, the city of lookout! Speed bumps and bollards . . . But now to home. The flat. Red brick, yellow insides. An entrance at the rear. Puddled with piss in summertime and blocked with adolescent bliss in wintertime. The lift gleams with spittle, the corridors with polish. Up on the sixth floor, the corridor, second on the left and in. Home, their home. Good-to-be-home home. Bence House, Pepys Estate, home.'

The joy of being out in the van. Banging heads in the gym. A corner of London that is all London. Andrew was a beachcomber of the southern suburbs. With a brown foam of strong cappuccino distinguishing his grey-flecked stubble like a petit mal seizure, Kötting recalls the distant wonder of banknotes: £7,000 cashmoney. In the hand. Down in Dulwich Village on the estate where Lady Thatcher lined up a retirement property, but couldn't bring herself to come over the river from Westminster.

'We got the nod from Metal Mickey. Put in an estimate for a decorating job for the missus of one of the Brink's-Mat mob. They were spreading out across London, into Kent, like horseshit on rhubarb. Shenley was favourite, A20 and over. Junction 2, M25. Keeping the property bubble going all by theirselves. With trickledown bungs for local craftsmen.'

Catching sight of tenders from the upmarket West London firms in opposition, Andrew cranked his own estimate from £3,000 to £7,000 – and Jo, the former page 3 girl, bit his hand off. He rounded up a few loose brothers to make a quorum. And they did a good job. Gold leaf in the snooker room. Gold taps like spouting dolphins.

The Dulwich family, a close one, were all Joes: Big Joe (dad), Joey (first son), JJ (number-two son), Mr Joseph (accountant son from first marriage), Jo (trophy wife), JoJo (her dog) and Joe Stalin (attack mastiff).

'Don't touch his soldiers, for fuckssake,' Jo warned. Lead soldiers, a museum-quality collection. Regiments, correct in every detail, occupied the shelves and cabinets of the games room. 'Insured for two million.'

When Joe took the fat roll from his pocket to settle up, he said, 'Don't count it, son. Any shortfall come down the yard.' That's etiquette. That's the social distance between Dulwich and New Cross. New Cross is on the Overground, Dulwich isn't.

The stretch between Surrey Quays and Queens Road Peckham is terra incognita, a miracle of high mesh fences, narrow paths, waste-processing plants. The railway is a dominant presence, but the substantial gap between Overground stations means that it's hard to read its effect on property development. If there are arches or caves beneath bridges they are motor-trade traditional: big doors, big dogs. Divorced from the street, the windows of working clothes and heavy boots that hover between function and fashion, the railway path has the exhilaration of the Regent's Canal, the muddy towpath, in the days when it was forbidden to civilians, those who did not have business with coal boats and lumber yards. Our parting from Lower Road is emphasized by a wall painting: a white male of the clerical type, bureaucrat policeman, suspended from a giant clothes peg. HUNG OUT TO DRY.

Railways cross railways. A felt underlay of scabby grass. The tall chimney of the processing plant. A single black tree stripped of its meat tilted over the permitted path, asset-stripped by the yellow spew of burning waste, gritty particulates you are free to absorb at no extra charge. SELCHIP, the South East London Combined Heat and Power Plant, squats the railway as the Enfield version, source of carcinogenic rumour, lurks beside the River Lea Navigation. The combined heat-and-power system was conceived, at no small cost, for a scheme that has never been implemented. Electricity – and bad will – are generated here. In 2002 Greenpeace activists, troubled by the threat of dioxins produced during the incineration process, took direct action by invading the main tipping hall and climbing the

stalk of the chimney. After this episode, and the attendant publicity, Liberal Democrats on Lewisham Council, and Peter Ainsworth, Shadow Environment Secretary, pledged their support. The looming presence of the plant, with the scatter of new-build estates, the dying tree, the silver tracks slipping under a double-arch bridge, evoked earlier journeys, our walk up the Lea to join the circuit of the M25 at Waltham Abbey. The same elements, the same mounting excitement.

London's smaller rivers, the tributary streams, visible, buried, or choked by refuse, flow by inclination towards the Thames, while the Overground, on this part of its circuit, drifts alongside the river, in parallel, a short distance inland. A rival. This unknown and previously unexplored Bermondsey landscape is made comfortable by its resemblance to the parts of the Lea complicated by never-resolved arguments between discontinued industries, converted gunpowder mills, expanding retail and storage zones, waste disposal, Ikea riots and the first stab at regeneration by means of showcase athletics.

PICKETTS LOCK FIASCO HEAPS SHAME ON BRITAIN bellowed the *Telegraph* in 2001. The author of this critique, scorning the political failure to erect a workable stadium while balancing the books, called the whole sorry affair 'an Ealing comedy'. 'Manifesto pledges have been broken, secretaries of state and sports ministers have come and gone and press officers have been plundering the thesaurus to construct obtuse and misleading language . . . Our ambitions are being butchered by incompetent ministers and lightweight, self-serving quangos.' Here was a prime example of the nay-saying negativism from certain elements of the media so furiously denounced by Lord Coe in the run-up to the 2012 Olympic triumph. The author of this scurrilous *Telegraph* diatribe was a certain Sebastian Coe.

Three or four hours of quiet, steady walking will do that, rub away barriers, borders, distinctions of north and south, past and future. Slipping into dioxin-clubbed reverie, arranging what is before us in terms of dystopian cinema, I am reminded of the way that film-maker Patrick Keiller associates trains with surrealism and privileged witness. In his essay 'The Poetic Experience of Townscape and Landscape' Keiller writes: 'The present day *flâneur* carries a camera and travels not so much on foot as in a car or on a train. There are several reasons for this, mostly connected with the decline of public life and urbanism.' South London is where Keiller's solitary and poetically inclined commuter gazes at an eternity of suburb without urb and thinks of Kentucky Fried Chicken outlets and Apollinaire. Apollinaire, when he lodged in this territory, spoke of 'wounds bleeding into the fog'. 'I began to think,' Keiller continues, 'it might be possible to predict the future by looking out of the window.'

The past is always ahead of us. Films like Keiller's seem to be documentaries about a future that is used up. 'The future,' William Burroughs said, 'is already photographed and pre-recorded.' All we can do is follow the image vine, the necessary chain of snapshots. Expose one frame, one image made without premeditation, and the rest follows. You pull in the string. Hoxton bleeds into Clapham Junction, into Willesden, into Kensal Rise, into Highbury & Islington.

I remembered what I felt, at the time of writing *Downriver*, about the way that accounts of the first railway age, Victorian boom-time confidence, overlaid the area we were now infiltrating. And how our present passage between trackside fence and high wall meshed with intimations of that earlier period. 'The viaduct blitzkriegs the market gardens of Deptford,' I wrote, 'recouping some of the capital investment by graciously allowing the punters to use the edge of the track as a rustic esplanade, catching glimpses of the meandering river, beyond the hedgerows and the mounds of rubble.'

As we crossed the tracks by way of a new bridge with neat ginger handrails and a roof of strengthened chicken wire (to deter jumpers), Kötting started to beat his chest and chant: 'Mill-wall! Mill-wall! Mill-wall!' Was this the right pub, the one where he met his mates before they marched on the Den? The shock for me when I first navigated the railway esplanade, on a recce undertaken before the Kötting walk, was the abrupt, out-of-nowhere confrontation with the notorious football stadium. I should have been better prepared. Living cities thrive on a proven equation: market, hospital, church. Limbic terrain fed by railway or motorway acquires different markers: prisons, megamalls, stadia. The Den, home of the Millwall FC wolf pack, is the obvious but unexpected destination of our railway path.

'Terry Hurlock,' Kötting intones. 'Teddy Sheringham. Tony Cascarino.' Fist thumped on heart for every hero. 'Football League, '88–'89 . . . Division One! Hurlock, Sheringham, Cascarino. Razor Ruddock, Les Briley. October, top of the table. Horne, Darren Tracy, Jimmy Carter.'

A stadium in repose is a bowl of latent noise, suspended emotion: unheard chanting, the ineradicable cheers of phantom crowds. Like that scummy afterglow left in a drained coffee cup. Here, right beside our path, is a Meccano cathedral with the roof sliced off. An emphatic structure under a dome of sky blue enough for a fatal space launch in Florida. And supported on complimentary blue pillars. A finished work-in-progress.

The embankment leading down to the turnstiles supplies an abundant source of almost-collectible junk: sodden jackets lacking one sleeve, microwaved vinyl by suspect bands, the usual divorced white goods. The sharpened tines of the protective fence have been embellished with nooses of barbed wire and a set of upturned yellow chairs cast in hard plastic. The chairs are potentially worthy of display in a Broadway Market window within three years.

Transport for London (Overground) have acknowledged their part in the curation of this Bermondsey esplanade with a wall map of the recently completed railway circuit and some propaganda about the ever-expanding city they are shaping. A guerrilla muralist – perhaps the person responsible for HUNG OUT TO DRY – has collaborated so deftly that the work now qualifies for exhibition in a show of art iconoclasm at the Tate. Even though it's hard to say who is the iconoclast, the original TfL designer or the spray-can bandit who added a neat *trompe l'oeil* chain to support the map and thereby turn it into a painting rather than a flat computer printout. Two stencilled yellow-tabard hardhats adjust the imaginary piece. One brandishes a clipboard: WE OWN THIS CITY. As soon as the map is drawn, territory is copyright to the map's commissioner. The 'Completed London Overground', like a trail of ginger gunpowder, reduces the complexity of the city to a whiteboard presentation.

We are heading south towards Peckham. The twin branches of the Overground split into a great V, exposing new mounds of exploitable turf, inter-rail estates, recreational dunes on which solitary males pose with their dogs. Passers-through scuttle in a miasma of unease, hunched into themselves against too much sky: the leaking chimney of the waste-disposal plant, the speedy thrust of the trains. A catalogue of opportunism unable to tolerate for long the notion of a railside path. A stencil artist with a signature that looks something like LOREITO has found a suitable piece for the grey concrete wall: an infant dressed

like a cosmonaut pushing a buggy containing a baby with a green alien skull.

We are expelled into a nowhere of cars with smashed windows, green glass in jagged patterns on soft grey seats. And messianic religions camped in garages and defunct factories: THE REDEEMED CHRISTIAN CHURCH OF GOD, WINNERS TEMPLE. A god of unrequired margins. Website faiths drawing an enthusiastic congregation in the way that, in earlier times, nonconformist artisans found their chapels in working zones outside the walls of the city. Where John Wesley launched his crusades, and William Blake, Daniel Defoe, John Bunyan were laid to earth, between Finsbury Circus and Old Street, the seething hub of Silicon Roundabout has emerged: digital traders, masters of robotics, radio freelancers worshipping that Cloud where all the miscellaneous information of the multiverse floats somewhere over India.

After the detours, the dips under railway bridges, now one side, now another, the windowless cars, the vernacular weirdness of places without a dominant narrative, we pick up the true path with another set of murals. The local artist, recorded at various points along the track from Surrey Quays, is ahead of us, making the Overground embankment into an elongated gallery. It's liberating, you can collect him through the simple act of walking. He has a satiric edge, after the fashion of Banksy, but he is choosing to show on ground where he is unlikely to be picked up by stray gallerists. Shoreditch lecture groups will not find their way down here just yet, but it will come. The Overground will bring them, chasing the ginger trail. This art is not designed to be read from trains. You have to walk the broken path to find it. A combat soldier on his belly, the penis barrel of his gun with terminal droop: THE WAR IT'S NOT A MAN'S THING.

*

Distance between stations induces desert hallucinations, the native oddity of a brief span without overt surveillance. Two black men stride down the centre of the road with large chairs, the exaggerated thrones of Bond villains, supported on their backs. The white arrow on the tarmac points right. They turn left. Or, again, around the point where that pilgrims' track, Old Kent Road, becomes New Cross Road, we wave at a ginger cow, the sacred beast of the Overground, as she teeters on her rear legs down the uneven pavement. The girl walking with this eight-foot-tall cartoon creature is not collecting for charity. They are chatting. It's hard for the soft cow, a star emblazoned on its throat, to bend down far enough to catch what's being said. I don't know where else in the world you could witness a sniff-and-shrug domestic between a pink girl with short dark hair and a talking cow with no mouth and huge unblinking eyes. As wide and white as death. With nobody on the public street paying them the slightest mind.

Andrew stalls for a moment, taking a surreptitious blow by looking back down Old Kent Road. He is frozen rigid, in contemplation of an unravelling mystery. As if some earlier self, in the first days of his intoxicated courtship of Leila, and the youthful freedoms of the city, should be revealed. He jumped back from the kerb, pushed by the slipstream of the ghost of his own motorbike. This was the route he always took, so he explained, on his return to St Leonards, after London tasks and adventures.

The Overground station at Queens Road Peckham is rewarded with another Kötting portrait. He has the energy to point: stout Cortez with his eagle eyes, none too silent on a peak in Peckham. But still managing to alarm a non-travelling vagrant, as he tried to make off with a pile of free newspapers. It says something about this station that they were still there, mid-morning.

Peckham improper, the definitive street of small shops, rank meat, trade, movement, goods, deals, arrives so suddenly and is so charged with bounce and collision, leftover civic structures signifying some dissipated claim to being a centre, that we miss it entirely; moving through in hot debate of our own, *without pausing to record Peckham Rye Station.* Thereby undoing the immaculate procession of our circular walk and disqualifying the premise of the image vine. (I charged back, a day or two later, to commit a selfie. By then Kötting was an absence, a loud ghost sprayed somewhere on the nether reaches of Old Kent Road.)

The station on Rye Lane was the grandest one so far encountered on our circuit; it required an etching press, not a digital camera. The nudge of recognition came from its association with the Lower Lea Valley and midwinter walks down the Northern Sewage Outfall. The architect was Charles Henry Driver, who was also responsible for Abbey Mills Pumping Station, that yellow-brick Moorish fantasy intruding on the Greenway path, breaking clouds, diverting storms, to disguise its legitimate function: housing engines to refine and reduce shit. Pumping stations and railway stations are in the same business: evacuation.

Peckham Rye Station, I subsequently discovered, was the epicentre of a major row about development. The promoters were in the grip of what they described as a 'Vision'. They started calling the commuter station a 'hub'. Suspect viruses advanced down the line. The journalist Alex Proud said that Peckham was now suffering from 'Shoreditchification'; entrepreneurial 'hipsters' and carpetbaggers in dark glasses were descending from Orange Line carriages to curate the buzz that leads to increased rents and spurious retail projects. These activities were forcing out the original (if not aboriginal) settlers. Network Rail owns the station, the land beneath the forecourt and all the arches leading to Bellenden Road. Following the Shoreditch/Hoxton example, they mean to make the best of it. So Peckham's railway zone was rebranded: The Gateway. It now sounded like a New Age religion.

We strain eagerly uphill, enthused by the way the short passage between the lowlands of railway Peckham, as tribal, immersive, loud, watchful as the former Kingsland Waste Market, and the nursery slopes of established Peckham Rye, demonstrates such a leap in real-estate values. Even a minor physical elevation comes with entitlement to upward social mobility. You don't need oxygen, but the modest ascent uses the Overground as a cultural funicular.

Muriel Spark might have composed *The Ballad of Peckham Rye*, but she'd be cut adrift in the contemporary action around the station, the railway lowlands. She treated the working district, in her slender, sharp-witted 1960 novel, as suitable turf for satire.

'Dougal turned sideways in his chair and gazed out of the window at the railway bridge; he was now a man of vision with a deformed shoulder. "The world of Industry," said Dougal, "throbs with human life. It will be my job to take the pulse of the people and plumb the industrial depths of Peckham."'

This horned Dougal, a genial Lucifer, presents himself as a teaser-out of local particulars, a scout in dim municipal libraries. He makes copies of unreliable facts, he raids friable newsprint. He has Mendelssohn composing his 'Spring Song' in Ruskin Park. And Boadicea committing suicide on Peckham Rye, 'probably where the bowling green is now'. He validates a dull present by inventing a ripe past.

Peckham Rye has chosen Bellenden Road as its engine of regeneration. A five-minute stroll from the Overground station. Tributaries with Hampstead aspirations: Elm Grove, Holly

Grove, Blenheim Grove. The estate agent's tactic of trifling with selected aspects of history that Spark exposes in her affectionate ridiculing of the pretensions of hilltop suburbia are extant in the rapid evolution of Bellenden Road into an elective Montmartre. Pavement cafés. Community bookshop. Authentic artisans stepping aside so that their warehouses and gated courtyards can be occupied by artists and printmakers. There is a well-kept sign pointing out that Bellenden Road was 'formerly Victoria Terrace'. A Victorian advertisement, like a supersize trade card, has been restored on an endwall: PRINTING OFFICE. FOR BUSINESS BUILDING. ESTD 1884. Here is an advertisement advertising heritage. And asserting the pedigree of the survivor.

In 1998, at the time of the conception of his *Angel of the North*, Antony Gormley had a studio here. Knighted now, a sculptor of international consequence, Gormley has followed the railway to the hub of hubs at King's Cross, the ultimate Eurozone of future development. Back then, I walked from Hackney to Peckham with a commission to produce an essay in response to the *Angel*. Blake was part of the attraction, his tree of celestial beings. Peckham angels were infusions of light, evanescent, but no more extraordinary than the colonies of parakeets in Wanstead. Less noisy perhaps. Alexander Gilchrist in *The Life of Blake*, first published in 1863, describes that famous episode: 'On Peckham Rye (by Dulwich Hill) it was, as he in after years related, that while quite a child, of eight or ten perhaps, he had his first vision. Sauntering along, the boy looked up and saw a tree filled with angels, bright angelic wings bespangled every bough like stars.'

Gormley's office-workshop, off Bellenden Road, shared a yard with the studio of the artist Tom Phillips. Phillips had been plundering the past, very fruitfully, by working over a

Victorian novel by William Hurrell Mallock called *A Human Document*. Pages of starchy narrative were defaced, isolated phrases emphasized, colour and pattern-making employed, to chart an adventure in concrete poetry. Phillips called the project *A Humument*. The original book was found in Peckham Rye, at Austin's, a furniture repository and accidental mausoleum of dead stuff that might now be dignified as 'architectural salvage'. Austin's was a major South London resource, somewhere in character between the Horniman Museum in Forest Hill and Nunhead Cemetery. Graham Greene references the place. He was a premature Overground man, testing the adulterous liaisons of *The End of the Affair* on Clapham Common. He furnished rooms from Peckham warehouses. In the days when Greene was making a fetish of not being filmed, he agreed to be interviewed, so long as his face wasn't shown: on a train.

Phillips visited Austin's in the company of R. B. Kitaj: School of London investigates a reserve collection of unoccupied beds, cupboards, chairs. A mad, uncurated heap of periods and submerged stories.

'Ron, I'll get the first book I find for thruppence and spend the rest of my life working on it.'

That book was *A Human Document*. A suitable case for the William Burroughs treatment: the masking, slicing, excavating of covert truths. Rivers of phrases. Pools and puddles of words. Enochian signs. Hypnagogic undertow. On page iii: 'a broken bridge and / photograph, betrayed . . . certain S-shaped iron ties'. Peckham as a site of divination, Mallock's novel as a reconfigured *I Ching*. Mundane narrative redacted, by the wit of Phillips, into poetry.

Like all of us who are responsive to place, determined to acquire a chorus of spiritual forebears, Phillips positions Austin's 'on Peckham Rye, where Blake saw his first angels and along which Van Gogh had probably walked on his way to Lewisham'. And where Muriel Spark located her own mischievous archivist burrowing into legends of freaks and mermaids. 'It will be necessary to discover the spiritual well-being, the glorious history of the place, before I am able to offer some impetus.'

Phillips ripped through numerous copies of *A Human Document*. The first one cost almost nothing. The one I sold him in 1981 was £8 (postage included). He sent me a postcard of 'Dante in his study'. The Peckham artist, the man on the far side of Gormley's courtyard, began by simply scoring out words to uncover the skeleton beneath the obfuscations of the dead author's controlling mind. Phillips used the found book as I was using London: a Tarot, a Book of Changes. He tapped it for confirmation: 'wanted. a little white opening out of thought'.

Tom's companion on that first trawl through the furniture repository, Ron Kitaj, shared this attitude towards a form of art recoverable by way of books as mediums. He favoured prints made of poets, philosophers. Walter Benjamin. Ed Dorn. The one-eyed Robert Creeley. The wall-eyed Robert Duncan. Kitaj's painting *Cecil Court, London WC2 (The Refugees)* is an epitaph for a vanishing trade, bookdealing. A paved beach and a court of windows. A memory-culture escaped from Hitler's Germany. A strip of London real estate soon to be priced out of existence. The painting has the noise and smell of Yiddish Theatre.

'I began to collect scarce books and pictures about this shadow world, the trail of which has not quite grown cold in my past life,' Kitaj said. He prowled book alleys. And the furniture repositories of Peckham. Street markets. Junk pits. But the submerged libraries of dealers who store everything and curate nothing have gone. Swept away in the slipstream of the

Ginger Line. Oxfam shelves, and all those other charity displays on dying high streets, will never supply the singular items with which Phillips and Kitaj worked, tracking wormholes through time. Some know-nothing dealer will be around to advise on what is to be kept: the bright, the current, the glossy pretenders. The rest is landfill. Austin's of Peckham has become Austin's Court, a nest of railway-connected flats. A desirable address. Old Alf Austin, the last of his line, had a catchphrase for first-time visitors to his warehouse. 'Gentlemen, everything is for sale.'

We sat in Gormley's office above the Peckham yard where a regiment of sculpted avatars, forked and naked, endure the season's showers, acquiring a weathered patina: *Invasion of the Body Snatchers* aliens bursting from the pod. Antony Gormley is monkish, long-limbed, an abbot of intent at the heart of a multinational enterprise; a global brand whose product is the marketing of copies, reworkings, extensions of his own body, cast by his partner, Vicken Parsons, and her assistants, who are sterile-suited in white like a forensic team newly arrived at the scene of the crime. Photographs of these procedures have a fetishistic allure: yogic discipline, the whiteness of the bandages, clingfilm body wrappings emphasizing every bump and gnarl. Private rituals servicing public art, with each stage of the process documented like *The Egyptian Book of the Dead*.

The *Angel of the North*, Gormley told me, was the realization of a dream. The sculptor's responses to my questions were considered, lengthy, and delivered after long pauses as he waits for the right word, the only word, to emerge from religious silence. I find my attention drifting to the window and the walk I made, up the hill to a small park, a stamp of green I associate with Blake's vision. I sank into the infinite emptiness Gormley locates within the human shell. His thin spectacles. That ink-black hair. The interrogator's quizzical tilt of head. The becoming stoop of a benevolent hierophant explaining years of rigorous discipline and practice to a layman with a hungry notebook.

Gormley saw his *Angel* as 'a concentrator of landscape', privileged above motorway and Sir John Hall's consumer hub, the Metro Centre. Why not in Peckham? Why not above the Ginger Line? The *Angel*, beginning as a peeling of self, travels out into the world to occupy a northern hilltop. Gormley's need to present his giant as the final flare of the age of iron, with heavy engineering complemented by digital technologies, is understandable, but marginal to the presence of the thing itself. The *Angel* is a Blakean archetype, a rusted automaton whose roots drop down into native rock. The steel sculpture is the focus for 'a field of energy': the tired eyes and wandering minds of 90,000 motorists, sealed in their metal bubbles, driving past every day of the year. They look at the blind looker. Who cannot return their gaze. The *Angel of the North* is the symbol of a symbol, logo for regeneration. Rooted and imprisoned where Blake's birds of light shimmer and vanish.

On the window ledge of Gormley's office is a small plaster figure, an angelic form of modest wingspan. The simple maquette exists somewhere beyond, and not before, the public clatter, committees and convoys of the Gateshead giant. It was made, Gormley explains, for the child of a friend. Seeing what he had achieved, the sculptor decided that the figurine belonged with him. It was the germ of the grand project. The *Angel of the North* should stand for at least 150 years. This warm-to-the-touch plaster thing could vanish tomorrow; its vulnerability is its release from the prison of time.

The benign emanation on the windowsill, looking out over Bellenden Road, was private. The inflated version, locked down in Gateshead, was an issue, political, cultural, economic, right from the start. If Gormley were to leave a memento, to pay his respects to a period on the south side of the river, it would be the commission from Thames Water to produce a series of manhole covers for Peckham. The project was stillborn, with the exception of a unique prototype installed at the junction of Maxted Road and Sandison Street, a short distance from the studio. The design is based on the sculptor's naked footprints, whorls and hard ridges of skin from miles tramped in London and elsewhere. A rectangle filled with a unique signature of self: the beating of the bounds. An iron mirror has been cast, as Gormley suggested, to look like ripples in a pond. 'You are invited to stand on it and feel yourself suspended, as it were, between the great infinity of the blue dome of the sky and this river of human ordure that it flowing beneath your feet.'

Ian Mansfield, a blogger, reported back, after making a pilgrimage to view the sacred slab. 'I doubtfully stood on the manhole cover and contemplated deep thoughts about how artists get away with such bollocks, and then darted swiftly away as this is a modestly busy road junction and standing in the middle of the street is a most unwise idea.'

Within days, the labyrinthine footprints, like blow-ups of a future crime, were gone. Some art fancier excavated the iron panel and took it away. The blogger came under attack, not so much for his adverb-heavy literary style, as for the injudicious identification of the site. The sewage hole was plugged by a standard Thames Water cover.

'It's all your fault,' Kötting said. '*City of Disappearances*, my arse. Leave well alone. Justgone and hasbeen. *Adiós*. *Adieu*. Goodbye.'

Peckham Rye to Clapham Junction

We shook the tree but there were no angels today, just the exposed angles of well-kept paths along which leotard women, blonde hair tied back in swishing ponytails, were chivvied by personal trainers; slim professionals in waterproof make-up, with fit black instructors monitoring performance against the stopwatch. 'Come on now, you can do it. Twenty-eight, twenty-nine . . . *Come on, last push*. Thirty!'

Threads of willow curtained the railway. Large houses, secure in the status of the hill, risked colour: dark bands of Arctic blue with a giant sun disk in marmalade orange, in salute to the Overground, the confirmation that a rail connection boosts property values. Height above sea level could be quantified in zeros on the asking price. Who's asking? The villagers of Peckham Rye are a community of morning athletes, yoga-improved, allowing few shops or commercial enterprises on the upper slopes: mother-and-buggy tea bars, choice vegetables, the latest electronic screens flashing behind work-from-home windows.

Among the imposing villas, copper beech groves, stucco, the views down long straight avenues to Camberwell – and the flicker of unease that comes with missing the moans of a railway muffled by discreet planting – the Kötting libido gives itself a good shake. He reminisces. Art-school days. Parties. Performances. Clattering and smoking around town, Penge to Putney, in a general dealer's van. Transporting some smitten, mascara-smudged student back to one of these hilltop houses. He recalls. Nests of flats with furniture under wraps, before the paintwork was taken in hand. We are carving across the footfall of Andrew's memory-map, firing reflex stories of punkish warehouse madness with lights and sirens and shuddery loops of film.

'I was a confusionist,' he said. 'If I couldn't find a thing, I'd make it happen. Then I'd drop my trousers.'

Something about the settled harbour of silent and desirable uphill properties jolts Kötting. Lovings and leavings. Herb smoke going sour in dirty saucers. Scratchy vinyl sounds bouncing and repeating on the turntable. And the way that old London sunlight used to barge through naked windows, firing bedspreads made from US flags. Nicotine glow of ranks of orange paperbacks: Greene, Orwell, Huxley. And one shoe to be retrieved after the barefoot return from a shared bathroom with an explosive geyser and black rust beard under a dripping tap.

One of the posh clients for Kötting, our Deptford painter and decorator, was the film presenter, archivist, collector Philip Jenkinson. A Northerner from Sale, Jenkinson got his first taste of showbiz by way of delivering juvenile George Formby impressions in holiday camps. An asthmatic child, he diverted his swimming money to illicit cinema trips. Then rinsed his trunks in the Gents before returning home. While lecturing at St Martin's School of Art, he was talent-spotted by a BBC producer and given a slot on *Late Night Line-Up*.

All of which served as useful preparation for becoming Kötting's front-room university, his inspiration. And eventually his patron. The growl of the 16mm projector, the cone of light on the wrinkled screen, taught the young director the value of creative befuddlement. He didn't know what he was watching, but it all meshed: Sam Fuller's bald-headed prostitute wielding a high-heeled shoe in *The Naked Kiss* and Russ Meyer's cheesy *Faster Pussycat! Kill! Kill!*.

'In amongst the cacophony,' Andrew said, 'was a story.' Finding that story and disguising it in discriminations of orchestrated babble became his signature method. And he never stopped giving credit for this to Jenkinson. Kötting's experience of chamber cinema in 1984 replaced the gilded and fading Alhambras still floating in my own memories of chasing down double bills in Streatham and Tooting and Stockwell in the early 1960s.

Appreciating Kötting's first primitive and energetic short film, *Klipperty Klopp*, Jenkinson dosed the youthful painter / decorator on shorts by Dick Lester and Bob Godfrey. Andrew did it all: running, jumping and standing still. He bullocked in and out of abandoned shipping containers, mounds of British rubbish, wearing silly hats and trawlerman's oilskins. Honouring the tradition of Bruce Lacey and the traction-engine survivalists of Philip Trevelyan's *The Moon and the Sledgehammer*, Andrew scavenged war detritus and relics of dying riverside industries. Over film stock shocked into silence, he imbecile-soliloquized, contradicting himself, scoring chaos into accidental poetry. Funny voices, warped sentiment and Millwall bluster lift and enhance the fogged footage of what would otherwise be an orthodox art-school product. The finished film looks like a rough cut.

'He'd run round and round in circles. He'd run round and round all the time. He'd wreck the grass and he made a terrible mess of himself.'

Andrew is rag-and-bone shamanic. With the emphasis on manic. A horseless rider of Mudchute steppes. He gallops around a spiral vortex laid out among overgrown bomb craters on the Isle of Dogs. Scorched lines look like a Stone Age premonition of the coming of the railways. 'He came out of this place where he was. And he wasn't at another.'

Jenkinson, tucked away on Kötting's side of the river, mentoring the spray of umlaut humour, opened doors. As we tramp towards Denmark Hill, Andrew stresses again the debt he owes to the man who knew just what to show him; what he needed to extend his ambitions. David Lynch's *Eraserhead* with the monster worm-baby, industrial-apocalyptic sets, the smoke. Frederick Wiseman's savage 1967 documentary, *The Titicut Follies*, shot in a Massachusetts hospital for the criminally insane. The inmates put on a talent show. It was hard to watch.

Kötting talked about these Friday-night screenings as 'The Strap'. 'It really felt as if we had been strapped in and weren't allowed to leave until Philip had shown us just one more film. All my early film noir experiences were there.'

The Kötting troop would straggle from the council flat in riverside Deptford to elegant Blackheath. Jenkinson was an uphill media figure; he danced in sailor suit on the *Morecambe & Wise Christmas Show*. He laboured through an interview with the professionally irascible and eye-patched John Ford, who behaved like an admiral pulling rank on a chorus-boy seaman.

Blackheath is not on the Overground. It doesn't need it. It's too long established in its village status, its green spaces saturated with historic traces of Wat Tyler and the rest. Tyler's betrayal by the young Richard II is a useful demonstration that this meadow is as far as revolting peasants are going to be permitted to march before they're turned back. Blackheath is part of that whalebacked line of Surrey hills, where white houses perch in safety above flood risks and riverbank piracy and the railway din of immigrants and street markets: Dulwich, Peckham Rye, Denmark Hill, Wimbledon, Richmond. A ridge from which to observe distant plagues and fires.

The right to trespass, to sprawl on Jenkinson's sofa with the grinding gears of the 16mm projector, confirmed Kötting on his life's trajectory: art, struggle, expulsion. Posing now beside a pickup truck – SCRAP CARS & MOT FAILURES WANTED – the sweating, heavy-suited film-maker highlights a path not taken. Or not for long. The Del Boy years of the other Peck-ham, *Fools and Horses*. We are reluctant to let go of our own myths. Through misremembered and improved autobiography, Andrew retrieves archival footage of a past capable of validating this long day's trudge. There are footprints in the ash.

He made films only to provide backdrops for performance. He called his act *Being Kärnal*. He supported himself as a market trader. He sold shoes to Derek Jarman. After he had put in a bid for a pitch at Camden Market, he would take himself off to the Scala in King's Cross for an all-night screening. That was the geography of cross-river London: constant transit, scavenging, cashmoney. Drawings made on flapping canvases with sump oil. 'This is where it began, all round here. It takes you right back.'

His destiny begins to make sense. He detects the faintest outline of a coherent narrative. So he leaves for South America with Leila. He is beside himself, he says, he is in love. Leila tells him so. And he knows it is true. They sleep rough and eat nettles in the New Forest. They're ready. They ship out. They find a ruined mining settlement in the middle of the Atacama Desert. He takes photographs. Then they come home to Deptford, Pepys Estate.

Denmark Hill reminds us that all the asylums, or factories for processing damaged psyches, are not on the outer fringes of London. They are not all decommissioned and converted into gated enclaves with cod-pastoral names and easy access to the orbital motorway. Will Self brought Friern Barnet, just outside the North Circular, back to life with a jolt in *Umbrella*, an immersive seance on modernism. One of the features of that grim hospital, recalled and reviled in so many memoirs, a hive of bad dreams and compulsive disorders, is the central corridor: a pedestrian circuit tramped into pilgrim smoothness by generations of white jackets and patient prisoners. A London loop for tranquillized hikers sandwiched between the M25 and the North Circular.

'That it's movement that's essential for the formation of memories,' Self writes. 'That memory is a somatic phenomenon, and so if a mind can no longer manipulate its body in space, it loses the capacity to orientation within time . . .' And he goes on: 'The ward is hot, the angled casements seem not to vent the sodium hypochlorite vapours and ruinous eddies, but only draw in the far-off shushing of traffic on the North Circular.'

The corridors ran for a mile around the intestines of the hospital. Agitated skeletons progressed, sleepwalked, snow-walked, crawled, crept, jerked, wall-touched, step-counted – like those outside, but without mobile phones – until their shot nerves demanded medication or the penance of reheated institutional food.

Self identifies the problem we face, as we collect graffiti, photographs of spray-can murals, fragments of torn advertisements. The catalogue of visual trophies, laid out, becomes the chart of a particular day, a journey. To stitch it together requires concentration. But the map can never be more than the map of a further map. Tighter and tighter, maps within maps, until our skulls split and we come to a dead halt in the middle of an attempted portrait of Kötting beside the sign for Denmark Hill Station in its Overground guise. The orange strip is the colour of the regular methadone prescription picked up by William Burroughs in Kansas City: medication for commuters. You *can* get away.

The rail halt, with its Xanax'd café, feels like a service hatch for the Maudsley Hospital. Paul Merton, a comedian who took his name from the district of London in which he grew up, checked in for a six-week stay, suffering from the side effects of Lariam, a drug taken in tablet form for the prevention and treatment of malaria. The active ingredient is mefloquine hydrochloride. Merton said that he was 'hallucinating conversations with friends'. Which was, despite the pain and loss of control, not a bad preparation for *Have I Got News for You*, where he became a regular panellist shortly after his release.

He no longer believed that he was a target for Freemasons. But he stayed in the cross hairs of Will Self, a luminary of the show, who told the *Mirror* that it was time for Merton and Ian Hislop to quit. 'All due respect . . . they're multimillionaires, plump middle-aged men sitting behind a desk making cracks about Clive Anderson's hairstyle.' The last time the TV show was any good, Self reckoned, was when he guested and 'ripped the tits' off Neil Kinnock.

The acknowledged side effects of mefloquine, leaking into the Denmark Hill landscape, and away down the Overground circuit, are anxiety, depression, suicidal thoughts, feelings of persecution, unmotivated weeping, aggression, forgetfulness, agitation, restlessness, confusion, nightmares, hallucinations. Apart from that: fine. The shakes are just swamp fevers, Deptford tremors, property envy.

Kötting's fingers were twitching so much he began to text, spattering predictive runes in the hope that some domestic crisis back in St Leonards would give him the excuse to pull out of the rest of the walk without losing face. He started rambling about the quality of blowjobs he had received in his alpha-male days as a *Being Kärnal* headbanger, supporting the Weather Girls at the Fridge in Brixton. Like having the marrow of your spine siphoned, he said, through a glass straw. He thought this had something to do with altitude: high-ceilinged rooms with big windows at the top of the hill, the upper reaches of Camberwell Grove.

The best advice, the Maudsley quacks reckoned, was: avoid being bitten. And sleep under mosquito nets. Kötting, I'm sure, had a set in his miracle pouch, along with energy bars, shards of rosy, sea-smoothed brick, crow feathers, comedy spectacles, a coverless copy of Beckett's *Happy Days*, and a slab of Kendal Mint Cake.

Mosquito madness was contagious. In January 1942 Heinrich Himmler gave the order for the creation of the Dachau Entomological Institute, with the covert intention of using mosquitoes as biological weapons. The protocols of the institute, ostensibly set up to find remedies against diseases transmitted by lice and other insects, allows no other conclusion. The master plan, never carried out, was to release malaria-infected insects into enemy territories.

Ruskin Park, with its wooded slopes, tennis courts, its outline like a dog's head (Disney's Goofy without the ears), belongs in a chain of soulful South London spaces, the captured gardens of grand houses offering relief from the endless grid of residential streets. In my first, confused days at film school in Brixton, I came on these green reservations with contained excitement: Brockwell Park, Tooting Bec Common, Streatham Common, Norwood Grove Recreation Ground. My attitude was provincial, a dawning recognition of the mysteries of gravel overlaying London clay. Maryon Park, downriver in Charlton, identified and exploited by Antonioni in *Blow-Up*, was the prime example of just such a site: a natural amphitheatre soliciting mime and ritual.

Even today, tramping with Kötting, we experience that sense of otherness, the way these parks invoke exiled French Impressionists in Norwood or Émile Zola wandering around Crystal Palace with a camera. The Overground tracks run between the northern border of the park and King's College Hospital. Paths and close-shaven slopes that seem deserted and outside time, on closer inspection are occupied by catatonic recreationalists on hard benches, and passerines on urgent diagonals, giving off powerful chemical signals: they are no danger. They are not sex-cruising, lurking, or itching to flash. They are going to work. Or railway station. Or hospital appointment. They are adequately medicated.

'All these big buildings,' Andrew says. 'It's an obligation to keep them supplied. Do your bit for the NHS Foundation Trust, fall out of a tree.'

John Ruskin, who lent his name to the park, lived on Denmark Hill. His parents, moving from Herne Hill, and holding firmly to the high ground, took the lease on a large, detached, ivy-smothered house in 1842. They were enthusiastic advocates of pre-railway suburbia. Ruskin promoted the new property as exemplifying 'dignity'; death's waiting room, a vantage point from which the old couple could stare with rheumy eyes out of their western windows into the captured darkness of the

noble cedar tree on the front lawn. John, commandeering the centre of the house for bedroom and study, woke each morning to inspect the latest formations of clouds, mingled with the democratic smoke of industry, over Deptford and Rotherhithe. A discipline he found 'inestimable for its aid in all healthy thought'. He draped his walls with a flush of Turners, including *Slavers Throwing overboard the Dead and Dying – Typhoon Coming On*. Lake District watercolours and refined topographical sketches imported a certain vision of England (depopulated, high-toned) indoors, elevating Ruskin's spirits and allowing the Oxford aesthete to congratulate himself on how swiftly an omnibus could carry him, by way of Vauxhall Road, from his Denmark Hill retreat to St James's Street and Cavendish Square.

We plunged, we dropped. The Overground got away from us. It was a long haul to Clapham High Street. Picking up the airs and graces of superior suburbia, high-ground halts like the hill stations of the British Raj around Simla, the railway declined to take on custom in low-caste Brixton. The whole diaspora of Brixton was station. The place was like a seething platform of hucksters, fast-food peddlers, jerk-chicken joints under bridges and pillars with sparking electrified cables.

Still under the influence of Ruskin, we failed to follow the railway string; we lost the Overground and blundered into Herne Hill, with its myths of stag-antlered forest gods. Herne the Hunter. Along the way, I noted Wellfit Street and a cash business soliciting copper, lead, brass, aluminium, electrical cable. White vans belonging to tribes we took for nocturnal railway strippers waited their turn to make a drop. No journey is worth undertaking, I told Kötting, without at least one fruitful detour. What is another three miles when set against unlooked-for discoveries?

Picking up our feet now in anticipation of a late lunch, we

arrived in Electric Avenue, Brixton. My original London. It wasn't quite a Proustian seizure. I should have been stepping down from the train, not dragging it behind me like an anchor tangled in gravestones. I remember, back in 1962, how the act of arriving here in wide-eyed innocence carried the imprint of a platform as exotic to me as New York City's Third Avenue El. You were, suddenly, without warning, above a street market, with its active press and squeeze and smell. But you were inoculated with resistant visions of Thames, council flats, green plots: the memory-film of the run out of Victoria Station.

I'm still reading Patrick Keiller's *The View from the Train*. Cinema for Keiller begins with the spectacle registered by a fixed camera on the Liverpool Overhead Railway, the first elevated electric railway in the world. There is no cutting away, it's a ride. A journey that runs for as long as the reel of film lasts; a ride that allows the sedentary traveller to experience shifting perspectives, numerous jolts and jumps of attention, incidents, revised alignments. A totality that Keiller associates with James Joyce's enraptured account of the city of Dublin in *Ulysses*, from sweep of bay at Kingstown, to bars, brothels and birthing places at the centre; to fat-frying basements, private schools, Martello towers, and cemeteries of the suburbs.

The poet Apollinaire, when he was still Wilhelm Kostrowicki, or Wilhelm de Kostrowitzky, visited Landor Road in Stockwell, a spit from the railway, in quest of a young woman called Annie Playden. 'The crowd moved about in all directions,' he wrote in 'L'Émigrant de Landor Road'. Kostro, as Annie called him, had proposed, when she was a governess in Germany, but she turned him down.

In May 1904, he caught the boat train from Paris Saint-Lazare to London Victoria. And on, it must be supposed, across the Thames. Annie was a big girl of firm opinions. An Apollinaire scholar tracked her down, in 1951, in the United States. So it was Annie who turned out to be the emigrant, not the poseur of the poem. 'Tomorrow my ship sails for America.' Apollinaire, wounded in the First War, died in 1918, on the day the Armistice was announced.

The writer James Campbell, like Keiller a committed retriever of the French in London, describes, in 'To London, for love', how he tracked down the addresses associated with Apollinaire, an Overground circuit of his own: from Oakley Crescent, off the City Road, to Chingford.

Campbell located an Apollinaire notebook that 'seemed to flash a momentary light on the cubist poet in Islington'.

retour à Angel
Tube en face poste
Demander Clapham Road
4d

Clapham Road Station is now Clapham North, right alongside the Overground. But not a stop. Train rides, with their voyeuristic glimpses, their enforced leisure, are a laboratory for the making of poems. Watch out for those notebooks, those iPads, those scribblers.

'And I shall never come back,' Apollinaire said. If you can take the word of a poet. I weakened. I relented. I did come back to the high, redbrick enigma of Electric Avenue. The curving, roofless arcade of foods and fancies between Brixton Road, the market and the station. A consciously modern street launched at the time of Jack the Ripper. Tall, narrow windows, two floors of them, reflect their twins on the far side, to recessive infinity. The butcher's shop, whose fatty reek saturated the linoleum stairs to the film school, was under new management: ZANA, QUALITY HALAL MEAT & FISH.

For me, Electric Avenue was the ideal starting point for half a century of London venturing. Cinema was doomed but not yet posthumous. Sublimated in train rides. Markets. Spicy lunches. Thump of sound: years before Eddy Grant's 1982 single carried the street's name right up the charts on both sides of the Atlantic. Atlantic Ocean, not Atlantic Road – which spilled into the notorious Railton Road; a battleground from the 1981 Brixton Riots, when more than 200 youths engaged with helmeted police foot patrols. A minicab was stopped and searched. Shops were mobbed and looted. A police van was set on fire. A street-specific local event, heated by festering resentment and mutual misunderstanding, escalated into guerrilla warfare, confirmed and exacerbated by newsreel crews looking for the image: urban apocalypse.

Atlantic Road is a conceit worthy of Apollinaire. A stone beach beside a thread of urban ocean. That's how it felt when I walked up the stairs of the film school. I arrived in the twilight of the first street market to be lit by electricity. There were canopies shading the shops. A walk to the door beside the butcher's slab was a daily experience of dropping into an invocation of Paris, the confidence to dress this arcade with manufactured light. Patrick Keiller places Electric Avenue on the route of one of his fictive pilgrimages in *London*, his documentary tribute to his years as a South London lodger.

Esther Leslie, in her 2013 book, *Derelicts: Thought Worms from the Wreckage*, has a photograph of Passage Choiseul in Paris from 1908 (twenty years after the construction of Electric Avenue). The passage is glassed over, but the commercial impulse is the same; a single spoke of a mercantile hub built for strolling. An anticipation of the much grosser Westfield supermall in Stratford. Which would be a fortress of commerce set *against* the city, rather than a seductive passageway through it. Leslie solicits Walter Benjamin. 'Benjamin writes of the arcades of Paris, as if he were writing of the labyrinth of the self, criss-crossed by paths made through encounters with others . . . The arcades are the stuff of recent history, but they have come to be experienced as ancient, once they – and the lives and relations they incubated – begin to pass into memory.'

The early promotional postcards of Electric Avenue have bulbs in trees, bedazzled windows, lights strung like stars from the canopies, but no pedestrians. Passage Choiseul, in 1908, is frozen: straw boaters of the men, a stopped regiment diminishing into the far distance, *all facing inwards, their backs to the windows.*

In April 1999, a man called David Copeland, crazed by his reading of the city, his fear of immigrants, miscegenation, homosexuals, his own impotence in the face of these challenges, placed a nail bomb in Brixton Road. He was hoping to ignite another riot. That old hunger for fire. That image-thirst. For sirens and helicopters. Burning buses. Torched warehouses. A market trader, sharp-eyed and wary of cameras, moved the suspect bag around the corner into Electric Avenue. The bomb detonated, injuring thirty-nine people. Copeland then shifted back across the river, and east, to position the next bomb in Brick Lane.

In my Electric Avenue days my inclination was to head north – Charing Cross Road, Camden Town, Belsize Park, Hampstead – chasing films, meeting friends in Soho coffee bars so uncomfortable in atmosphere they had probably been cursed by William Burroughs. It took a few months before I found Liverpool Street and the 149 bus to Dalston Junction and the Rio Cinema, for Joseph Losey's *The Criminal*. But even then I recognized a connection, crumbling civic pomposity and imported Marxist rhetoric, between the two proud 'loony left' boroughs, Hackney and Lambeth. Town Halls thumped down like monolithic bookends. Both boroughs were denied a direct

link with the Underground system, a punitive cultural prophy-
lactic. As if they were zones of contamination. Socialism might
be catching. Thatcher was not so much interested in abolishing
the Greater London Council as abolishing Lambeth and Hackney. In the meantime, it was enough to make it as difficult as
possible to get in and out of the renegade boroughs.

Angela Carter opens her final novel, *Wise Children*, with a
riff on 'two cities divided by a river'. Her ageing music-hall
twins are marooned in Brixton. 'The rich lived amidst pleasant
verdure in the North speedily whisked to exclusive shopping by
abundant public transport while the poor eked out miserable
existences in the South in circumstances of urban deprivation
condemned to wait for hours at windswept bus-stops . . .'
Carter's feisty old sisters, with their bittersweet Hollywood
memories, were not unaware of my film-school street: 'The
whirr and rattle of the trams, the lights of Electric Avenue
glowing like bad fish through a good old London fog.'

Hackney, flogging off Shoreditch landholdings, tearing down
Georgian properties for the benefit of development packages tied to Overground links, lifted the curse. They kept the
white temple of the former Town Hall as a photo op for
Saturday-afternoon weddings, while throwing up more glass
and steel than Stansted Airport for the new municipal offices.
Old, loud, close-packed markets were downgraded or destroyed
by overregulation, while farmers' markets and foodie extensions of Borough Market were promoted. The arrival of the
Overground, taking up tracks unused and allowed to rot in the
Thatcher period, signalled the political emasculation of Hackney and its rebirth as hip boomtown. House prices of terraces
condemned in the era of the tower blocks doubled, then tri-
pled, overnight. Locals, mesmerized by daily offers, couldn't
decide whether to stick or bust.

Brixton, we felt, although it was moving upward, was not

quite ready for Ginger Line dinner parties. There was a healthy dose of edge to the streets. This was still a parish infected by poetry and the lives of poets who came, perched, passed through, suffered incarceration. Many of the luminaries of the 1960s and 1970s paid their respects to Professor Eric Mottram in his Herne Hill house. Among them Allen Fisher, then a Brixton-based plastic-pipe salesman, later another peripatetic professor. Fisher's *Place*, a serial publication undertaken through fugitive presses, was an epic of local history, international conceptualism, conceived in the spirit of Charles Olson.

> before us a land lying waste
> not 1026 acres of pasture
> but a row of streets
> strung out in rhythm with the railway

Back in the day, I visited Fisher for a meal in his compact flat, up the hill, not far from Brixton windmill and the prison. There was not enough room for two couples to eat together. Our hosts went first, before our arrival. Then, if memory serves, we sat on a cleared patch of floor, at a low table, while Allen's partner brought out plates for their guests from across the river. As my wife recalls, the cooks perched on the top of the bookcases. Space was required for production. Allen was a painter and publisher and Fluxus artist as well as a poet. Books that had been exchanged with other writers piled up. And books for research. A slim poetry volume such as *Brixton Fractals* came with a five-page bibliography, running from Theodor Adorno's *Theses against Occultism* to Ya Zeldovich's *Giant Voids in the Universe*.

The flat was a beacon among the southern slopes, linked by tom-tom of electric typewriter, stencil cut, silkscreen chemicals, punch of stapler, with others of similar persuasion, in a network of anarchic cut-up urbanists. Or 'future exiles' as I called them, knowing they would have to leave town, pushed out in the early Thatcher years by rent hikes and diminishing employment opportunities. Poets are always the first redundancy. *Brixton Fractals*, a farewell to Lambeth, was published by Aloes Books in 1985. 'Brixton,' Fisher writes, 'is that part of southwest London extending south/north geohistographically from its prison and windmill down through the high road to the police station on one axis, and from the employment exchange to Coldharbour through the market to the Sunlight laundry factory east/west on another.'

Fractals are intended as a useful device: 'to sharpen out-of-focus photographs; to make maps of the radio sky; to generate images from human energy'. In the wake of riot. The dance of flame. The prismatic spectrum of petrol stains on shattered glass. In advance of civic disorder. And the tumultuous voodoo whispering and threatening down the rails of the Overground from Dalston Junction to Croydon. A conceptual railway system, showcasing virgin territory like an estate agent's CGI travelogue, is a three-dimensional extension of mobile phone technology. Inside the orange-flashed London Overground torpedo, they are all confirming, all tapping and stroking. *I'm coming. I'm delayed. You're there, are you? I'm here. We're stuck.*

'Steel wheels on steel rails,' Fisher said, 'run through the lounge.' Visible crime is street-easy, it confesses and asks what you are going to do about it. Police responses are more comfortable behind locked doors, vans and cells. It's a closed system with a long tradition, understood by both sides. It's ugly, yes, but it's a familiar ugliness, susceptible to translation into popular television. The angry boil of Fisher's map of crime is about to burst, to recalibrate, become fractal in the banking system. When you can see the ice sculptures of the City of London from the windmill on the hill, the pyramids and dildos and giant toasters, it's too late to do anything about it. 'The irrational State insists on control.'

Bill Griffiths, another terrifyingly prolific producer of texts, drawings, pamphlets, had connections with both Hackney and Lambeth. He spent time in Brixton Prison in his youth, after warrior days with Hell's Angels, the Harrow Roadrats. Bill rode a red Ducati.

When he heard the word 'Ducati', Andrew perked up. He had listened dutifully to my tales of poets, the more obscure (to his way of thinking) the better. Sometimes he accepted copies of their books. It washed over him. Motorbikes were another thing. He swept across Romney Marsh to his teaching duties in Canterbury like the spectre of T. E. Lawrence. The poetry of movement. He probably got served that stuff in school. Ted Hughes and Thom Gunn: foxes in the attic, leather boys on the roar.

I saw affinities between Kötting and Griffiths, the two bikers, in the way both men scored for multiple voices. Bill wrote about his Brixton incarceration in a rush of scorched phrases, broken police statements, hallucinated epiphanies. 'Like let someone ask you how Angels fight.' The prison is houses, rows of houses. 'They make a real noise they say is baiting of me.' The usual misunderstandings with authority over language, bureaucratic rictus against choke of breath. Warps and wraps of unreliable evidence. Taken down. Against the seizures of poetry that are the only true echoes of place itself. 'Smacking at my head And what / will i say to you court folk what can i say to you whos world it is.'

When I heard the soft-shouldered Griffiths, with his tattoos and biker's jacket, the beard at which he constantly scratched, read for this first time . . . *Reality*. He wheezed and sang, travelling a beat or so behind words fresh-minted and liberated from reflex usage. Jeff Nuttall spoke about Bill performing 'with the light hesitancy of a hunting thrush . . . His voice, grey with roll-ups, skips in a series of syllables and short gasps along his perfectly tuned lines.'

Griffiths moved in the same spontaneous and validated bird-skips across the territory, away from childhood Kingsbury, which he called 'Thatcherite London', to prefabs and anarchist squats in Whitechapel, to a narrowboat at Uxbridge (lost with his papers to fire), to Seaham Harbour, where he died in harsh poverty. At work. Engaged. Picking at origins of language: Old English, Norse, pitman dialects.

None of the poets are there now. Moved on, moved away. And I'm no longer present in these Brixton streets. A youthful intruder fading from photographs. I don't see myself on the flat roof at the back of the film school, with milkless coffee, yellow cigarettes, and the morning conversation of mature Dutch, Portuguese, Egyptian students; the only British male in the place. Afternoon witness to silent German epics by Fritz Lang. We are offered no film stock, outdated or otherwise, to record our visions of place. *I am another.* Brixton stranger. Bus passenger. Regular patron, after a short walk to Stockwell, of the Northern Line.

The twin sisters, Dora and Nora Chance, dancers, soubrettes, of Angela Carter's *Wise Children*, are old Brixton personified: resting actors behind every privet hedge, successful comedians shoring up rental property against the inevitable turn of the tide. 'Brixton, before the lights went out over Europe, hub of a wheel of theatres, music halls, Empires, Royalties, what have you. You could tram it all over from Brixton.' Tall, narrow houses stuffed, as Carter has it, with goats, dancing dwarves, the wanted and unwanted regiments of switched-off performers. And legitimates who 'considered themselves a cut above'.

After a big night in Croydon, loss of virginity, first tacit acknowledgement from famous thespian dad, Dora doesn't take the tram (the whispering remnant of which has been brought back to the town centre as a symbol of regeneration). She cabs it home. And stops at the top of Brixton Hill to walk. Only walking will do it. 'The sky was the colour of a gas jet.'

Dora's descendants are out there now, among us, on the orbital walk. Smart girls, hard-shelled, making the best of it, setting the style by copying whatever they fancy, striding out. And the old ladies too, slightly skewed, one heel shorter than the other. They're fine in Streatham, on Brixton Hill, in Atlantic Road market, but they keep away from the tracks. 'It's never the same,' Carter writes. 'Even the railway stations, changed out of recognition, turned into souks. Waterloo. Victoria. Nowhere you can get a decent cup of tea, all they give you is Harvey Wallbangers, filthy cappuccino. Stocking shops and knicker outlets everywhere you look.'

It's a boost to be among a thrash of walkers whose sudden swerves are impossible to predict. They flinch away, some of them, from unsanctioned meats, others from brands of butchered orthodoxy of which they disapprove. There are even those, Carter tells us, who cross the street if they notice a florist; fingers in ears to mute the scream of cut daffs. Back-parlour naturists awkward in layers of outdoor black.

And then there are no pedestrians; greasepaint Brixton, chummy and herbal, with an undertow of justified resentment, morphs into narcoleptic midday Stockwell. Hanging on to the railway brings us down Ferndale Road towards Clapham North, where the Overground does not halt, and Clapham High Street, where it does: a generous splash of orange on old yellow brick.

Now there are only the ghosts of earlier Stockwell walkers, European lodgers who misread the signals from the landlady's daughter. Apollinaire returning to Landor Road. Vincent Van Gogh, polishing his top hat, to stride out from 87 Hackford

Road to his employment with the art dealers, Goupil & Co, in Covent Garden.

Clapham High Street has come on us before we are ready for it. Another urban village, well stocked with overspill of Pimlico and Chelsea, looking with yearning across the river. A knot of politicians finding Clapham convenient for the House. For late, boozy dining. And, in some cases, nocturnal adventures among the pick-ups on the Common. This triangle, bordered on all sides by streams of agitated traffic, has never had much appeal for me. Or for Kötting – who is running low on anecdotes, a long way from Deptford, stomach rumbling with mustard-basted panini, and getting ready for the next hit.

I tried him with an account of my visit to John Bellany's house on the north side of the Common, when I wanted permission to use his painting *Time and the Raven* on the cover of my first novel. Early Bellany, fuelled by Calvinist folk memory, Port Seton fishermen, bloody labour, and a good hard stare at Max Beckmann, was primal. A slopping, seething bouillabaisse of tentacles, octopus crucifixions, love's claw, bible-black Munch wakes, wax suns, scarlet dagger tongues, pelican beaks, seagulls and accordions. Drink was part of it. His liver was shot, but not yet replaced. There was a yellow tinge to his eye. The stacked paintings had the DTs. They hallucinated a retched vision of the history of European art. They reeked of turps and fish oil. It was like opening a smokehouse of eels and kippers inside an immaculate Clapham Common villa.

Jock McFadyen had a story about the two of them, Scots boys, out on the Serpentine in a rowing boat, after some art opening, whisky bottles clinking in coat pockets, drifting in circles. He thought Bellany looked like death. Brian Catling, in his days on the art-school circuit, remembers John, liquid-lunched, fired up, grabbing him by the lapels and thumping him against the wall, ordering him to *do it*, make the work, bugger the rest. Painting and drinking: life.

Time and the Raven. The bird's predatory beak. The stopped clock. The operatic gush and spill of brothel red. The suicide of Juliet, Bellany's second wife. The version I used on my book was a watercolour, a swift recapitulation of the oil-on-canvas version from 1982. It's a hard painting to live beside. I told Bellany how his work fed, in a way I didn't really understand, into the last section of my novel, the funeral of Sir William Gull. How the royal surgeon stands on a hill watching the procession carry his coffin to the churchyard at Thorpe-le-Soken. Maybe that name, Gull, was the link. Or some residual Scottishness on my part. A rip in the direction of Nordic expressionism.

'I can see the man walk out of the woman. Voiceless, steps on to a beach of tongues, live fish . . . When the double departs, there are only three days to live,' I quoted.

'Aye, aye,' he said, cutting me off. I was telling him something he knew. He got all that without having to read it. 'Oh aye.' And he turned away. Back into the art mob of the coming Hackney, warehouse as gallery.

Bellany's success at that time was marked by the move to Clapham, this house, and by the way he dressed, white deck shoes and cableknit cricket sweater. He's sporting it in the portrait by Lord Snowdon. I don't know if it was a gift from Ian Botham, but it has the same colours at neck and cuffs as the stout figure in the painting. This strange and unbalanced account of the cricketing hero, a National Portrait Gallery commission painted at the house of Tim Hudson, Botham's rock-star agent, was in evidence, resting on an easel in the Clapham studio. Like subsequent celebrity portraits undertaken by Bellany, such as the wild stab at Sean Connery, the head is too small, propped on a solid body, as if shrunken or boiled in a bag. Like an alcoholic potato balanced on a sack of grain. Botham admired the intensity with which the portraitist studied his prey. It was just the way he himself sized up a batsman, probing for weakness. The sweater, I surmise, bears the colours of Hudson's private cricket ground.

Reacquainted with the Overground, stations appear at regular intervals. It has been said that Clapham experienced a social dip in the late nineteenth century, when public transport made the village more accessible. The grander houses around the Common were nudged by terraces thrown up to lodge the common man. The broad avenues, as we head north towards Wandsworth Road, are having none of it: they speak of established settlement, sustained property values. A nodding relationship with a sunken railway that has been adequately screened.

There is a spectacular mansion at the bottom of Brayburne Avenue, right beside Wandsworth Road Station. Paint is peeling; it might have been close to ginger once, laid over many coats of rusty brown. Odd windows. Single chimney stack, off to the side. Dutch roof, tiled. It's not a ruin, but it hankers after that status, a lurch into the Gothic.

Kötting scowls. He props himself on a convenient bin – before trapping a flustered woman on her way up the steps. She is gripping the ginger rails with scarlet talons, wrestling with knapsack and laptop and wheelie case. In no mood for ordinary madmen: survey-taking clipboarders, charity muggers, religious hit squads.

'Are you a Ginger Liner?' Andrew bellowed.

'I'm sorry . . . ?'

'The Overground.'

'Oh, the bloody Overground! Its very existence means I can no longer travel from Wandsworth Road, one minute and thirty seconds from my front door, to Victoria. The journey to work used to take me seven minutes. And there was, you know,

95

a lovely pre-Beeching feel about the service: two carriages, twice an hour, from a station with no ticket office which one approached up a slope with a glorious shrub-filled flowerbed to one side. The drivers used to wait for you if they saw you running. And now . . .'

She gestures at the orange-tipped stairs, the matching stair rails like a walking frame for legless heroes.

'Give me your petition, I'll sign. The only way to get to Victoria by Overground is to go in completely the opposite direction and change at Clapham Junction. Honestly!'

'Anywhere around here for a decent Scotch egg?'

It was a weary trawl to Clapham Junction. The Overground attempted a sharp left, declining to cross the river to Victoria as the irate traveller required, and keeping its distance from Wandsworth Road and Lavender Hill, in favour of a dullish passage through storage facilities, metal mountains, aggregate alps, allotment strips with tumbledown sheds and roofs held in place with tyres. There were hidden yards stacked with caravans and modest railway terraces. Helicopters from Barclays London Heliport at Battersea clattered overhead, sky-rickshaws for impatient commuters.

The branded aerial taxis followed a prescribed figure-of-eight circuit at around 1,000 feet, seeking, so they said, to avoid noise pollution (and a degree of shake) for owners of new flats in blocks that were bursting forth along the Thames. The connection with Clapham Junction, however unlikely, is flagged up. It struck us that low-flying helicopters were not compatible with the dense forest of ever-taller construction cranes. A morbid prediction brought into the headlines on 16 January 2013, when a helicopter, diverting to Battersea in bad weather, clipped a crane on St George Wharf Tower and bombed into Wandsworth Road, not too far from where we were now walking, and closer still to the MI6 fortress designed by Terry Farrell at Vauxhall. One man died, nine others were injured, as the helicopter became a fireball, a few yards from where Wandsworth Road ducked under the railway.

Chloe Dooknah, a nineteen-year-old witness, said: 'There was metal flying everywhere. It narrowly missed a train that was going over the bridge. The whole road was on fire, people were screaming and lots of people were trying to help.'

The helicopter pilot, Peter Barnes, was a trained ski instructor who had moved on to the advertising industry. A sketchy newspaper biography that has the smack of J. G. Ballard's *Millennium People*. Barnes was employed as a pilot by the organizers of the 2012 Olympics, where numerous flights were made transporting dignitaries over the site and rehearsing Danny Boyle's big night. The chopper ace ferried David Cameron, the Dalai Lama and Simon Cowell. He worked on a number of films, including Spielberg's *Saving Private Ryan* and the last James Bond vehicle to star Pierce Brosnan, *Die Another Day*. The previous Brosnan Bond, *The World is Not Enough*, showcased a sequence launched with exploding money at the MI6 building in Vauxhall and registering a powerboat sweep downriver to the Millennium Dome. Here was a high-concept promotional travelogue for the new London involving the usual helicopter footage (otherwise known as 'surveillance').

At this point, we go with the flow. A little slower now, I drag my feet and trip over invisible obstacles. Kötting headbutts persons who are not there, not blocking his way. He makes those urgent *whah whah* sounds boxers with broken noses let out at the end of a session on the heavy bag. There are florists, hairdressers, cafés, restaurants, but we don't want to stop, everything is pouring into the long-established hub of Clapham Junction Station. The theoretical halfway point in

our journey. If we were on the Overground, we would have to change platforms. And look out for the spectre of Oscar Wilde, jeered at by the mob, while he waited for the connection to hard labour in Reading Gaol.

Lavender Hill invokes the London of market gardens and lavender beds. Catherine, William Blake's wife, came from a family who worked this land. But despite Andrew's best efforts there is not much of an Ealing comedy, no *Lavender Hill Mob* high jinks, about our progress, until we discover a fancy junk-shop with a few books out front. Nothing I want to carry away, especially not one of my own from the give-away rack. Andrew pounces, demands a signature, and goes into the full routine.

'This man is a writer. He says he wrote this book all by him-self and now he's scribbled in it, so you have to give it the treatment. Go on, put it in a bag. That's a pretty colour. Now put it in the window. Are you gay?'

The shop flagged up a certain shift in social indicators. Kötting preened, in the way that David Hemmings congratulates himself, in *Blow-Up*, on discovering a little antiques place with a wooden propeller alongside Maryon Park, on the fringes of Woolwich. Wandsworth Road was shrugging against the traffic, against smacked-out pubs with English flags instead of windows; carbonized burger pits, potted palm trees choking on diesel fumes. The modest gradient towards Lavender Hill teased out restaurants with Parisian ambitions. And new names every season. Screens of bamboo and a thick-tongued plant to screen off the cars.

'This man's sources are innumerable,' Kötting said, pressing the willowy dealer in the Dr Who scarf back on his velvet throne. 'His erudition is profound. And, truth to tell, a mite tedious. He does not mince his words. They slide out of him. Do you have a chocolate biscuit to hand?'

I was backing towards the door, navigating by blind touch through cases and cabinets and overloaded shelves of unwanted stuff. The smell of unsuccessful resurrection, weak grass, joss sticks, shedding fox fur, brutal furniture polish, made me claustrophobic. I flicked through the pavement books again while Andrew crunched digestives and made friends.

'I had a donkey who was gay in France. I don't know what he was like in England. He choked on one of my socks.'

The book Kötting bought, to reward the dealer for his tolerance and biscuits, was a paperback by Bruce Chatwin. *What am I Doing Here?* A collection of essays and travel bits. I flicked through it. 'Man's real home is not a house, but the Road and how life itself is a journey to be walked on foot.' I thought the capitalization of 'Road' was a little pretentious.

The Fourth Guest at the Table

We crossed over the river to the other side. The river lies between
Brixton and glamour like a sword . . . Comedy is tragedy that
happens to other people . . . Memory Lane is a dead end . . . Why
don't you sell it to that library in Texas?

– Angela Carter

Our trudge along the length of Wandsworth Road towards
Lavender Hill brought back Thursdays in summer when I
packed the car with boxes of books, unsold stock, folding
shelves, old rugs, and drove down, as soon as the market was
over in Islington, to play cricket on the common, right opposite Wandsworth Prison. I was a ringer in a team of architects
who were then going through a bit of a dip between generic
municipal projects and the coming revival of the City, the push
of Docklands. The upper echelons were around for several
seasons; junior draughtsmen and site managers were culled. A
sabbatical Aussie might be pressed straight into service: confident boasts, fancy cap, modest performance. A Jamaican social
worker from Brixton shared the donkey work with me: he put
the frighteners on, pacey and erratic on unpredictable surfaces,
while I trundled in with a frowning Angus Fraser predictability.
Then we gave it a cheery bang in the twilight.

There was a condition these cricketers, working up a thirst
with a bout of eccentric Twenty20, shared with architects in
Ballard novels: they had no interest whatsoever in architecture,

never mentioned it, beyond the grudge of office politics. They were, for the most part, men of the suburbs. My fellow sportsmen, unlike Ballard's deracinated professionals, never dreamed of firebombing video stores or crashing cars on the Westway.

The drive down Wandsworth Road got slower every year, certain checkpoints monitored my progress: Lambeth Palace, Lord Archer's penthouse, the MI6 building at Vauxhall Cross, Battersea Arts Centre, the Arding and Hobbs Department Store with its 'landmark cupola', Clapham Junction Station. And the side road with the house where I visited Angela Carter.

I pointed this out to Kötting as we passed, but he was engaged in attempting to describe the particular smell of the Bruce Chatwin paperback he'd acquired.

'What is it? You're a bookman, book-bibbler, word-dribbler. Confabulator. Have a sniff.'

He sneezed.

He said that he thought the book was just the right size to block a crack under the door of the hut he'd built inside the sailmakers' loft he used for a communal studio in Hastings. It was cold in winter. In his swan-encrusted cardigan. And his seasonal stubble, hoar-frosted, chiming when he scratched. Eggshell and breadcrumbs spiked around his blistered lips until the spring thaw.

The Chase. That was the name of the road. Right-hand side, I remember, running up to Clapham Common, closer to Wandsworth Road Station than Clapham Junction. A friendly basement kitchen. Sitting down there, among kites and painted plates and cookbooks, with large mugs of tea. Angela Carter was amused, a plosive cackler, swaying and nodding her approval, from somewhere inside an abundance of thick grey hair. I'd come to take away some of the books. She had multiples of *The Infernal Desire Machines of Doctor Hoffman*, and she was happy to sign them at her kitchen table. I was very new, then, to paid publication and had weird assumptions about the relationship between publishers, authors and the backlist.

Imagine. First editions from 1972 in mint condition, signed by author, brought to a book fair and released in strictly limited quantities, so as not to flood the market. In the author photograph, Carter's head is on the tilt, studio trapped. She is carefully made up, unsmiling, with wide-spaced eyes and short, curled and premeditated barnet.

I first came across Angela Carter, as a poet, in 1963. She achieved a 'recommended' status in a stapled mimeo student magazine published out of Leeds. Her poem was better than that, formally and in substance, ripe with the catalogue of surreal detritus that would make its reappearance in the junkshop of her first novel, *Shadow Dance*, which was published in a shocking-pink dustwrapper in 1966. With supporting quote from Anthony Burgess: 'A capacity for looking at the mess of contemporary life totally without flinching.' The mimeo poem listed: 'a selection of plastic-ray-guns and space-helmets with flashing lights on top' and 'a mechanical monkey which played the xylophone and excreted water'. The poem's sophistication is way ahead of the more obvious prizewinners. 'Angela Carter is completely new to us. She is a student at Bristol University. Her letter was funny too.' Bristol, the editors remark, is a hive of potential poets, devouring the ephemeral magazine as soon as it reaches them and hammering out entries for competitions.

Carter, newly married, poses with cat on lap, in rocking chair, for the author photo of *Shadow Dance*. She chose to give up her work as a reporter on a provincial newspaper and moved with her husband to Bristol, where she read English. Bristol was the right place, trading in long-established bohemia, the utopian dreams of Samuel Taylor Coleridge, Robert Southey and the Pantisocrats – and pioneer nitrous oxide gas sniffers like Humphry Davy and Thomas Beddoes at the Pneumatic Institute in Clifton. The geography was right, with the gorge, the wells, the stately terraces. And the social and industrial history of docks, cigarette factory, zoo. Substantial wealth was generated by the slave trade. This was just the kind of place, in later times, for the Blairs to invest in property.

The poet Charles Tomlinson, at the university, helped turn eyes towards America. There was a scene. Certain bars and cafés were favoured. Old houses crumbling or multiple-occupied fed congeries of junkshops. Carter's author notes, for her first Bristol novel, confess that she plays the English concertina 'and collects Victorian rubbish'. There were leather-jacket poets around, folk musicians holding court, and figures of local interest like the sculptor Barry Flanagan. Soon the Carshalton émigré Chris Torrance would be assembling materials for his first book of poetry, and cutting grass in parks and commons and drinking wine on Brandon Hill. Bristol favoured days on the drift, sunflowers dying in sunless yards. A good city for dope smokers with a head for heights. Angela Carter is fastidious in her notice of all categories of human stain on fancy-dress uniforms in yellow satin. Those who wash too often and those who live for years in one set of clothes.

In my discriminate scavenging of South Coast book pits and doggy-damp upstairs chambers in Norwich and private back rooms in Bury St Edmunds, I came upon most of Carter's novels, her stories. I kept examples of all of them and parted with duplicates.

Out of my usual territory, and coming home, after a hunt through the rubbish spread under the flyover at the rough end of Portobello Road, I noticed that Angela Carter and Elaine Feinstein were signing books from a new imprint in a neighbourhood shop. They were launching Next Editions, a stiff-card series, spiral bound, marrying text and illustration. There was a

Notting Hill flavour to the enterprise, fired by Emma Tennant, and featuring a selection of her former lovers, including J. G. Ballard and Ted Hughes. And the local sprite, spirit of place, Heathcote Williams. Who was famous for a failed levitation act. And infamous, according to Mike Moorcock, for painting Mike's phone number on walls around the area, after Moorcock broke off his affair with Tennant. She hurled every potted plant given to her by Ballard on to the front path of the property she owned on Blenheim Crescent, where Moorcock rented his overstocked flat.

In her memoir, *Burnt Diaries*, Tennant writes about how, when she was involved with an earlier magazine, she wanted, 'most importantly', to find Angela Carter, whose 'extraordinary, scented prose' she had encountered when browsing in the basement of Better Books in Charing Cross Road. Carter delivers, like musk or some hallucinogenic secretion, the words that Tennant aches to achieve. The two women meet and become friends. There are garden parties, crowded thrashes in a Tennant yard.

'Angela's fascination is so great that it doesn't matter how long one has to wait for the tentatively begun sentence – this broken into by the chisel of high laughter, or the power-drill of an indrawn breath, for she is as amused as any by the kaleidoscope of thought processes which interrupt the consummation of her sentence.'

The interconnections here, through place, patronage, magazines, dinners, meld together some of the best writers of the period: Ballard glances off Angus Wilson, Moorcock seeks out Burroughs and Borges. There is an attempt, before London Overground circuits and orbital motorways, to form a hub, a new vortex; fertile ground where the charting of inner and outer can begin.

Ballard arrives in a white suit and shades carrying maps. 'He is one of those rare beings,' Carter says, 'who talk in grammatically correct sentences.' Emma Tennant, meeting Ted Hughes, thinks of an Easter Island statue. 'I am against my better judgement reminded of Angela [Carter] and her passion for wolves, for hairy men who will suffocate her with their embrace. Has Angela . . . I wonder . . . and it comes to me that she said a few months back when I spoke of Hughes's sudden nocturnal visit to my basement kitchen that there had been "something" between them.'

When *Black Venus's Tale*, the book that Carter will be signing in the Notting Hill bookshop, was being solicited by Emma Tennant, the editor took her potential author to lunch at a restaurant called Thompsons. Tennant reports, in her diary, talk of Baudelaire and Jeanne Duval: 'silence filled with half-thoughts'. Philip Roth emerges from the shadows to congratulate Carter on *The Sadeian Woman*. 'Angela's flaming cheeks evincing the mixed feelings a compliment from such a quarter must provoke.'

There was, as yet, no queue in the shop. I was free to mumble my own compliments and to receive an inscription in my book, signed with a characteristic squiggle of wavelets beneath the author's name. Angela was, after all, born in Eastbourne, smelling the English Channel. Her mother, also a mythmaker, said that she had her pregnancy confirmed on the day war was declared. I felt a distant kinship; Angela was three years older than me, the age of my sister who died as a baby. Her father was Scottish. And there was time spent, escaping the London bombing, with mining relatives, on her mother's side, in the Yorkshire coalfield. The name on her birth certificate was Stalker. Which set the tone for much that followed. Tarkovsky made to dance through the ruins.

The period around the time of the publication of *Shadow Dance*, Carter's 1966 novel, produced a flush of picaresque, oddball tales of seedy-suburban and off-season-coastal-resort lives. Stories by young women with black stockings and panda eyes who turned up in publishers' offices with unexploded typescripts. And angular, challenging ways of sitting and not speaking. And who wouldn't go away. Or were they just good writers, with certain tastes in common: European cinema, English Gothic, fairground surrealism, narcoleptic pubs, marionettes, sour locked-in daddy males and Byronic peacock boys in velvet flares and dark glasses, like premature avatars of Michael Moorcock's Jerry Cornelius?

Ann Quin's *Berg* (1964). Shena Mackay's *Dust Falls on Eugene Schlumberger* (1964). Rosemary Tonks with *Opium Fogs* (1963). Things did not always go well for these novelists. They were no sisterhood. The terrain was mildewed: communal bathrooms, sinister cats, burnt food, weak tea, weaker booze, show-off clothes, incest, murder. Austerity England was given the treatment: attitude, colour, a ripening of the senses. 'All this sitting about in cafés to calm down / Simply wears me out' Tonks wrote in her poem 'The Sofas, Fogs and Cinemas'. Ann Quin, whose books are now reissued by the Dalkey Archive Press, was sidelined in England as an 'experimentalist'. The experiment being to write off-balance novels seriously. She swam out from Brighton Pier in 1973 and drowned herself. Tonks, shortly after this, vanished from sight into rumours of a conversion to Fundamentalist Christianity. She lived privately, spurning contact from family and friends, taking no calls. Shena Mackay carried on and by 1992 achieved wide recognition with *Dunedin*. Angela Carter persevered and thrived: Germanic forests, urban shamanism, post-feminist polemics, memoirs, films, fashion and food.

Behind those feisty novels of the 1960s, I registered the necromancy of Muriel Spark and *The Ballad of Peckham Rye*. A steady pressure of intent in conjuring with fate in drowsy, unsuspecting places. Allotment sheds and unlit windows seen from suburban trains. The arrival of some devilish outsider. And Spark's sprightly, sardonic tone. 'The Rye for an instant looking like a cloud of green and gold, the people seeming to ride upon it, as you might say there was another world than this.'

I knew about the next Carter signing in advance. I came prepared with the classic shopping bag of first editions. Forbidden Planet, specialists in science fiction, comics and associated ephemera, geek stuff, were then in Denmark Street, 'Tin Pan Alley'; queues for signings by cult figures like Moorcock could run round the corner into Charing Cross Road. Angela Carter, being literary and independent, didn't quite fit in the boys' world of the bagmen collectors. Forbidden Planet set her up as part of a double-header session and it was modestly attended. But she did much better than when Alan Moore arranged my first attempt at such a thing before a reading I was supposed to give in a Templar church in Northampton. Nobody came, not one book sold. I was with Paladin at that time and acting as a theoretical poetry editor. 'Why don't we have any poetry in the shop?' I asked the local rep. 'Do we publish poetry then?' he said. 'Amazing what gets out these days.'

What hit me, when I put the embellished books back on the shelf – Carter tucked in, comfortably, between Djuna Barnes and L.-F. Céline – was the sequence of image changes in the author photos. Author as performer. As starlet in a cinema of self. A graphic autobiography above a growing list of works and awards.

Shadow Dance: profile in long shot. Rocking chair like Russian sledge. And the monster cat I mistook for a baby. Carter's expression is wary. Everything behind her is on the tilt. As if the house were caught at the start of an earthquake. With the white wall, the chair, the picture, the girl, the reference to a still from Jean-Luc Godard is evident.

Some writers let the same portrait run for decades. Others work their way up to a session with Jerry Bauer. Carter re-presents herself every time: new book, new woman. The second novel, *The Magic Toyshop* (1967), has a severe, turtle-neck, close-cropped look. Dark helmet of Sorbonne hair and the passport strain of trying not to blink. Asked about herself, Carter says, 'I'm fond of cats.'

Can it be the same woman on the back of *Several Perceptions* (1968)? Left profile, big Wyndham Lewis hat, spectacles. Bloomsbury fierce. Watch out, boys.

Heroes & Villains (1969). Thinner face. Wire specs. Combat jacket with epaulettes. Feminist communard. By way of Porto-bello Market. Maoist-period Godard.

Love (1971). Womanly. Mock formal. Studio. Carter describes this novel 'as a tragedy of contemporary manners'.

And so on to Fay Godwin (if it's not Jerry Bauer, it's Fay). *The Bloody Chamber* (1979). The real person – performed – at last. Generous lips, smiling. A garden. A captured moment in a conversation between two women.

For *Nights at the Circus* (1984), Carter is again mid-sentence, stopped in the mode of hesitation Emma Tennant describes. Serious comedy specs and a conspiratorial smile. Hair straight and running free.

In the portrait for *Wise Children* (1991), the hair is now grey. This is the last novel. Later publications, *Expletives Deleted* (1992) and the rest, are posthumous. The Tara Heinemann author photo runs on. For *Burning Your Boats* (1995) there is a smiling, hurt-eyed variant with copious swathes of hair.

I met Carter, with the opportunity for a different kind of conversation, at a party for the *Guardian* Fiction Prize in 1988.

She was on an upper level, among excited courtiers and ten-percenters, a silver-maned Gloriana. Beryl Bainbridge, in a little black dress, smoked to something less than essence, clinked on the next perch. So brittle you could flick her with your nail and she would ring like Waterford crystal. They were as necessary to the occasion as the Chance sisters in *Wise Children*. No literary gathering would be complete without one or both.

Angela made a gracious descent into the pit. She really did feel like the godmother for a better class of subversive writing. Through her late novels, I saw our city as a beautiful monster, a mythical being as deformed, heavy-bodied, flighty, vulnerable as her swan-winged *aerialiste* Fevvers. Carter wrote of Michael Moorcock's imagination as 'a vast, uncorseted, senti-mental, comic, elegiac salmagundy . . . so deeply within a certain tradition of English writing, indeed, of English popular culture, that it feels foreign'. She could have been describing herself, books like *Nights at the Circus* and *Wise Children*. Moor-cock and Carter, South Londoners both, and world-travellers too, ran the newsreel of history back to music hall, through war traumas and the tricks and feints of bureaucrats and bul-lies. There was an absolute respect for working lives, an autodidactic love of Shakespeare and the English classics, with no pious whispers in the pews or bowing to established dogma.

I was walking with Moorcock one time when we came, from the north, unexpectedly, mid-conversation, upon West-minster Bridge. He froze. I had a car parked on the other side in Lambeth. I'd have to fetch it and return to pick him up. He would not cross the Thames; it was a kind of death. And yet he writes with tender exasperation of his childhood in Norbury. Maybe that's it: the memory-place should remain fixed. The attitude to the great sprawl of the metropolis is verging on Oedipal: *Mother London* for Moorcock and *Wise*

Children for Carter. 'Nothing could be more magical than the real fabric of the city,' says Carter, defending Moorcock's brand of myth-making. 'He takes you on a grand tour of the forgotten, neglected parts of London, as far as Mitcham in the South, but always coming back to W11.'

Angela had no transpontine qualms. She made the required visits to W11, but she lived and worked in Clapham. She died too soon, much too soon, to partake of the imposed psychogeography of the Overground. It might have inspired new fictions, stories of Honour Oak Park, Shadwell, Kensal Rise. Her game old ladies, the twin Brixton troopers from *Wise Children*, made play with trams and buses and taxis. On special moonlit nights, they walked. Transport systems incubate different forms of writing: the babble of double-deckers shunting to hospitals, or late-night suburbs, with chemical aggravation. And sudden Jacobean assaults. All the action played out in real time on monitor screens like gallery installations. Trains incline to reverie, Keiller meditations on housing and decaying industrial stock. The bass telltale throb of a cab pricks sexual fantasy, pre- or post-coital, a sealed-off interlude of unearned respite, under the eyes of the voyeur, with his running commentary, as he watches you in the driving mirror.

A taste of what Carter might have brought to the poetry of London Overground can be got from *Nights at the Circus*. Her changeling superstar, Fevvers, buys 'one of those nice big houses off Lavender Hill' for the family. Escaping from a sacrificial encounter with a hellfire occultist, and still naked, she makes her way home from the country. 'Then I went from covert to covert, always concealing myself, until I came to the railway line and borrowed a ride off a load of freight . . . for I needed the railway to guide me back to London. To my delight, the train soon steamed through Clapham Junction and I nipped out just by Battersea Park, to make my way with all speed through the empty dark up the Queenstown Road ducking behind the privet hedges as I went until I got at last happily home.'

To The Chase. To the home where stories are cooked. To the kitchen table, and the kites and plates and retrieved junk-shop bits, and photographs. Angela should have, but doesn't need, visible wings. She already possessed the spirit, the energy. The words, when she's on a run, take flight. It's like the technique William Burroughs describes of trying to hit the shutter of a camera at the instant that allows you to photograph the future. You're not freezing anything. You are anticipating a pre-ordained set of circumstances. Preordained, pre-written: found footage of possession.

As I lift my mug at the Clapham kitchen table, in that basement of chosen objects, it strikes me that the room is an extension of all the fabulous Carter sets, the kitchens in her books. And now, years later, going back on my incomplete memory-film of that afternoon when I took tea in her house, I realize that the Wandsworth Road junkshop where Andrew Kötting picked up his Bruce Chatwin draught excluder belongs with the junkshops of Carter's novels. Metaphors are promiscuous. They leak and spill. There is no way we can walk around the collar of the Overground without animating latent fictions, hitting invisible tripwires, downloading poems we have never read.

It was perceptive, and ahead of the game, dowsing the state of early Thatcherite London, the time of the strong woman, to call a novel *Nights at the Circus*. The Thames riverbank would, in a few years, become a circus, with Ferris wheel, chair-lift rides, millennial (discon)tent on the East Greenwich swamps, and a shockheaded mayor as public clown, swinging from wires or falling off a trick bicycle.

After the *Guardian* Prize affair, the luminaries of the publishing world, the nicotine ghosts, Russian cultural attaché, William

Golding, honourable Grub Street irregulars, Angela invited me down to Clapham to buy a few books. That was still my trade, but I was beginning to venture in fiction.

We talked. Even Carter, with her status assured, entrained, at regular intervals, to a job in the creative-writing factory in Norwich. She shouldered, I feel sure, more of the grind than was strictly necessary. Her attitude was playful and undeceived about the ultimate value of such exercises: the real writers would write whatever. She gave value for money, listening, encouraging, demonstrating, distributing proper levels of cynicism.

She took off with her man, whenever they could, to a narrowboat. I think she said it was parked in Camden, somewhere near London Zoo. Did she lie in her tight bed listening to the lions and the shrieking birds?

Carter went upstairs to the reserve collection and brought down a bunch of pristine copies of her unsold but desirable stock. It took me time to appreciate that items highly prized by collectors, who had few dealings with the everyday world, meant nothing to the publishing industry. Often a single fanatic could sustain a reputation and keep prices buoyant, as traders scramble to buy from each other, all the way up the food chain. Along with the bag of Hart-Davis titles, *Love* and *The Infernal Desire Machines of Doctor Hoffman*, Carter threw in some early Ian McEwen items and a couple of others from the UEA hothouse. She was never, she implied, going to return to those pages. A boy on the make, McEwen didn't need her blessing. Which is just as it should be.

Then a Norwich friend, the academic and fellow writer Lorna Sage, arrived. The kitchen conference was unbalanced around the gossip they wanted and the single empty chair. I thought of a phrase of Carter's I'd read in one of the late books: 'the fourth guest at the table'. The absence, the Banquo space that is cousin to Eliot's 'third who always walks beside you'. Mortality. Shadow dance. 'Those who sit in the style of contentment, meaning / Death.'

For my transition, like a slow fade never fully accomplished, from bookdealer to author, Angela Carter was the white witch, invaluable in her support. Providing quotations for dustwrappers. Talking to editors. Writing a substantial piece for the *London Review of Books* on *Downriver*. It launched me by bringing a fresh eye to territory then unfamiliar to most of the scattered literary and academic community (those who had not yet bought into Hackney, Bethnal Green, Limehouse, Leytonstone). The essay starts with an ascent from the Underworld, Eurydice in Whitechapel. 'This reviewer is a South Londoner, herself. When I cross the river, the sword that divides me from pleasure and money, I go North. That is, I take the Northern Line "up West", as we say: that is, to the West End. My London consists of all the stations on the Northern Line, but don't think I scare easily . . . Nothing between Morden and Camden Town holds terror for me.'

Carter, like my earlier film-student self in Brixton, functioned along the black vine of the Underground system, the Northern Line – which suffered from one drawback: fall asleep and you are in High Barnet or Edgware, one of those remote places now supplied by Tesco and Waitrose vans, allowing commuters to order online and never have to venture into a supermarket again. Shopping as a travel accessory.

'To enter, Orpheus-like,' Carter writes at the end of her first novel, 'the shadowed regions of death.' To enter Whitechapel, with its dark history, its toughness, as she comes up out of the tube at Aldgate East on one of her expeditions to Freedom Bookshop in Angel Alley. The bookshop is closed. 'I felt quite the country bumpkin, slow-moving, slow-witted, come in from the pastoral world of Clapham Common, Brockwell Park, Tooting Bec . . . It was an older London, by far, than mine . . . I smelled danger . . . I was scared shitless the first time I went to the East End.'

London Overground, transporting Clapham bumpkins to Whitechapel, Shoreditch hipsters to Denmark Hill, jobbing Willesden actors to Wapping locations, undoes post-historic dread: 'the intangible difference in the air of places where there has been intense suffering', as Carter qualifies it, quoting Patrick White. The railway smoothes history into heritage, neutralizing the venom. Every halt absorbs the last, until the necklace achieves a uniform, dull sheen. Faked pearls on a ginger string.

I was invited by the people at the *LRB* for a lunch to celebrate the publication of Angela Carter's piece on *Downriver*, which was that issue's cover story. One of the chapters in *Downriver* is called 'Living in Restaurants'. It was the end of that era, the munching with editors, the scheming with agents, the wild three-bottle promises of publicists, the kiss-off for some television commission. This gathering, four at the table, in a close-packed Italian place, Trattoria Bardigiana, happened alongside Russell Square Tube Station on 28 February 1991. I know that because Angela inscribed my first edition of *The Magic Toyshop*. At the end of the meal. A slip in her dating of the year gave it a troubling numerology: 19111. Add up the digits, unlucky thirteen.

'In Britain an enlightened interest in food has always been the mark of the kind of person who uses turns of phrase such as "an enlightened interest in food" . . . An enthusiasm for the table, the grape, and the stove itself is a characteristic of the deviant sub-section of the British bourgeoisie that has always gone in for the arts,' Carter wrote, in a review that provoked a furious reaction from native piggies. 'Many a serious scholar would consider the reading and creation of fiction a frivolous pastime,' one of them harrumphed.

I wonder if John Lanchester was listening. Before he took an enlightened interest in money markets and the state-of-the-nation London novel, Lanchester enjoyed a great success with *The Debt to Pleasure*. A portrait of a person with the satirical name of Tarquin Winot who progresses quietly around France offering up thoughts on the cuisine, while revealing himself, incrementally, as a monster, a Wilkie Collins villain. Lanchester went on to write foodie pieces for *Esquire*. Back in 1991, he worked as an editor for the LRB.

It's likely that all the group at the trattoria table wrote about food, cooking, ethnic experiments; about analysing and describing the stuff they put in their mouths, as they did it, pre-digestion. Restaurant as theatre: a period sidebar, along with creative writing, to the freelance life. Nobody has a divine right to indulgence for inflicting contrived fantasies on the public. But somebody has to produce the necessary chaff for academic institutions to winnow: issues, big themes, novel topographies.

The stuff on the plate was fine. London lunchtime-speed service, with tomatoes and curly pasta, as you'd expect, and rich red wine. Did T. S. Eliot pop out from the office around the corner for a morsel of fish? Or did he snap a cream cracker at his desk? If he did not dine, solemnly, at the club. With bishops and bankers. And poets touching him for an advance on their way to Fitzrovia.

I was early, so I had time to think about this. And about the whole late-Bloomsbury/publishing/Hawksmoor church/university nexus. I thought about William Burroughs in his strange, submerged years of London exile, checking out mummies, Mayan glyphs and death cultures in the British Museum. I thought about the film *Deathline* (aka *Raw Meat*), in which plague-infested cannibals emerge from the tunnels beneath Russell Square to snack on unlucky Tube passengers.

This was not a topic of interest for Susannah Clapp, Carter's editor at the LRB, and another former Bristol student. She was next to arrive. She told me that she was working – the project took many years – on a biography of Bruce Chatwin, a slippery subject.

Angela was the last, a flurry of bags, scarf, hair, bus, bad connections from distant Clapham. But she was the star of the show, the Fevvers figure, settling her invisible wings, amused by everything, talking in eloquent bursts and ripples: the representative of what this literary, serious-fun, periodical-producing coterie should be. Head girl.

I hadn't yet adjusted to the idea that somebody would let me publish a book and pay for it. It felt as if I'd nipped out from one of the Bloomsbury hotel book fairs, for a drink and a sandwich, and stumbled on a table of potential signatures. But, as Angela talked, that new identity settled. It was just a job, like any other. The city, London, was the engine. You could feel the beat of it in the simple exchanges of this restaurant, in the tunnels under us. In the old churches and temples of cultural plunder. Writers writing about writers. Walkers colliding and swerving, drawn by the gravity of power in the fossil-crusted stones.

Memory Lane is a dead end . . . Comedy is tragedy that happens to other people . . . Shortly after this lunch, I heard that Angela Carter was ill, lung cancer. It felt completely wrong. Even the news of it was a physical shock. Recognition had arrived, late, and the work was in flood. The last novel, *Wise Virgins*, lived out, so convincingly, in every creak and jolt, in voice and gesture and bloody-mindedness, the old age in an old city that Angela was never to enjoy. A lovely book that should have flounced off with the Booker. Instead, what is remembered from one of those ceremonies is the episode when the telegenic person who used to be Selina Scott asks Carter who she is and what she does. Which is not so much a criticism of Scott, caught up in action for which she is ill-prepared, but of the notion that prizes, the winning and losing, are a spectator sport fit for an audience who have no intention of reading the books.

For a few months Carter crossed the river to the Royal Brompton Hospital for treatment. She died in February 1992. Lorna Sage wrote the *Guardian* obituary, telling us how 'Angela somehow understood, not just theoretically but sensuously and imaginatively, that we were living with constructs of ourselves, neither false nor true but mythical and alterable.' And she was right about that. As those books live and prove. They inform and inspire our city.

Clapham Junction to Imperial Wharf

At Clapham Junction, we came through an unconvinced retail tunnel, lacking that whiff of open-table stalls, and out into damp air with a promise of river. Transitional malls, such as the shopping centre at Dalston Junction, work a compromise between indoor market and overlit generic shop. Low-paid security guards confirm the impression that the managers and promoters regard all through traffic as potential shoplifters. The smell is: badly cured leather, popcorn varnish, tired feet, acid rain steaming from disnatured wool. The threatened open-air market at Ridley Road is dizzy with forced fruit, glossy bags, meat and fish dicing with food inspectors: it's real, it's loud, it works.

Clapham Junction is overprescribed, a little shaky on its feet. If we trundled along at this elderly speed in Dalston, we'd be flattened. Everybody up there has learned the art of looking as if they know just where they're going. They're shrugging and twisting and patting themselves down, fresh from the latest stop-and-search confrontation. The twin streams, urban hipster and recent indigenous, don't see each other. They weave, sharp shoes swerving from angry shoulder-rollers who come straight at you. All parties use the width of generous pavements, relics of promenading times, to avoid the sorry legions of substance-abuse beggars and damaged solicitors of single coins. The casualties of cuts and expulsions who are barely tolerated, as invisibles, in the microclimate of station-confirming blocks with pointless water features and thrown-up-overnight estates.

Arding and Hobbs, an imperious department store, a shopping experience kept at a polite distance from the station, is presently occupied by Debenhams. Who thrive by offering something off everything. And then something off that. And setting up outstations in places like mid-town Hastings. The urban regenerators have used the Ginger Line as the excuse for imposing, right opposite Debenhams, a ginger-themed block with slim window slits and metallic trim: TRAVELODGE.

The railway part of Clapham Junction, with coffee outlets, fast-food kiosks, numerous platforms, blue-roof and grey-roof trains hissing and hustling, is immense and relevant and active. Comings and goings between systems: junction and terminal. Achieve Clapham, having come across the Thames from Hackney, and it seems right – like a change of horses – to pause, rest, take refreshment, realign. Before going on over Battersea Reach, by railway bridge, to another kind of London entirely: the pyramid on the tower at Chelsea Harbour, the oligarch's whim of Chelsea FC at Stamford Bridge. Start again. The circuit is broken.

The rear approach to the station, up against an embankment of goose grass, blue cans and empty burger cartons, is secure ground: for cars. Pedestrians are not required. As so often in zones undergoing the blessing of regeneration, the signalled footpath runs straight into mesh, a blocked bridge, an unspoken invitation to step out into headlong traffic. It's fortunate that Clapham is not yet a cycling colony. The pavements, if you make it out of the station, are free of two-wheel racers, and the sort of aggrieved and entitled off-road pedallers who punched a protesting citizen in Bournemouth and killed him.

We're happy with Falcon Road; even under the hoot and snarl of cars and white vans, the falcon can still, if he works at it, hear the falconer. We slouch towards a pit stop on the curve of Battersea High Street. It is coming, the Overground guarantees it: ranks of Barclays bikes (for which the bankers are no longer footing the bill) will soon be installed. A docking station on Grant Road, a tributary to Falcon Road, is promised. Symbols of future docking stations fall from the map like a shower of hot-air balloons. If the elevated orbital railway were a cycle track it might work. For the moment, ranks of blue, set up to obscure sightlines for motorists, do nothing more useful than clog highways with the support vehicles required to service this monster fleet. They confirm the status of new stations around the Ginger Line. When I paused, back home in Hackney, to inspect the scale of ground given over to empty Barclays docking racks, a neighbour told me that local rumour had container-loads of blue bikes turning up in Africa. Which part of Africa she didn't stipulate. I'd seen a few, in the days of their novelty, being joyridden, two or three up, along the canalbank and through the estates. Now, like everything else, the bikes were an investment opportunity for the export market.

Another kind of bike becomes a topic of conversation: Kötting's motorized steed, the machine on which he ramps out of London and weaves across Romney Marsh in a delirious interval between tasks. Hot-metal release: cold hands, aching back. And the English road. Swaying into bends. On the motorbike you are in landscape, in weather.

So Andrew says. So he promotes the romance.

'A red BMW R1200GS. German like me.'

Russell Motors on Falcon Road is a riot of folk art and a colourful riposte to the accumulation of generic enterprises around Clapham Junction, station and shopping centre. As ever with these colonized crossroads, the theoretical centre doesn't hold; it's an illusion, a courtesy title. The term 'centre' when attached to 'shopping' implies a centripetal force: that everything pours inwards, to a locus that is not really there. The centre has no *centre*, it's all corridor leading to nothing. A chasm of prostituted windows and secure doors, goods that are like advertisements for digital versions of themselves. You buy into what they represent, not the actual objects – which are inevitably diminished, faded in attraction, by the time you get them home. Very often, addicted shoppers carry the purchase straight back to the store. Another journey, another railway adventure.

Raw and primitive: RED! A hand-painted, heart's-blood splash. Surrounding a leathered and helmeted biker hurtling through a laurel wreath. Heroic British names in traditional calligraphy: NORTON, BSA, ARIEL. MOTOR CYCLES & SPARES. It makes you proud to be on the loose in the city. On the wrong side of the river. We are experiencing the buzz Antonioni located in places like Stockwell, when he discovered blocks of Mediterranean colour on grey English walls, for the driving sequences of *Blow-Up*. Submerged areas of South London, for their own reasons, commercial or mundane, love to enhance brick, to challenge the prevailing drizzle and drudgery of endless pavements with slaps of Iberian red, midnight blue. Intimations of the Portuguese immigrant communities Patrick Keiller identifies and salutes. Tribalists dug in among driving schools and flying-saucer spotters.

Russell Motors is a proper family business in a proper London street. A street that is ordinary and exotic, spillage of infinite cultures. The shop was established half a century ago, a few years before I moved to Hackney. I've never needed it, but it's been there from around the time I left South London. The founder, Bill Myers, came out of the RAF in 1945. He specialized, so he says, 'in ex-war-department spares'. A trade operated, with less legitimacy, by many others on this side of the river; some of whom rose to be notable scrap dealers and property speculators; some of whom employed Kötting and spare brothers as painters and decorators.

★

Afghan Road. Khyber Road. Cabul Road. We're tramping through the high passes of imperial history, the old mistakes and fated incursions dignified with real-estate speculations; desirable terraces thrown up against the curve of the railway as it slides towards Battersea Creek.

Hunger calls up recollections of previous pit stops, memorable coffees; hard crumbs of biscuit, lodged between the teeth, remind us of past pleasures. I had a place called Mazar in mind for lunch: Lebanese and Continental Cuisine. It was on Battersea Square and it suited me very well; quiet, roomy, with friendly unobtrusive service, rich thick treacle coffee in decorative silver-thimble cups. My consoling reverie lifted me above present discomfort, the regular thud of Andrew's heavy tread. I recalled another excursion, a view on a conceptual square, like a vision of something in a French provincial town rudely sliced by through traffic, with just enough going on to tease your interest.

A young woman on her mobile phone, in light drizzle, described a generous circle around the paved pedestrian area. Her attitude was initially playful. Orbital loops: clockwise, then counterclockwise. After perhaps five or ten minutes, the circles tightened. There was more tension in the shoulders, kabuki gestures of exasperation. Where the early circuits were flirtatious, and took in the potentialities of the entire square, the new loops favoured the south side: round and round a parked car. Soon I felt, now wholly engrossed in this movie, she would beat on the bonnet. The circuits straightened into lines about half the length of a cricket pitch. Like being condemned to pace a cell instead of the prison yard, the nunnery garden. I pictured relationships crumbling, betrayal, tearful confession. I pictured the phone dialogue as a grinding Ingmar Bergman breakdown, detail by remorseless detail, existential and unforgiving. She might have been enjoying a coffee in Mazar when the phone shrilled. She stepped outside, pleased at first, to be in the sunlight, then concerned, alarmed, furious.

A regular came in, distracting me with her chat, blocking my sightline as she gossiped with the obliging manager.

'He gave me some unusual Christmas presents: a lunch box and two tea towels. Then for my birthday he got a bumbag. And books. *Books*. He's got no idea.'

She moved, just in time to allow me to see the irate, possibly suicidal phone victim dart through a door. When I paid my bill and headed back out, I couldn't resist crossing the square to see where the woman had gone, half expecting the door to be still open.

An estate agent.

Another Battersea estate agent! The woman was at her desk. Some hot deal had fallen through. A victim of one of those personally addressed 'we have several serious buyers actively looking for properties in your area' letters changing his or her mind, pulling out, staying put. 'You might be surprised to find out just how much your property is worth today.' *Without you in it.*

Andrew couldn't wait for Mazar. My stories of previous walks carried no conviction when set against the now-rapturous pangs of hunger. Falcon Road narrowed into Battersea High Street with a demographic shift of gear, a few paces closer to Chelsea. Refuelling was a necessity, before we detoured to Battersea Bridge for our river crossing. Galapagos Foods seemed to fit the bill. I wasn't altogether convinced. The name was too overtly Darwinian: would they be serving giant turtle or other prehistoric evolutionary accidents?

A pint of fruit crush with ginger and a well-stuffed crayfish baguette with all the trimmings will have to hold the man in the steaming tweed suit. Dew drips from his stubble as he shakes himself down, salty droplets ping into the surface of my soup. The food is excellent and will carry us on towards the twilight of Willesden. The owner, challenged by the intrepid Kötting, Chatwin paperback in fist, says that he is from Ecuador. Quito. Have we heard of it?

'My favourite city in the world!' Andrew seizes him in a thornproof embrace, a scrape of sandpaper cheek.

Bonded! Memories pour out from both sides of the counter. The South American expedition with Leila, country to country, city to city, mountain to desert to surf-crashed shore. The Ecuadorian replies with a tale of a cult in his home country, a tribal group who dress in white trousers and sandals made from adobe. They weave textiles from llama wool and sell them to Gucci and Prada.

Back at our perch in the window, I begin to appreciate how a day's random tramp around London turns into a travel journal: tourism without the air miles. Werner Herzog would approve. I heard the reed pipes of Patrick Keiller's strolling musicians from *London*. The most valuable imports are exchanges in cafés and launderettes. Quito imposed on Battersea. Without the intrusive heliport. They say the pilot in the fatal Vauxhall crash was reaching across to his laptop.

Enough miles have been covered in this half-day's walk to call up a discussion about circularity, the Homeric voyage of adventure and return, against the grander reach of the diurnal cycle, an eternal and unchanging figure. Night chasing day chasing night. The abacus of the stars. The eye of heaven orbiting *under* the dish of ocean, as Charles Olson says in his *Maximus Poems*: 'through which (inside of which) the sun passes'. The drawing together of the circle is our faith in that model of the universe. And our love of it.

Kötting wipes his lips. And gives my stumbling justifications for the miles over which I am dragging him a Beckettian spin. 'Life's an interval between whatever and wherever. Every day away from the sea is a day lost.'

On a wall, suspended from barbed wire, is a book that the scavenging Kötting pounces on: *London Falling* by Paul Cornell. 'Only they can see the evil.' A red pentagram for a cover. Not only is London falling but this paperback looks as if it's been bombed from a helicopter or flung from a train. A forensic analyst discovers the ability to see ghosts. This gift or curse, known as 'The Sight', initiates four police officers into a 'metaphysical' parallel world. The sort of hallucination that often occurs for walkers on motorway verges heady with diesel fumes. The author emerged from his own parallel world, television, where he found employment hacking at *Dr Who*, *Coronation Street*, *Holby City*. Andrew slips the Cornell into his poacher's sack alongside the Chatwin. *London Falling* had been positioned quite artfully above a crude aerosol graffito: TORY SCUM.

Battersea High Street is now the kind of place where housemovers stencil FURNITURE LOGISTICS on the sides of their vans. The elevated tracks of the Overground are having an immediate effect. We pass a couple of young bucks in quilted jackets who look ready for presenting a programme about renovating country houses. A handsome redbrick mansion is in the process of being adapted into a holding facility for 'eligible' infants. OPENING SEPTEMBER: RAILWAY CHILDREN. This is the first establishment, crèche, nursery, playpen, we've noticed that is specifically targeted at the new railway demographic. The poster depicts a set of smiling pink-faced, golden-haired blobs waving from the windows of toy-town carriages on a bumpy track. Here, in prospect, are the first children of the railway, the Midwich Cuckoos of London Overground.

★

St Mary's at Battersea, a white church dwarfed by cliffs of river-facing flats, is a site of abiding significance. This is where William Blake married Catherine Boucher, daughter of market gardeners. Blake moved to the neighbourhood in July 1782 to stay with relatives and establish residence before the marriage ceremony. Catherine, who marked the formal certificate with an 'X', accompanied Blake through all his shifts, helping with the colouring of his proofs, cooking, keeping house, singing – and, like Leila (Kötting) McMillan, making her husband's clothes.

I have been inside this church and appreciated the bounce of light from the river, the way it polishes the soft leather seat of the old chair associated with Turner – and the claim that he kept it here, dragging it outside to paint when sunset visions, upstream, took his fancy. I don't think it matters so much what these London luminaries actually did or did not do; the tables, beds and addresses supposedly sanctified by their presence. There are so many ghosts present in these quiet buildings; unregistered, obliterated from gravestones. We dowse for traces, for special sites to confirm the mystery and magic of the city. Ruin becomes rune. Eloquent absences sustaining our faith in the continuity of stubborn visionary experience. Against everything that is permitted or accountable. The belief in progress. Investing in the future. Serving the community.

St Mary's invokes the spirit of Catherine more than that of William. He came to her. He responded to the empathy she demonstrated over the way he had been spurned by an earlier love. She may or may not, at that time, have been literate. She was parted from Blake for only a few days in the forty-five years they were together. He never had reason to write to her. His letters were matters of business, solicited commissions, sleights by patrons. 'To the Eyes of a Miser a Guinea is more beautiful than the Sun, & a bag worn with the use of Money has more beautiful proportions than a Vine filled with Grapes.'

SPIRITUALLY SEARCHING SINCE 693 AD. OPEN CHURCH OPEN HEART. New apartment blocks, new Battersea: locked church door. Even when the interior is off-limits, the memory of it remains potent. The temenos, the scoop of ground, retains its quality as a riverside retreat, a mooring with an exposed beach of silt, clay, broken bricks, returned plastic. A sanctuary set against the non-denominational pyramid-tower of Chelsea Harbour on the north shore.

The temenos for Carl Jung had aspects of the peyote shamanism promoted by Carlos Castaneda in his books about the Yaqui *brujo*, Don Juan: a secured area of ground in which it is 'safe' to attempt feats of meditation or magical workings for the renewal of self. 'I was the noisiest walker,' Castaneda wrote, when he resumed his apprenticeship after a break of four years, 'and that made me into an unwilling clown.' Jung's temenos was the squared circle, the mandala garden with a fountain at the centre. A site in which to confront one's shadow. In a degraded form, this was the ambition behind our orbital tramp. To be attentive to the voices; to walk beside our shadow selves. To reverse the polarity of incomprehensible public schemes, the secret motors of capital defended and promoted by professionally mendacious politicians capable of justifying anything.

We walked down to the foreshore, which was granular, rough under our tread, like a beach made from cracked nutshells swept from a parrot's cage. Hanging from the grey-blue wall, at the slipway leading to the river, was a votive display of single shoes, drowned trainers, slime-encrusted boxing boots and scarlet football slippers. They rocked against the rising tide on leather straps and coloured strings. They reminded me of Maltese churches decorated with crutches and callipers, offered as evidence of miraculous cures. This Battersea installation invoked a troop of one-legged marathon runners swallowed

by the Thames. Kötting, who had more experience of provincial art galleries, half-cooked conceptualism, put it down to sex, gay trysting. 'They're all at it down here. Six-foot hulks with five-o'clock shadow looking for Cinderella's glass slipper under the railway arches.'

I'm not convinced. I saw trees on mountain passes in California thick with a harvest of unmatched trainers; much cleaner, it's true, than this shoreline crop. Crossing Hungerford Bridge, one time, making a considerable detour with the intention of connecting with the District Line at Embankment, to ride east to Whitechapel, for the sole purpose of coming home on the Overground, I looked down, as jumpers do, and noticed a great spread of shoes dropped on one of the piers supporting the bridge. There must be hundreds of barefoot pilgrims out there, following the river, and paying their dues before crossing to the other side. That made more sense: the slipway in Battersea and Hungerford Bridge were points of transition. Give the ferryman his due. Take off *one* shoe before you enter the next chamber of the city. Limp on, urban sadhu: one foot, encased, touching the ground, and one foot, bare, cleansed in the river. Every step a penance, every step a memento mori.

Battersea Bridge confirms the distance now separating us from the Overground circuit. Shallow arches, alternately black and white, harpoon directly into the alien aggregation of the Chelsea Harbour development. Our footfall bridge is a Turkish fantasy, nicely managed, playing games with scale, under thunderous skies already stained with sunset. We are conscious that the five-span bridge with its seductive cast-iron detailing, its rose-pattern screens throwing shadows on the path, is a relative newcomer, a Joseph Bazalgette replacement of 1885, taking trade from the original ferry. Coming over by boat allowed time for adjustment. There are claims that this was the point of the Thames, then sluggish and fordable, where Julius Caesar made his crossing in 54 BC.

   Alongside the statue of Whistler, in a little riverside alcove, is a bench of respite, where pilgrims can follow the exiled artist's unblinking stare back across the Thames to St Mary's in Battersea. A gaunt figure, in a greasy trilby, was slumped, panting, recovering, legs gone. I noticed that he was wearing a shroud-like garment, a hospital gown or unlaced straightjacket, under his long brown coat. Andrew was too tired to bother with memorials. The American impressionist, master of tone, moonlight on river, silver on luminous black, left him cold. He was flinching from the sudden wealth of Cheyne Walk, the compulsory blue and brown heritage plaques like posh people's satellite dishes. He spoke of cycling down here, not really knowing where he was, and making deliveries to pioneer production companies. He didn't have the puff, at that moment, for his usual interrogation.

'Four miles to Mortlake,' said the man on the bench. 'Must be at least that, wouldn't you say?'

He spoke as if he knew me. The trick is never to stop moving. Just smile and nod. I nodded.

'You could get the Overground from Imperial Wharf to Clapham Junction, then the train,' I said.

'I don't employ buses. Or trains,' he replied. 'One never knows who one is going to have to sit beside.' He gave Kötting a meaningful glare.

The distressed walker reminded me of a character out of Sebald, a revenant squeezed from the sepia juices of old photo albums, incubated out of friable press cuttings, translated and mistranslated into the contemporary world. He called up the Sebald laboratory assistant in Manchester, the one who absorbed so much silver that he became a 'kind of photographic plate'. Face and hands, exposed to bright light, turned blue. Then other selves, earlier portraits, came up through his skin: a carousel of death masks.

Sebald, I was reminded when I came to check that reference in *The Emigrants*, also had something to say about the dangers of a morbid obsession with train systems. Which sometimes led in his manipulated histories to acts of ritualized suicide, head on tracks, spectacles laid aside, shadowy form approaching as a terrible sound: mortality. 'Railways had always meant a great deal to him,' Sebald wrote, 'perhaps he felt they were headed for death.'

Our man hunched forward. If he moved, the pain would be unbearable. His brown brogues were unlaced; in fact, they had no laces.

'It hurts too much to bend down.'

He had no socks and his ankles were like wrists, all knob and hairless bone.

'How far have you come?'

'Brompton.'

Long walks, at certain points, throw up messengers from parallel worlds. You see them when you need them. Perhaps, in some strange way, they need us too: confirming absence, confirming the validity of a confession that has to be made, over and again. I've come across old women supposedly picking up litter in Kentish woods who saved me miles by putting me back on the right path. Wise men waiting in birdwatchers' hides near Whitstable. Snake-tattooed stoners on narrowboats with keys to forbidden locks.

Kötting took the chance to massage his own ankles, but he wouldn't risk removing boots that were beginning to slurp with burst blisters and the cheesy secretions of feet that had never quite recovered from the rats and mud of his swan voyage up the Medway.

The vagrant's story emerged in fits and starts. The Mortlake room, in a house overlooking the graveyard where Sir Richard Burton, the saturnine adventurer and eroticist, pitched his stone tent sepulchre, was the motivation for this desperate hike. The man without socks lived between river and railway. The light of one. The sound of the other. He wasn't well, but who is? Blinding headaches, white light. Pressure on the basal ganglia. Eventual collapse. Local quack. Ambulance with siren screaming. Hospital on the wrong side. Brain tumour. Power drill splits the scalp.

'They always say "size of a grapefruit". More like a moderate-sized lemon. And good riddance.'

He discharged himself in two days, against advice. And is now walking back to his Mortlake room, his papers.

I told him about a person who sent me a bag of notes, diagrams, X-rays. He superimposed the outline of his tumour, the size of a Christmas pudding, on Clerkenwell. The notion being to walk the shape as a healing pilgrimage. He dedicated the exercise to Rahere, the monk who founded the hospital of St Bartholomew in Smithfield. He died within a month of the attempt. I left out that part of it. And we took our leave, wishing the outpatient well.

It's unfeeling and predatory to dwell on such incidents, but the encounter with the man on the bench gave our steps a certain lift, as we discussed and debated the veracity of his account. The wounded walker didn't remove his trilby when we raised our hands in a farewell salute, but I saw no evidence of hair beneath.

Heritaged artists of former times, now approved as enhancers of real estate, dominated this stretch of the river. Along with parking space for superior houseboats under threat of eviction, to make room for the yachts of oligarchs. Here were moorings where bohemians hung out in swinging London films of the 1960s. John Osborne, at the time of his triumph with *Look Back in Anger*, was tied up at Chiswick. In more recent times, Damien Hirst customized one of these floating islands to the highest specifications. He was part of a co-operative of barge owners trying to buy the Chelsea Reach moorings, before the owners could sell the land for £4.75 million. The Cheyne Walk spectres of Sir Thomas More and Sir Michael Jagger nudged us towards the Overground. We would all live on the river if we could, waiting for the rains of *Schadenfreude* to wash us away. Climate is another word for conscience.

Turner, Whistler, Dante Gabriel Rossetti, George Eliot, Mrs Gaskell, Hilaire Belloc, Philip Wilson Steer, Sylvia Pankhurst,

Ian Fleming: quite a party. What a roost of entitled egos blue-badging enviable properties.

Lots Road, losing the impact of the Thames behind the domineering bulk of the former power station, is a useful demonstration of how London can switch gears in a blink. *Don't look back.* Lot, the Old Testament fugitive from Sodom, his wife recently converted to a pillar of salt (valuable commodity), was condemned to wander in desert places. The name 'Lots Road' reverberates; tight terraces, now brightly painted, sound like *Lost Road*. Like Los, Blake's 'Prophet of Eternity', manifestation of the spirit of poetry.

Andrew does look back to days editing early films in production houses that advertise the transition from dirty (and useful) industry to artisanal latte, retrospective orthopaedic chairs, and property sharks wanting to price anachronistic residents out of the market.

And I look back too. We are salty enough already, sweat dripping down our collars. The power station was still in play, 1964, and I was home from France, roofless, in company with Ivan Pawle, later to achieve cult status with the psychedelic folk group known as Dr Strangely Strange. The usual West London floors, around Cromwell Road and Notting Hill, were not available. A riverside drift brought us to a boarding house in Lots Road, hot bunks for shift workers at the coal (and later oil-fired) power plant. This brief Orwellian moment made me aware of what the city offered if you were without employment or money in your pocket. A view of smoking chimney stacks and a penitential wall.

The original task at Lots Road was to supply electricity to London Underground. The generating station, built on Chelsea Creek, became operational in 1905. It burned 700 tonnes of coal a day. In 2013, the developer Hutchison Whampoa

Properties took over the eight-acre site. Boris Johnson tooled down to give his blessing to the rebranding as 'Chelsea Waterfront'. Plans are afoot to build the new (and ill-conceived) Thames Tideway super sewer right alongside. A case of excessive sanitation for promised but as-yet-unbuilt apartments.

Much of the former electricity-generating plant has been adapted into space for desirable cushions, drapes and other necessary but expensive accoutrements of fashionable life. Most of the former pubs and corner shops have adjusted to the coming climate. Newish antiques of the better sort. Auction houses far grander than the plunder they are attempting to flog. Hand-woven rugs from the margins of war zones. Tables that cost more than three of the terraced houses of the 1960s.

Everything is pouring into the definitive non-place that calls itself CHELSEA HARBOUR. The approach to this fortunate enclave, beyond a rank of waiting taxis for those who won't be braving the Overground station at Imperial Wharf, is a sheet of glass down which water constantly pours. I read it, one letter lost in my own shadow, as CHELSEA ARBOUR. A bower. An orchard of millennial balconies. A brochure come to life without the human element. You can go in, but you'll soon subside in a coffee outlet like a canteen in a fading television franchise.

The original Chelsea Harbour tower with the witch's hat, where Michael Caine was rumoured to be in residence, a formidable early-morning walker, looked astonished to be surrounded by so many other buildings. If the tower were to be pictured as a person, it would be Don Quixote in the paintings by Honoré Daumier. A windmill, in a silly helmet, tilting at itself.

And that is what we are now, Don Quixote and Sancho Panza: my ridiculous, head-down charges at illusory enemies and Kötting's more grounded clowning. The whole picaresque extravaganza of treating the railway as a metaphor was collapsing around us. Chelsea Harbour put satire out of business.

I flipped my Cervantes and stabbed a finger. 'These Preparations being made, he found his Designs ripe for Action, and thought it now a Crime to deny himself any longer to the injur'd World, that wanted such a Deliverer.'

Millennium People

You wonder why Princess Di, in Oxford-blue FLY ATLANTIC sweatshirt, long bare legs, white socks, morning-after diva glasses (anticipating funerals), at the wheel of her dark green Audi Cabriolet, schlepped all the way from Kensington Palace to borderline Fulham, out of Barbara Cart-land into J. G. Ballard-ville, to work up a becoming flush in a leisure centre open to all manner of indecently wealthy riverside casuals with time on their hands, as well as the occasional over-entitled rugby professional from the other side, from middle-class Barnes, or Putney, where resting actors play at domesticity? Was she slumming for romance? For a trademark toss of the floppy mane and stutter of tribute from fellow member Hugh Grant – who is busy sipping ethical coffee and skimming the tabloids for actionable sleights? Anyone for tennis?

Chelsea Harbour was a late-Thatcher dragnet for new money, commissioned with a champagne party, in April 1987, held on two pontoons floating rather precariously on the newly flooded 'marina'. Invitations went out to representatives of sport, celebrity, business; all the opportunists prepared to decamp to a triangular island between the Thames, Counter's Creek and an active railway embankment – which featured, at that time, no stopping point to let off proles until you reached West Brompton. Therefore: excellent parking facilities for gym members. And no bicycles, not then. Ranks of Audi Cabriolets, sleek BMWs, Chelsea tractors. Diana could have availed herself of the private gymnasia reserved for royalty, but she was drawn, without much resistance, to the pre-breakfast, body-image narcissism of the coming millennium people: semi-retired thesps, televisual travel promoters, cosmetic surgeons, fashionable dentists, Olympic oarsmen waiting on a sufficiently visible role with one of the better charities. As much as anything, Di's commute was to do with the enactment of that eyes-down scuttle between open-top German motor and the secure entrance to Chelsea Harbour Club.

For brief periods, boats called in at that harbour. A river service connecting outreach Fulham with choice bits of the heritage city – Charing Cross, Tower of London, Greenwich – was in operation when I passed through at the period when I was researching *Lights Out for the Territory* in the mid-1990s. This was a voyage that never failed to lift the spirits, as powerful craft surged, low to the water, offering unrivalled vistas of historic real estate. *Without commentary.* The river trip was a boost to the senses, not a feat of endurance. Now, dragging myself to the deserted pier with a mute Andrew Kötting, on a necessary fact-finding mission, I learn that the padlocks won't be coming off the gates until the Harbour-dwellers are ready to return from City and Docklands. River transport is exclusive to the rush hour. Chelsea Harbour, in the afternoon, is funereal. It has outlived its time. Novelty, when it goes just off the boil, is oppressive and slightly embarrassing: like yesterday's fashions before they achieve retro cool.

Princess Diana, handsome, burnished, high-bred, but amputated of those boring 'Royal Highness' trappings, was a star without a confirmed project. Her in-development movie was conceptual, a modelled walk from car to gym. Camera-vultures were allowed to perch on ladders, at a safe distance, simmering their *Sunset Boulevard* fantasies, and shouting vulgar encouragement. The young woman who commanded the world's attention trotted gamely through to the next entanglement like a promotional clip for a David Lloyd Leisure Club. Most of the male population of Britain, it seems, confessed to dreaming, lasciviously, about either Margaret Thatcher (as Ballard did), in an SM scenario better not imagined, or the offering of a strong shoulder to the spurned princess.

Eager courtiers acquired from Chelsea Harbour exercise-machine proximity, and elsewhere around town, if taken one at a time, by profession and appearance, fit nicely within the Mills and Boon template: surgeon, riding instructor, motor-trade salesman, personal-security muscle, art broker, England rugby captain. The talent list, as an erotic collective, with most of them married, indicates a pattern of behaviour that belongs to Ballard's 'Chelsea Marina': the casual, off-kilter sexual collisions and shifting alliances of his 2003 novel, *Millennium People*.

At the Harbour Club, freed from her tiresome husband and his coterie of toothpaste-squeezing attendants, his fusty obsessions with architecture and organic farming, his obligations to an inherited regime of duty (with sidebar entitlements), Diana opted to go American. A nice reminder of what those colonists did to George III. If she gave the FLY ATLANTIC top a rest, she favoured a white variant branded with HARVARD. The firm-calved blonde in the dark glasses, in perpetual transit between place of exercise and coffee outlet, with a detour to drop off the kids, is ersatz US East Coast summer season. In the Diana years, Chelsea Harbour was the place to chill between holidays. It had to look like you were always a week back from the Hamptons. And waiting to get on court for a knock-up with Tim Henman.

But the more telling revenge on Diana's unfaithful husband was instinctive, not plotted: it was architectural. Chelsea Harbour, ambitious infill from a generic brochure ('luxury' apartments, 'luxury' hotel, offices, showrooms, bijou marina), was top dressing on the rubble of an ex-British Rail coal yard and a Victorian coaling dock. Black mounds to feed the trains up on the embankment. Generations of dumped contamination provided the right radioactive compost for mushroom development, with room for a seventy-five-berth marina, apartments, commercial space, and that witch's hat stack with the pyramid at the summit. The signature Belvedere Tower, visible for miles, was a building in translation; a draughtsman's joke made literal.

The royal letter-writer, HRH, disgruntled of Highgrove, would have abominated the whole speculation, encroaching as it did on the Thames of Turner and Whistler: if he had recognized it as being architecture at all. The scope for carbuncular metaphors and references to East Berlin secret police barracks was limited. Chelsea Harbour was post-vernacular, pre-postmodern. Another nice gig for Bovis Homes Group and the P&O & Global Investment Trust. Maritime operatives contriving a fabulous harbour, an upstream Gibraltar with cruise-boat facilities. It would make perfect sense for Chelsea Harbour to align itself with Crimea by voting to join the empire of the oligarchs. It's twelve minutes' walk from Stamford Bridge and the citadel of Roman Abramovich. Unfortunately, Ambramovich's yacht is too big to fit into the marina. To compensate, several of the blocks pastiche that floating-gin-palace style.

Oliver Hoare, a man from the shallows of the art trade, schooled in discretion, was a millennium person out of the pages of Ballard's Chelsea novel. Even his name has the authentic Ballardian stamp, English as a hard biscuit, but caught in a double bind: puritanical first name, libidinous surname. Officer class, privately educated, no distinguishing features. Ballard's remedial professionals – architects, makers of commercials, doctors, spookish bureaucrats – don't actually work; they're recovering, in remission, sitting on the balcony. These are men of means living in secure compounds with access to the gym by 7 a.m. Which is where, at the Chelsea Harbour Club, Hoare met Diana. He flogged Islamic art to the world's biggest collector, Sheikh Al Thani of Qatar. When the broker was caught up in an investigation into financial irregularities, it emerged from forensic examination of invoices that he had supplied the Sheikh with artworks worth more than £20 million. Under threats from his wife, heiress to a French oil fortune, the dealer broke off his friendship with the Princess, an alleged consummation of shared exercise regimes and fine dining.

On the darkening February afternoon, when I stand beside Kötting, rubbernecking through the window of the Chelsea Harbour gym and swimming pool, there is no way of recovering the ambiance of the urgent 1990s, when this windswept approach was staked out by photographers. Diana must have relished getting them up so early. Now the gym is deserted and the pool is occupied by a good father, a dark, powerful man lapping steadily, backstroke, with one arm, a small boy clutching his chest. The stump of the missing arm is cupped in what looks like a black silk stocking. Despite this handicap, and the burden of the perfectly calm child, he barely disturbs the clear water.

This is not London, or not the London of coal docks and power stations and the dumping of contaminated materials, and women renting narrow bunk beds in dormitories on Lots Road. Chelsea Harbour, attached to the artery of the Ginger Line by the new Imperial Wharf Station, trades on its separateness. Today, at this curfew hour, the spaces beneath the glazed domes, like newsreels of Riviera hotels and baroque casinos, are empty. Showrooms heaped with carpets are proofs of their own redundancy. Even the birdhouse chatter of mobile phones has died away. The fantastic aviary of tasteful design, every drape and lamp required for decorating a riverside apartment, has been abandoned, as if to some Ballardian catastrophe. The crystal world fairy tale of Chelsea Harbour has put us all to sleep. A late-afternoon chill from the sluggish reaches of the river makes our daggers of breath tinkle like glass.

When the nicotine wars at the gym were over (to smoke or not to smoke), and the women who drifted down in their Jimmy Choo shoes and fur coats had been banished, the Harbour colony fell into a lethargy too deep for fiction. There are zones along the Overground undone by encounters with visionary novelists. Brixton, charmed by Angela Carter, decided against attaching itself to the Overground promotion. Chelsea Harbour, fixed at the turn of the millennium by J. G. Ballard, accepted a railway halt as the price for release from the mythology imposed upon it.

The ramp leading from the reality of Lots Road to the Overground is a causeway of unconvinced interventions, not quite sculpture, not quite propaganda. For a couple of hundred yards, the Imperial Wharf approach is the drive into town from a new airport in a new country, using up its Euro budget.

A line of taxis, engines thumping. A giant pair of severed grey hands dumped in a mesh cage for potential refurbishment. Green-and-blue periscope towers. Novelty flats built in expectation of the railway effect. Blind roundabouts. Contradictory road markings. Humming vaults where machines are housed to keep the whole complicated ecosystem breathing.

Chelsea Harbour is not Ballard's Chelsea Marina, but it stands in the same relation to railway London. Ballard's disaffected middle-class terrorists don't do trains, they have the suburban fetish for car ownership. For muddy weekends in Gloucestershire and Norfolk. When the winter rains came, flooding the Thames Valley, turning Shepperton roads into rivers, Ballard's drowned world was realized. The meteorological catastrophes of his early novels overwhelmed the place where so much of his work had been contemplated, cooked, produced. In the way that Mortlake is marked by the presence of the Elizabethan magus Dr John Dee, and the destruction by fire of his library, Shepperton, without the living Ballard in Old Charlton Road, is obliged to confirm those feats of imagination. Droughts, floods, Heathrow paranoia, motorway catastrophes: reality limps along, trying to keep pace with the exiled author's handwritten pages. Ballard extracted future scripts from the amniotic reservoir of his spinal canal.

Chelsea Harbour was a set, built as a set, refusing cultural memory. Colonists were slow moving, subdued, tranquillized by a lack of affect: actors waiting for their words to be delivered. There was none of the repressed discontent, the eros of incipient revolutionary action, Ballard locates among the community of Chelsea Marina in his satiric novel. Investors who had bought into this riverside package failed to live up to their fictional avatars, they didn't have that energy.

Millennium People is the central panel of a triptych of interrelated novels. It is bookended by *Super-Cannes* (2000) and *Kingdom Come* (2006). Locations shift but the moves are established: an ordinary sensual man, suffering from loss, anomie, in a drifting second marriage, is drawn into the subversive, potentially lethal games of a messianic psychopath, rogue scientist. A sweat-drenched driver in leather flying jacket or slept-in suit. A haunter of airport slip roads and long-stay car parks. 'The areas peripheral to great airports,' Ballard told me, when I interviewed him in 1998, 'are identical all over the world ... two-storey factories, flat housing, warehouses.'

Some commentators, at the time of publication, were wary of this return to London, unsure about Ballard's take on gated communities, the sinister interconnections of police and Secret

State. Ballard, they felt, was not to be trusted as a critic of St John's Wood, the National Film Theatre, Tate Modern, the London Eye. They were quite wrong. As *Millennium People* demonstrates: *Ballard is the London eye.* Witness to a city in the process of losing its soul. The distinction between drowsy riparian settlements of the Thames Valley and the colonists at Chelsea Marina (neither in Chelsea, nor a marina) was meaningless. Ballard imported suburban anxieties into a capital traumatized between the anti-metropolitan stance of Margaret Thatcher and the bogus piety of Tony Blair and New Labour. War apologists operating with the dangerous notion that pantomimed sincerity is sincerity, that conviction is truth.

Ballard's deranged biker-vicar, addicted to the afterburn of whippings he has endured, is a revenant among the doorstep assassins of SW3. Fundamentalism of every stamp, including the fundamental decencies of the old Surrey stockbroker belt (now given over to Russian oligarchs and Premier League footballers), is suspect. Bourgeois marriage is a lie. Property is debt.

'The major problem for contemporary civilization,' Ballard said, 'is finding somewhere to park.' So firebomb a travel agency. Trash a video-rental store. Leave a fissile art book on the open shelves of the shop that is the true hub of Tate Modern: surrealism jumping off the page. 'A vicious boredom ruled the world, for the first time in human history, interrupted by meaningless acts of violence.'

One aspect of Ballard's years of apparent retreat in Shepperton – actually a strategic withdrawal to cut out inessentials and facilitate a ruthless production of texts – was his virtuosity with the telephone. Afternoons are passed in dialogue with some remote and unseen interrogator. Ballard riffs around rehearsals for the novels: provocative takes on US politics, Vietnam, Iraq, oil, pornography.

'I sometimes think we're entering a New Dark Age. The

lights are full on, but there's an *inner darkness,*' he told V. Vale in 2004. 'The flight of reason leaves people with these partly conscious notions that perhaps they can rely on the *irrational*. Psychopathology offers a better guarantor of freedom from cant and bullshit and sales commercials that fill the ether every moment of the day. One can almost choose to indulge in a mode of psychopathic behaviour without any sort of moral inhibition at all.'

David Markham, the narrator of *Millennium People*, shares a special kind of *visual* addiction with the film-maker Luis Buñuel, an interest in the erotic potential of psychosomatic disability, his wife's use of walking canes as a weapon of power. Cinema, infecting Ballard all the way back to childhood expeditions in Shanghai, through afternoons avoiding medical studies in Cambridge, becomes the defining aspect of millennial London: a prompt for acts of urban terrorism. Like the motorcar, cinema was a twentieth-century phenomenon: its usefulness was over, the heroic period was done. A sentimental attachment to past masters is now registered as a badge of bourgeois self-satisfaction.

'I remembered the quirky young woman I had met at the National Film Theatre, and invited to a late screening of Antonioni's *Passenger*,' Ballard writes. Seduced by the lizardly sexuality of a film-studies lecturer with posters of Kurosawa samurai and the screaming woman from *Battleship Potemkin* on the walls of her unruly flat, Markham is soon a passenger of another kind, a participant in attacks on the institutions of riverbank culture. He becomes part of the outer circle of the group responsible for a bomb left in the National Film Theatre. If the Overground railway is a rough democracy, all classes, all tastes, then the oil-company-promoted galleries, theatres and cinemas of the South Bank are an exploitation of the river.

The Thames is a hierarchy of power and property, from the downriver towers of *High-Rise* to the bungalows of Shepperton, by way of Chelsea Marina. The circuit of the orbital railway, like the M25 motorway, links east and west, ghetto and suburb. Train journeys mingle inner and outer topographies; cinematic reveries in the spirit of Patrick Keiller with a neurotic picking at iPhones and Kindles. Chelsea Harbour is about stasis and false memory. Ballard's translation makes that concept into a fever chart of incipient violence, a spill point for embattled investors.

Readers who had tracked Ballard's work for years, and taken his published interviews at face value, trusted him as a guide to the airport margin, the terrain covered by those lists he delivered: science parks, retail parks, golf courses, executive housing, pharmaceutical-research facilities, motorway junctions. The internalized geography of the final Ballard novel, *Kingdom Come*, was the apotheosis of the M25. A supermall is the ideal setting for a mirthless comedy of messianic consumerism. *Millennium People* was more troubling because it played its fate game in a city that Ballard had always told us was devoid of interest. A suitable location for apocalyptic fantasy of the sort previously contrived by Richard Jefferies in *After London* (1885). Jefferies imagined his own drowned world, a poisonous swamp occupied by stunted inbreeds. Ballard, at the start of his career, concentrated on what would happen on the far side of ecological cataclysm: London frozen, burnt, returned to the Mesozoic era. He compared his favoured Westway overpass with the ruined temples of Ankor Wat: 'a stone dream that will never awake'.

'I regard the city as a semi-extinct form,' Ballard told me. 'London is basically a nineteenth-century city. And the habits of mind appropriate to the nineteenth century, which survive into the novels set in London in the twentieth century, aren't really appropriate to understanding what is going on today.'

Horror is incubated in the labyrinth of an estate agent's glossy brochure, in CGI panoramas of estates that will never be built, populated by smiling people who have never lived. Victor Gollancz, Ballard's formidable early publisher, took him to lunch at the Ivy, telling him how much he had enjoyed *The Drowned World*, even though it was stolen from Conrad. At that time, as Ballard admitted, he had read nothing by the Polish author. Influence can act through sensitivity to place, as much as through close reading. The Chelsea bombers of *Millennium People* inherit the virus from the Soho anarchists of Conrad, as displayed in *The Secret Agent* (1907). The microclimate of Köt-ting's Deptford, as exploited by Paul Theroux in *The Family Arsenal* (1976), is part of the same lineage. Sedentary writers, coming to terms with the unquantifiable mystery of London, discover an inclination towards nihilistic violence. 'If you think blowing up Nelson's column is crazy why did you put the bomb in Euston?' says one of Theroux's characters. Reports of anarchist incidents, random killings in quiet Berkshire towns, bombs in department stores and railway terminals, shape the trajectory of literary fiction; fictions that, by some inexplicable magic, become mantic, prophesying – *and making inevitable* – future disasters.

A hypnagogic foreshadowing of tabloid headlines is one of Ballard's disturbing gifts. His aerodynamic prose has journal-ists ringing him for quotes every time there is a car crash in an underpass. The framing material of *Millennium People* is built from a close reading of recent outrages: the unsolved murder of the television presenter Jill Dando on her Fulham doorstep, the Hungerford killings by Michael Ryan, the massacre of six-teen children and one adult at Dunblane Primary School on

13 March 1996. Ballard's Chelsea Marina cultists, disaffected middle-class professionals, treat the Dando assassination as a re-enactment. The prose has the inevitability of that archive clip, the CCTV footage of Dando forever emerging from a Hammersmith store with a newly acquired stapler. Ballard's rogue paediatrician, Richard Gould, heretical prophet of the group, makes regular pilgrimages to Hungerford.

The names Ballard gives his actors are always significant. What do we make of David Markham, the mediating consciousness of *Millennium People*? Is the 'Markham' bit a nod towards Ballard's early supporter and Hampstead friend, Kingsley Amis? Amis, under the pseudonym 'Robert Markham', wrote the posthumous James Bond novel *Colonel Sun*. The sun, seen as part of the Japanese flag on the cover of *Empire of the Sun*, has a symbolic role to play in *Millennium People*. There is an epiphany for Richard Gould, after the doorstep shooting of the Dando character in Fulham, when he lifts his arms and salutes the burning gold orb behind the canopy of shivering leaves in the trees in Bishop's Park.

After Ballard's mad clergyman has thrown his revolver into the Thames, he vanishes 'into the infinite space of Greater London, a terrain beyond all maps'. At that intersection of time and place, when books and charts can no longer be trusted, a pared-down narrative becomes uncanny. Five years after the publication of the novel, there was a tragic incident in Chelsea that could have been lifted straight from the pages of *Millennium People*. A barrister, Mark Saunders, living in a quiet residential square, just off King's Road, fired his shotgun indiscriminately at neighbours. The police were called. One of the eyewitnesses, Jane Winkworth, was in the square's private garden, working on shoe designs. Her clients, newspapers reported, had included Diana, Princess of Wales, and, more recently, Kate Middleton. A police marksman returned fire and

Mr Saunders received a fatal wound. *The incident happened in Markham Square.*

'The sirens sounded for many days,' Ballard wrote, 'a melancholy tocsin that became the aural signature of west London.' Producing his novel, right on the hinge of the new millennium, he demonstrated, yet again, a gift for travelling both ways in time, teaching us how to read the runes and how to confront the best as well as the worst of ourselves.

Before we took our leave of Chelsea Harbour and returned to the companionship of the railway – rails that whispered of Haggerston, Whitechapel, Surrey Quays – we inspected the misconceived piazza in which we found ourselves; a town square with no town, a non-space bereft of humans but overlooked by an infinity of blind windows with a bluish glaze. The open square felt committee designed, with no casting vote, and all options still on the table: herringbone-patterned bricks on which to walk, stock bricks the colour of dried mustard for the walls. A low-level lamp standard was hung with globes like Christmas-tree decorations. It was the season of uprooted forests; dead evergreens dropped under railway arches near London Fields.

There was a shop, with a trade name blazoned on three awnings, offering lamps and lamp-holders: VAUGHAN. I thought of the poet of light and of borderlands between worlds, the haunted hours between night and day, Henry Vaughan: 'Rove in that mighty and eternal light / Where no rude shade, or night / Shall dare approach us.' And I thought of another Vaughan too, the 'hoodlum scientist' of *Crash*; the one whose windshield is set at an angle to express an 'oblique and obsessive passage' through the open spaces of Ballard's troubled consciousness.

Imperial Wharf to West Brompton

We left the colony of the barely living, Chelsea Harbour, and we moved on towards a much more substantial enclosure, a city of the named dead, those who fought to stay with us, to make us aware of their suspended narratives.

Reconnecting with Lots Road, we registered a specialist trade in tables too distinguished to be dirtied with food, oil paintings of questionable pedigree, and all the displayed plunder of forages through gardens and libraries, kitchens and bedrooms; the residue of persons of property who no longer had any use for it. They would not be burying it with them. Auction houses like private banks. Coffee enclaves, draped in subtle greenery, in which bidders and vendors debated percentages. And yawned. And fingernailed digital wafers. There were mews entrances to secret yards, quiet offices and spaces that hovered between top-end retail and sneering exhibitionism.

Here was a subterrain in which neither of us was at home; it lacked, as we did, serviceable anecdotes. We pushed through the confusion of King's Road and Fulham Road, as they sprinted competitively, in parallel lanes, towards their point of abdication at Putney Bridge. You haul in the necessary connections until you arrive at some wholly unexpected destination: Sloane Square or the Royal Brompton Hospital (and painful recollection of Angela Carter's gruelling sessions of chemotherapy).

The Overground, after crossing the Thames – all change, please, at Clapham Junction – has a revived identity: high on its embankment, or down below, now screened by strategic planting, viewed over the lip of an established bridge, a rounded

149

ledge of lichen blots and cracks filled with mosses. The line has been coerced into the orbital promotion, splashed with ginger, but it retains its older inclination, as a track for transporting coal; a link with the railway-harbour at Willesden Junction; a boundary marker for Kensington and Chelsea; a western rim for Brompton Cemetery.

Before venturing into the burial ground, by way of South Lodge, we made a detour to its hollow neighbour, the Stamford Bridge football cathedral, autonomous province of the oligarch Abramovich: West London's Crimea. The citizens here, paying heavily for their role as obedient spectators, voted some years back to throw in their lot with the exiled Russian billionaire, his associates and political connections. A fools' plebiscite allowing them to do no more than clap in approval at the loss of identity.

We noticed, at the perimeter of the deserted stadium, a wall on which a representation of a Euro-triumphant Chelsea team had been projected. A well-behaved queue, fathers with sons in branded shirts, was waiting its turn for the chance to pose for a photograph that would place a humble fan among the demigods, the Terrys and Drogbas. The emptiness of the high bowl, attended by security guards, gazed upon by devout pilgrims, was buffered by development: executive flats, two hotels, restaurants, bars, megastore. There was an attempt, which never took, to rebrand this plot of captured Fulham ground as 'Chelsea Village' or 'The Village'; in just the way that upwardly mobile knots of Hackney, parasitical on parks or railway hubs, try to sound neo-pastoral by slapping an Oliver Goldsmith title on to a concrete mall or a bleak and windblown Barratt Homes piazza with spouting water feature. Locations without locality. The careless exuberance of Ridley Road street market becomes a 'Shopping Village', roofed over, policed; while at the same time, by some curious irony, grass-roots protestors, challenging the firebombing and inevitable demolition of a Georgian terrace, say that they are fighting to preserve the ambiance of a threatened village, a community of many faiths and origins.

Chelsea football managers are appointed like provincial governors, hired, fired, paid off. Sometimes, like José Mourinho, they come back, in new outfits, with reconsidered (and greying) hair, and new lines in obscurantist banter. Sometimes, like the unfortunate Spaniard Rafael Benítez, tainted by his association with Liverpool FC, former managers become non-persons, exploitable for a few months before being shipped out to Naples.

Kötting was restless. It was at least two hours since we had eaten with the man from Ecuador, two hours since there had been anyone worth interrogating. I couldn't sell my companion the close relationship between geology, railways and football stadia. How Stamford Bridge was connected with his beloved Millwall and the Den. How Stanford Creek once flowed down to the Thames along the way now occupied by rail tracks. In the early days of territorial exploitation, there was an attempt to sell the land on which the stadium was built to the Great Western Railway Company. Stamford Bridge had its own small railway halt, lost after Second World War bombing raids. Great dunes of London soil, excavated during the construction of the Piccadilly Line, were used as terracing for standing spectators. Railways, rivers, stadiums, cemeteries: there was always traffic between them, acoustic whispers, mass cheers and whistles of derision, the scream of trains slowing for West Brompton, drifting over the layered and dignified silence of the nature-reserve burial ground.

The lodged dead absorb and soak up the restless movement of the city. They manufacture calm. Contemplation. And a measure of gratitude: that we are still on our feet. We are going home. This time. We are allowed to saunter, without challenge, down the broad avenue of an enclosed space laid out over a market garden as an open-air, non-denominational church. A pantheist temple roofed by West London sky. In death, inequalities are emphasized: from grandiose mausoleums, follies and vaults, to half-erased slabs and squares of turf marked with twigs or numbers. And patrolled by crows.

The design of Brompton Cemetery, seen from above, is like a thermometer with the bulb of the Great Circle to the south. Or like an elongated ankh, symbol of life. Andrew is inspired by this set. He sees possibilities for future interventions. He wants to return with his pet photographer, a former student who goes by the name of Anonymous Bosch, and who has mastered the pinhole camera as a device for capturing interactions between movement and stillness, past and present, the

living and the dead. Elective accidents. Leaks of furtive light. Mortality as a lens fault. A sudden blurring of focus confirming future disease.

The lime avenue short cut between Fulham Road and Lillie Road is an oasis for wildlife and certain specialized subspecies of the human tribe: amateur antiquarians, canine accompanists, relatives paying their respects to the dear departed, gay men patrolling the outer circle, and wild-haired, barefoot vagrants setting down their burdens in shady alcoves. What attracted me was the sense of being somewhere with a rich history about which I knew very little. Among the colonnades, Andrew was a silent stalker. I told him that this was the favourite cruising ground of William Burroughs in his first, mysterious London days, when he practised the cult of invisibility in the old Empress Hotel at 25 Lillie Road. He was cruising for silence and a connection with the reservoir of memory as much as for sexual partners. Bill liked to spread a rug over a convenient tombstone and picnic on sandwiches and wine from a paper cup. He made a number of recordings.

The dead are a logistical nuisance in expanding cities. They offer a poor return for short-term property investors. In Brompton the concept was always theatrical architecture; an aspect stressed by the designer Benjamin Baud, in order that this railside halt could compete with the rustic attractions of suburban burying grounds like Nunhead and Highgate. Brompton Cemetery was a city of extinguished Londoners built for 250,000 souls. Victorian cemeteries were the original garden cities. A demonstration, perhaps, that utopian theme parks for the good life are much better suited to citizens who will never move again. Here was a sculpture garden dressed with 35,000 eccentric monuments to the wealthy and the established (almost all of whom are now forgotten).

A former colleague of mine in the illegitimate book trade, a self-assembled eccentric who went under the name of Driffield, wrote about hearing a radio programme on the wildlife in Brompton Cemetery, and being inspired, at once, to go there, after equipping himself with a large tub of ice cream and a pint of fruit juice. Driff was a man who slept under suicide-watch conditions: lights on, World Service playing all night. Waiting for the dawn knock on the door.

But the aspect of Baud's plan that appealed to me was the circle of colonnades (with catacombs beneath) at the approach to the Anglican chapel. This lidless temple, rimmed by Piranesi walkways, memorial tablets obscured by occult geometries and sexual solicitation, is a forest of calcified classical figures: stumps, pillars, crosses. The carbon-encrusted skulls on the fading stones are a vanitas, a stern reminder of the penalty for thinking too well of ourselves. Here are the platforms, ramps, vaults, of a ghost station from which no traveller returns.

The intrusion of metaphysics into our tramp dressed the colonnades in Shakespearean velvet: *Hamlet*, Act V, Scene I – A Church-Yard 'What is he that builds stronger than either the mason, the shipwright, or the carpenter?'

A brisk female photographer fussed around a senior actor, who was being invited to hold up one of those circular sun-reflecting disks. Like a provincial aristocrat expected to catch his own head after he has been guillotined. She rushed and flustered to exploit the golden hour.

'You must tell me about the hair,' the man said, patting it down. What there was of it.

'I can always retouch.'

He is in a white jacket for an uncivil day, a midnight-blue shirt. Dressing for the Med, in the way some big performers favour: as if coming ashore from a cruise liner. And expecting the day to be ten degrees hotter than it actually is. Dark glasses and straw hat optional.

I know the actor's face, his mannerisms, the timbre of the voice, but the name takes a few hours to shake from my sluggish memory-file. I'd seen him do Polonius. And, if not, he should have done, he had the right look: asymmetrical, one eye more hooded than the other; successful, well fed; a babbler of unwanted advice with a streak of irony running down his spine, like Blackpool rock. Courtier, minor duke, king's uncle. Now required to turn out in a cemetery, to be herded and primped by a photographer the age of his daughter, if he had one. Lear and Cordelia. Where Lear is fond, confused. And Cordelia can't keep still. This man was more obliging about the process than Ballard when he was trapped on a traffic island in Shepherd's Bush in the rain. 'One more, Mr Ballard.' Sodden, nagged by back pain, threatened by traffic. 'I'm off.'

Oliver Ford Davies. The name popped into my head, a couple of hours later, and three Overground stations down the track, as we skirted a flashers' wood on the margin of Wormwood Scrubs. I saw Mr Davies do a turn as Duke of York to David Tennant's king in *Richard* II. Serviceable. But playing well within himself, the senior company man. This other performance, gracious among the tombs, was a ruder assignment.

The whole spectacle of the colonnades, figures vanishing into alcoves and secret exits, broad steps leading down to the underworld, makes Brompton Cemetery one of London's most Jacobean retreats. The empty grave of the Sioux warrior Long Wolf proves this quality of other-worldliness. The burial site, on the left-hand side as you approach the chapel, is a bed of lavender. Long Wolf, who is reputed to have fought against Custer at Little Big Horn, died when he was performing with Buffalo Bill Cody's troop at Earls Court in 1892. In September 1997, the grave was opened. There were two caskets interred on top of Long Wolf: Star Ghost Dog, a two-year-old Sioux girl who fell from a horse in Cody's show, and an anonymous

Englishman. After tribal ceremonies, a feast of venison and buffalo meat, Long Wolf was returned to South Dakota, to the Pine Ridge Reservation of the Oglala Sioux Tribe.

The long straight avenue leading to Old Brompton Road was a meditative walk through a gated community where all the temples had shrunk and the towers were occupied by owls and ravens and the multifarious wildlife with which Driffield wanted to become acquainted. There were names and dates on doors and relief portraits like selfies taken with a marble camera. Emmeline Pankhurst, suffragette. Dr John Snow, pioneer anaesthetist. James McDonald, co-founder of Standard Oil. Bernard Levin, journalist. George Henty, novelist. Constant Lambert, composer. George Borrow, writer and wanderer. And thousands more in this huge West Brompton boarding house, this alternative Empress Hotel, of all the trades and professions. With a notable repertory company of players and stage folk, gypsies of the halls: Sir Squire Bancroft, Richard Tauber, Brian Glover, Benjamin Webster, Sir Augustus Harris, Walter Brandon Thomas.

Anonymous Bosch, when he came here on assignment, lumbering his tripod and pinhole camera, found a story I had missed: the burial place of a faded celebrity photographer, Bob Carlos Clarke. Like to like, camera drawn to camera, I thought, with the two image-makers as compliant accessories. Bosch, in shaping his record of the grave, was invited to complete a portfolio begun, years earlier, by a very different operator. Carlos Clarke was hard-edged, a cataloguer of women as fish. Bosch sculpted smoke.

Clarke loved the garlicky Gothic, cemeteries as sets: relief from private spaces where fetishized young women, glossy as seals, were trussed in latex and perched on dangerous heels. He was troubled and of his time: beyond surface, surface. A presentational skill ambitious of critical respect (without the hurt, the risk). Black mirrors of narcissism. Portraits of Keith Richards and Marco Pierre White as stoned refractions of himself. Most of the subjects are invited to glare back at the invasive camera.

Objects were auditioned from the foreshore of the Thames; bent cutlery swabbed down and removed, to be recorded under laboratory conditions. When mortality first rattled his bones, Carlos Clarke acquired a powerful BSA 650 motorbike. He said he would ride it off the roof one day.

On the morning of 25 March 2006, the photographer left the Priory Hospital in Roehampton. He had been there for a fortnight and was thought to be responding well to treatment. He walked north down Priory Lane and Vine Road towards the Thames; a route buffered by green acres: golf course, tennis courts, rugby ground. Woodland screening the tracks of the

commuter line. At the Barnes level crossing, Carlos Clarke ran out in front of a train.

Having recently sold his Battersea studio, he said that he made more money from property than from a lifetime's photography. The Clarke archive, postmortem, was relocated to a rented lock-up in World's End.

Driffield was initially drawn to Brompton Cemetery, not by radio wildlife, nor by death (another of his interests), but by I. CLARKE MARINE STORES, a superior junkshop offering boxes of loose porn, replenished daily. Kensington dustcarts disgorged every afternoon. Driffield was on hand to forage, while listening to the *Jimmy Young Show*. He once walked away with a silk top hat. The junkpit serviced the cemetery like an unlicensed version of the Tate Modern gift shop. The tombs were the exhibits: sculpture, architecture, bandit graffiti. The shop flogged grave goods, the rubbish of our lives, the stuff that survives. And is taken up by living hands, re-narrated. Thanks to I. Clarke, the ranks of the Brompton dead were given a special status, made into honorary mariners. Inland watermen of the Styx.

Now, as we discover, the shop is gone. The cemetery perimeter has a transitional feel, local estate agents trying to catch an uncertain wave are daunted by the mass of Earls Court Exhibition Centre, a once-popular venue for trade shows and circuses, fed by the railway. Ballard's middle-class Chelsea Marina terrorists from *Millennium People* came here to subvert a cat show at Olympia, the other railside behemoth shed. And the sex-death cultists of *Crash*, enervated by petrol-fume excesses – blood, semen, X-rays – visited the motor show at Earls Court, in order to parade their combat wounds – scars, scrapes, callipers – while hoping, against the dazzle of corporate novelty, chromium and celluloid, that 'something obscene might happen'.

Earls Court was Buffalo Bill Cody's marquee, a metropolitan space where his rough riders and reservation warriors could deliver a spectacle of the old west to the new west, to the emergent suburbs, the railhead. Cody – looking like a trial run for Colonel Sanders, the Kentucky Fried Chicken rancher, but without the sinister spectacles – mixed showbiz with dollar biz; he worked the brand, franchising pre-cinematic clichés of wagon-train battles before John Ford had the chance to invent them. Sitting Bull and his Sioux ghost dancers, with other landless shamen, drummed the gods of earth and sky, the diurnal cycle, into London sawdust. Earls Court Exhibition Centre opened in 1887, one year before the Ripper murders in Whitechapel – at which point, Cody was in town. Conspiracy theorists, taken with the way immigrants escaping Russian and Polish pogroms came ashore by Tower Bridge and settled in Whitechapel, believing they had made it to New York City and the New World, decided that there must be a link between First People re-enacting the slaughter at Little Big Horn and the brutal sacrifices of East End prostitutes.

Earls Court and Olympia were born of the railway. 'Waste ground', which politicians and promoters love to carve up and rewrite, was available. And would soon become a tangle of metal tracks. An interim performance zone before the imperial trade fairs and the construction of the great white sheds. In 1895 an observation wheel was installed for the Empire of India Exhibition, a precursor to the South Bank's London Eye. The recent Eye, that symbol of surveillance, being a Ferris-wheel device for allowing tourists to experience aspects of air travel (queuing, security, a circuit of the Thames) without stomping carbon footprints all over the heavens. Virtual travel is the smarter future. Earls Court Exhibition Centre grasped that from the start. The 1935 rethink, the swaggering Egyptian-cinema modernism of C. Howard Crane, had its traditional elements: it ran well over budget and it came in late.

The old gods were expelled from Olympia. And the lords of enterprise culture ejected from Earls Court with the erection of Richard Rogers's New Labour tent on Bugsby's Marshes, East Greenwich. Smart money moved east: more waste ground, fewer regulations. Kensington was covertly decanting into the kind of ghost town left behind by gold-rush fever or a dry oil well. The stucco was as frosty as ever, villas and mansion blocks intact and unravished, but the former inhabitants had been priced out, or replaced by remote investors. The Royal Borough was a manifestation of Monopoly mania, a property-speculating, money-laundering board game: the right to buy and not occupy.

The commentator Simon Jenkins, who lives in the area, described the recent changes: 'Luxury cars untaxed in basements. Gated "communities" are like eerie sets for *The Stepford Wives*. Streets are empty at night . . . This part of London is like Hamelin after the piper left.'

The Earls Court Exhibition Centre, overtaken by the O2 Arena (and the novelty of the Jubilee Line station forced through for the millennium-night fiasco), is deader than Brompton Cemetery. It enjoyed a final flourish by taking on the volleyball originally advertised for the Olympic Park in Stratford. The Earls Court pool, an indoor sea comprising more than two million gallons of water, once home of the Boat Show, has been transferred to the ExCel Centre, alongside Royal Victoria Dock, in the eastern development zone. A bigger shed serviced by a newer, brighter railway. Tighter security and more space for arms fairs, displays of weaponry, manacles, cattle prods.

Earls Court faces demolition. And potential development into the standard blend of residential flats, retail outlets and a convention centre. On 3 July 2013 Boris Johnson approved the plans and waved through a proposal for four new 'villages' and a virtual 'high street'.

We couldn't find a corner shop for ice cream and candy bars and energy drinks to keep Andrew ticking over. Forced to pull away from the comforting tracks of the Overground, we followed the curve of Eardley Crescent, another dusty passage of abandoned and now skeletal Christmas trees and communal houses that gave nothing away. I suggested a minor detour to the former Brompton Road Underground Station, but the swollen-footed film-maker was having none of it. He was eager to tramp on towards the oasis of the Westfield supermall in Shepherd's Bush, where he had heard that fast food of every nation was readily available. And that our disreputable appearance would not disqualify us from vacant stools in the street of snacks. He might also break his habit of pissing the mortar from the bricks of shady corners and avail himself of a stall in one of Westfield's admirable toilet facilities.

Our disorientation, afternoon slump, was due in part to the way that the Overground walk was becoming confused by the layers of a labyrinthine underground system pulling us in the wrong direction, away to the east. I'd never been able to work out the best method for navigating a route through Earls Court, where all the coloured spaghetti strands of Tube lines knot and unravel. The abandoned Brompton Road Station seemed to hold a clue, if not a TfL minotaur. Its status was unconfirmed. Development pitches were in the air; a sale for £53 million was mentioned. It was also said, as part of the myth, that Rudolf Hess, Hitler's cracked deputy, had been brought here for interrogation. The disused station was commandeered by the Ministry of Defence, who initially favoured an interval as a heritage attraction: before the site passed to property speculators for re-visioning as executive flats. The Qatar royal family, who never tire of rescuing spare slabs of London, and an unnamed Ukrainian billionaire, are among the rumoured purchasers. The MoD spokesperson, Andrew Morrison, is at pains to stress that the authorities take their role as 'custodian of the nation's history' very seriously. Monies raised from the sale will be returned to the defence budget.

I've not written much about this area of London, because there are no memories to exploit. There are no memories because I haven't walked these streets enough to initiate a dialogue with the buildings, the spaces between buildings, the stations, plat-forms, bus stops, cafés and pubs. But now, in a winter twilight of orange lamp-blisters on the yellow wall of Kensington (Olympia), and the candle-flame glow of the interior at West Brompton Station, and the notices ordering customers to TELL US WHAT YOU THINK, and Kötting posing with his lopsided ursine grin beside a poster advising him to SWAP COMFORT FOOD FOR COMFORT FITNESS, and even though it's inconveni-ent to stop and fumble with gloved hands for my notebook, I have to record how the neutered husks of Olympia and the barrel-roofed mead halls of Earls Court do provoke memory. They summon disconnected incidents and flash-frames from some sealed archive at the sump of consciousness. Walking does that. Walking inhibits reflex systems of censorship. Andrew talks or clowns or forages for books and bricks to carry home, to confirm memory, to make a record. When he has processed this material in his warm hut, within his chilly sailmaker's loft studio in Hastings, it will begin to make sense.

In an odd and rather submerged period of my life, between

my last years in school and my temporary migration to Greyhound Lane in Streatham, after leaving Dublin, this was the area of London where I found a bed or couch or portion of floor. As we pound towards Shepherd's Bush, listening for the sounds of the railway, involuntary memories flood back. A hitchhiker couple I picked up in Glasgow – what was I doing there? – and brought all the way to a basement flat not far from here, to which I had somehow acquired a key. A single narrow bed. And their voices in contrapuntal disagreement, all night, before I turned them out with invented phone numbers.

Or, again, returning with a London friend, late, unexpectedly, after an abortive trip to Belgium, and falling asleep behind a high sofa while he went out to search for his partner. And being woken by whispers of confession, tears, solicitous words, soothing actions: *no no no, yes, no, yes, oh yes, oh oh oh*. Brief and vigorous: bed, floor, sofa lovemaking. More tears, more petting. And away. It was my fellow traveller's girlfriend, the one he had left behind, and another man. The one entrusted with looking after her. Gone, both of them, before the frustrated searcher returned.

I used to see clusters of agitated young girls hanging around outside the property in Emperor's Gate, off Cromwell Road, where John Lennon, who was supposed to be a bachelor boy, lived, up six flights of stairs, in a three-bedroom flat, with his new wife, Cynthia. And young baby.

Earls Court: I was brought to trade shows, Ideal Homes Exhibitions, with my parents. The warm smell of the Underground. The crowds. I remember some *Eagle* comic space pod for which I had to dress in a silver bin bag for a simulated voyage to the stars. I remember getting a certificate for doing a jump from a parachute tower.

The emptied vaults of these buildings, visited by so many people, trigger unreliable recollections without structure or chronology. I came to Olympia on the whim of a girl who had been told about a fortune-teller who saw it as it was. The decision to dress up, go out, make this expedition, turned into a performance. There was a subtext that I barely understood: how the relationship she was in was not working: her life, the basement flat, London. She was soliciting permission to behave badly. She'd been brought up as a Catholic, a good system for wiping the slate and carrying on regardless.

She came out buzzing. The old woman in the tailored charcoal suit – probably twenty years younger than I am now – had no theatrical props, beyond a fistful of rings. She looked as if she might double up with a stall of antique jewellery in Camden Passage. The cubicle, with its creaking plastic chairs and smell of embrocation, might well have been shared with an alternative chiropractor. She sussed me right away and played back all the things my actions and attitude were telling her. (I would never again undergo such a fraudulent experience – until, fifty years later, Alejandro Jodorowsky pulled out his set of well-used Tarot cards.)

I would fulfil my ambition to write, the fortune-teller confirmed. But I had no such ambition. I wanted to make films. Writing was something like eating and walking and sleeping. *And I would come back*. She said. That was her throwaway line. I marched out of the booth, telling the girl how good the fortune-teller had been. And how wrong. I was never coming back. Not to her, not to Olympia. Not anywhere west of the park. My future was Ireland, America.

West Brompton to Willesden Junction

The next passage, as afternoon thickened around us, was our Sargasso Sea. The Overground was still present, but its vigour, its tendency to promote a strip of satellite development alongside the track, was countered by older, more established patterns of exploitation. The action was underground, in the shuffle and skitter of torpedo containers worrying through hot clay wrappings: the shuddering oven of transit by through-travellers, backpack antipodeans, casual bar staff, and legions of babbling, map-devouring tourists. To keep the district in balance, all this subterranean action was flipped by the somnolence of the streets between Earls Court and Shepherd's Bush. Warwick Road and Holland Road were boulevards down which nobody strolled.

Respecting public avenues, feeders for the Shepherd's Bush roundabout, while staying on the west side of the railway, we found ourselves in Sinclair Road, running into Sinclair Gardens. A nameplate Andrew took as permission to shake up, unscrew, and glug down, Adam's apple bobbing like a cork, the vial of purple caffeine-sugars he'd found in Earls Court among disapproving redbrick mansion blocks from the 1880s. This enamel-rotting stuff, sold as a budget sex aid under the rubric of something like HOT ROD, SUPER STUD, BIG UP, coursed visibly through his veins like a barium meal. A liquefied spinach substitute fizzing and spitting and causing tired muscles to cramp and swell to shirt-splitting proportions like a Popeye cartoon. Pinhole pupils behind dark glasses glowed vampire-red in steroidal bliss-orgy: eyeball Viagra. He was himself again.

Bruise-blue Maori ankle tattoos, phantom socks made from ink, rippled like electronic signage.

'We're a long way from Deptford,' Andrew said. 'And my last remembered rapture. Oh yes! If I tell myself the Pyrenees are just around the corner, nothing will stop me.'

Hammersmith air is bottled air, drained of all virtue; snow-ploughed by stalled traffic, and coughed into a choking fug by the exhaust pipes of anxious vehicles held at the lights for sadistically calculated intervals.

Walkers are spies for truth. Drawing imaginary lines from Deptford, and our starting point in Hackney, to this railside halt, we are at the sharp point of an isosceles triangle. And, therefore, in some mystical-mathematical way, at the limit of one chapter of our journey. We are equidistant from our respective bases. Go any further and we'll enter the unknown, trusting ourselves to orbital tracks, symbol of the diurnal cycle, darkness into light.

Thomas Taylor, the Platonist and inspiration for William Blake, considering the Eleusinian and Bacchic mysteries in 1816, wrote of the soul coming under the influence of Saturn like a 'river voluminous, sluggish, and cold', merging herself in fluctuating matter, before becoming one with the sea, that emblem of purity.

Quitting the protection of the now-achieved triangle, Andrew's stories and mine arrow back to source: we are shipwrecked. Peckish as crows. Taylor speaks of intellectual nature, without bearings in sublunary darkness, navigating by match flares, 'and continuing the pursuit into the depths of Hades herself'.

Within the scheme of our day's walk, Shepherd's Bush as railway hub, road hub, severed village green, mother of malls, was our nominated Hades. Or plastic paradise. Take your choice. I had spent time visiting Westfield, the huge retail hangar waved through by Mayor Ken Livingstone, when it was newly opened. And I'd written about the experience in a book called *Ghost Milk*. Andrew, having sampled the few paragraphs in which he appeared, avoided the rest: so he came to this bright island in a spirit of optimism. Food. Drink. Micturation in a pristine trough.

'You're such a grouse,' he said. 'Muttering and moaning and chuntering words of Brandoesque nonsense like Kurtz in *Apocalypse Now*. With your polished skull and your T. S. Eliot and overlandunderground rumbles. And what's wrong with people enjoying themselves at the Olympics? I'm proud to be a British German, a roastbeef Englishman with an umlaut.'

Kötting was confusing the feudal field system of the western Westfield, where the 1908 and 1948 Olympics were staged, with the new eastern park, which will eventually be opened to the public, after being landscaped as a backdrop to the shining memory of the 2012 Olympic city of Stratford. A forgivable mistake. When parking space is at a premium, build slots for cars and the public will come: you might as well stack shops and coffee halts up above.

Our own marathon trudge around London Overground was no more eccentric or arbitrary than the route of the 1908 run to White City Stadium. The old distance of twenty-five miles was extended by a mile, so that the race could begin at Windsor Castle, and it was tweaked again to have the athletes line up under the window of Princess May. British officials made a final adjustment by moving the finish line to a position immediately beneath the Royal Box. Thereby setting the now-established distance of twenty-six miles, 385 yards. Andrew, in his pomp, lacking credentials, inserted himself into the London Marathon and ran the whole gasping route as a self-sponsored free-floater. His training runs out of Deptford took him through the fume-tube of the Rotherhithe Tunnel, shoulder to shoulder with white vans. Which explains a lot.

Veteran brownfield acres left over from the Franco-British Exhibition of 1908, and the Olympic summer when the original White City was known as the Great Stadium, gave way to usage as a railway depot. Railways, like wildlife on the central reservations of motorways, flourish in places where the curious can't get at them. No vistas are more appealing, and less available, than the tumble of dereliction, shed cults, covert industries, squatted warehouses, spray-painted walls, train-seeded knotweeds and glimpsed canals of railway-terminal approaches. Or those unexplained halts when the carriage trembles and passengers yawn and inspect their watches, before gazing without recognition at some wilderness snaking between busy carriageways and motorway spurs. Which is why the Defoe entrapment of Ballard's *Concrete Island*, a car spinning off a Westway interchange and hurling an architect, Robert Maitland, into a no-man's-land pit, was a necessary stage between White City's railway stagnation and the rebirth of Shepherd's Bush as the prime port of entry for the Westfield supermall. The Piraeus to the Athens of the Overground.

'The apex of the island pointed towards the west and the declining sun, whose warm light lay over the distant television studios at White City,' Ballard wrote. Now those studios were as doomed and ghost-freighted as the acoustic echoes of the 60,000 spectators at the 1908 Olympics, and the characters of the dog-track era that followed. The wide boys who don't work out of lost novels by Robert Westerby.

One fine summer afternoon, coming away from a meeting in Bayswater, I drifted west through streets and crescents in which I find it easy to get lost. I've never quite worked out how those Westbournes and Ladbrokes and Landsdownes and Elgins contrive their mazy circles, complicated by private gardens, around a theoretical centre, which may or may not be of psychogeographic significance. Choices of artisan bread and fine-ground coffee, both of which I needed to carry home, were overwhelming. The villas of Holland Park invoked so many generations of literary figures – Ford Madox Ford and Violet Hunt, Wyndham Lewis, Hackney's upgraded Harold Pinter, J. G. Ballard ducking into the Hilton for a Chinese meal – that I was confirmed in my tourist status. I kept my head down, hugged my grainy loaf, and stepped it out until I was safely positioned on the Ginger Line platform at Shepherd's Bush; waiting nervously for a connection to the railway loop that would carry me back to Highbury & Islington. Then Haggerston. The known world.

Safely back among my books, I dug out a copy of *South Lodge* by Douglas Goldring, his account of Ford and the *English Review* circle, published in the year of my birth, 1943. I was surprised to find the story opening with a letter from Goldring to Tommy Earp, in which he hesitates 'to try to estimate the number of miles of Dockland pavements we have tramped together in the course of our riparian wanderings; the number of noisy East-End pubs in which we have exchanged ideas'. So the compulsion must always be there: to go out of your knowledge, cross the river, scrape off a little of yourself in areas so obscure that every encounter becomes a potential fiction.

I was sharing the platform with faces I knew and didn't know, half-familiar characters waiting to be assigned roles I had failed to invent for them in abandoned novels. They were like cousins or uncles seen once at a family funeral in a suburb of Peterborough, a cold wedding in a flapping Dorset tent. Something had gone wrong in the intervening years. Wrong with me, my eyes. My index system. These men were the mirror of my own decline. Even the physical size wasn't right; they had shrunk somehow. The flesh tones were too high. Hair was thin and overbarbered. Actors of note, evidently. TV drama recidivists. Staff officers of White City. You've shared your sofa with this trio as paranormal investigators, forensic scientists, colonial administrators, East End godfathers, hitmen waiting in a basement for a word from Harold Pinter. I wasn't a casting director, but the names would surely come.

Where the eastern rim of the Overground, Haggerston to Shoreditch, was infested with image cannibals, photographers taking photographs of photographers taking photographs, the western corridor, Brompton to Willesden Junction, was populated by actors in civvies. They were everywhere, tour guides without a script. In my part of town, on any morning circuit of Victoria Park and Regent's Canal, you might witness actors being actors, doing their job: alfresco breakfasting, resting in caravans. The east is London's local-colour location; the west is where the performers live (the ones of a certain age and status).

By the time we were settled in our Overground carriage, the rolling credits came to me. The subdued performers were returning home after a hard day under the lights in the BBC studios: Tim Piggott-Smith, Bill Paterson, Kenneth Cranham. No courtesy cars. The enforced democracy of the Ginger Line. In spite of a nicely underplayed nonchalance about the prospect of being recognized – or, worse, of not being recognized; or, worse again, of one of the others being recognized first – nobody did. Fellow commuters were slumped behind free papers, finger-jiggling screens, earplugged to playlists. And if travellers did acknowledge faces that belonged on something grander than a CCTV surveillance monitor, they were too polite to make anything of it. Respectable actors should be quarantined within the magic rectangle, not expelled to the 3.39 p.m. shuttle on the Overground.

They were around my age, these men, even a few years younger; or, in Cranham's case, a year older. After a punishingly early start and a day shoehorned into costume, they were dressed down in casual jeans and jackets, but with visibly good wristwatches. They exchanged inconsequential remarks, giving the impression of having been thrown together for a particular job without being close friends or neighbours.

'I was travelling up to Leeds,' Piggott-Smith said, 'and they booked me second class! I upgraded to first. Even with my Senior Railcard, it cost forty pounds.'

Cranham, flushed, stroking a grey beard, gasps. He breathes hard, hanging on to the ginger pole as the train lurches. Piggott-Smith and Patterson managed seats. 'We can catch up, Tim,' Cranham says. 'We can catch up at Willesden Junction.'

Willesden Junction is where they exit. Willesden Junction, and the rail-serviced diaspora of Kensal Green, Kensal Rise, Willesden Green, is a reservation for actors and filmmakers. Substantial villas, screened by leylandii hedges, gardens generous enough to contain cricket nets, were once available at competitive prices. Drifting out from Hampstead and Notting Hill, upgrading from Acton and Kilburn, actors with families, second families, dependants, followed Peter O'Toole, a pioneer Willesden Green migrant.

If we decided, at some future date, to make a mad Kötting film about the orbital walk, would we secure sufficient budget for the three Shepherd's Bush actors to play themselves? Andrew, in full flow, could be persuasive. He got Dudley Sutton, in smart tweed three-piece, out on the plastic swan. He made Sean Lock swim the English Channel. He hypnotized Freddie Jones, the King Lear of *Emmerdale*, into chugging enough 'interesting' coffee to rip through a heart-rending recital of poems by John Clare.

Within the year, it was revealed that the Willesden Junction actors were responsible for starting the First World War. If the war ended with the Armistice of Compiègne, signed in

Marshal Foch's railway carriage parked in a forest siding, after the German delegation had been brought, by private train, to this secret destination, it launched in Shepherd's Bush.

Tim Piggott-Smith played Asquith, the prime minister. No wonder, staying in character, he felt entitled to a first-class ticket. Kenneth Cranham was John Burns, trade unionist and radical. In life, Burns came around our tramped London circuit: born in Vauxhall, schooled in Battersea, arrested after a demonstration on Clapham Common. In retirement, he developed an obsession with the matter of London. He is credited with first voicing the future TV cliché: 'The Thames is liquid history.' The diminutive Patterson, all Scottish frown and calibrated intensity, played Lord Morley, the Liberal and anti-imperialist. Morley and Burns were the two cabinet ministers who opposed war and who resigned when it was declared. The programme was called *37 Days*. It felt longer.

The Shepherd's Bush Westfield drome achieves a critical non-mass. It's an all-year-round winter wonderland made from synthetic ice. The scale and density is manageable without an induction course. The compass is not wholly subverted. Treat the skating-rink floors and celestial ceilings like a walk-through park and it's harmless. The heavier Stratford version is much more of a black hole, a Gormenghast swallowing life as we know it for a dole of recycled air. The permanently interim quality of the surrounding post-Olympic terrain is a microclimate of choking dust – gouged pits, septic ponds, rubble dunes – mingling with infinitely small particles of sand from the Sahara. Already, this speculation is sub-zoning into knots of hanging-out/non-attending schoolkids sucking cans, lost souls from the rubber corridors of decommissioned hospitals, and misdirected travellers condemned to endless circuits while they search for an exit to daylight.

The Shepherd's Bush Westfield is kinder, but Andrew decides that he isn't so hungry after all. And he'd rather piss in the woods on the edge of Wormwood Scrubs. We pass through the supermall, the former rail depot, and on to Wood Lane. I am astonished by the suspension of corporate sensitivity, post-Savile, responsible for a large hi-definition poster on the side of the BBC studios, where a crowd of unticketed folk are waiting to be let in as noise-makers for a games show. A twinkling octogenarian hoofer is tight to a very young blonde woman with a glitter ball in her hand. The pattern of reflections within the facets of the magic ball make it appear to contain multiple reproductions of the shrunken skull of Sooty the glove puppet. This sinister charity triage is completed by a bandaged cyclopean bear with jaundiced fur and a weak smile.

Pausing in the echoing vault beneath Westway, thrummed by constant traffic overhead, and conscious of the fact that this pillared slab of concrete modernism is a barrier, a frontier before our trudge into the darkness of the Scrubs, we rested for a moment. Kötting rolled up his trouser legs. He massaged the knots out of calf muscles still pulsing with the energy drink that hit his exhausted meat like a jolt of Frankenstein's stolen lightning.

Revealed flesh, under the septic light of the motorway cavern, is a book, a graphic novel. Manga madness reminding me of that moment in *Moby-Dick* when Ishmael first encounters Queequeg. 'It's only his outside,' Ishmael decides, 'a man can be honest in any sort of skin.'

Never shy of a photo opportunity, Andrew explained: 'An abandoned self-adornment diary project.' Maori tattoos adapting images and symbols from locations that formed part of his backstory. He had turned his arms and legs into an illuminated

173

gospel, decorated with the comic strip of his life. Here is his daughter's first drawing, an angel. And here some cave paintings from Scandinavia (where he worked as a lumberjack). Stone carvings from the South American odyssey. Along with natural wounds and scars. And teenage hurts exorcized in carved flesh. All this harm: before he discovered the solace of the sea, the numbing hours when the mind detaches from the punished body. Now he swam, I walked. Limped. Dragged. Floated.

Road and railway and woodland merged as we came, in clammy early-evening darkness, burned at the edges by mean spill from light poles and urgent beams from cars, like a necklace of flaring and furtive cigarettes, along the sudden, mid-stretching width of Wormwood Scrubs. Surely one of the most evocative names in London. Like the title of a rejected novel by Evelyn Waugh. A public space dedicated to decline and fall. And weekend football noise. Peter Ackroyd, the living embodiment of literary London, gives interviews a Gissing spin by speaking of growing up, with a single parent, on a council estate 'a stone's throw from Wormwood Scrubs'. There is more poetry in that beginning than in acknowledging the claims of East Acton.

The prison block is heritage-lit in the twilight like the ruins of a Norman castle. Part of the mystique of a reliable English penal institution is to have the right measure of dread in the name: Dartmoor, Belmarsh, Wormwood Scrubs. The suggestion of swamp or remote Conan Doyle moor is an advantage. We like this scrubby interlude, the shrouded path through the woods and the open land beyond. There is room for three of the architectural categories that have defined our walk: prison, hospital, football stadium. They are all clustered on the southern perimeter, facing Westway.

We have tracked the silence of stadiums around the Overground, from Millwall's Den to Stamford Bridge and Queen's Park Rangers at White City. If we followed the Ginger Line spur north from Willesden Junction for three stops, we'd be at Wembley. There are prisons too, visible from the train window, or just out of sight: Pentonville, Brixton, Wandsworth, Wormwood Scrubs. It might be time, I tell Andrew, to establish a new lexicon.

FOOTBALL STADIUM. *A large, unexplained oval structure left empty for much of the time. Often unfinished in appearance, scaffolding seemingly integral to the design. Numerous designated parking bays but few cars. The stadium is never the right size, either too small for anticipated capacity (and revenue stream), or too large (club in decline, waiting on overseas investment). If a desired capacity is achieved, the owners will lobby for a move to a better site, preferably the unwanted shell of some Olympic ghost or legacy power station. The Football Stadium should therefore be understood, not as a focus for local passions, but as a property speculation; future apartments trading on the club's mythology. A sideline in scattering the ashes of supporters allows the club to forge links with a suitable crematorium.*

PRISON. *Inconvenient real estate in which the boarders refuse to pay their way. Solidly built and expensive to demolish. Suitable for privatization and outsourcing. If possible, as at Oxford, where the old castle prison has been rebranded as Malmaison, a boutique hotel, use some imagination. 'Don't worry about doing porridge,' the brochure says. 'This is the one hotel in Oxford city centre where you'll be happy to get a long stretch!'*

HOSPITAL. *An instrument for inflating bureaucracy. Scandals justify enquiries. Failed enquiries demand further enquiries. An infinite process. Rationalize, close down, leave in limbo until the property market takes an interest. See St Clement's, Mile End Road: Victorian workhouse, asylum, arts venue with tunnels for urban explorers, major regeneration project (with minor public housing element). Promised public housing = Achieved public relations.*

We found numerous abandoned umbrellas in this strip of woodland, and alongside the railway embankment, when we emerged on Scrubs Lane. It was as if a regiment of well-prepared walkers, perhaps striding as we were towards the station at Willesden Junction, encountered English weather for the first time and flung away their token instruments of protection. At the first gust, these black satin bells blow inside out. Funereal silks, punctured by thorns, have parachuted into the railway corridor, alongside the usual blue cans and unrequired newspapers. I thought, again, of Will Self's Man Booker-shortlisted novel: we had accessed a theme-park trail that would lead, inevitably, to the great central corridor of Friern Barnet asylum. 'Any symbols – words, numerals, pictorial – were experienced as a sort of map, one that if concentrated on became a map of a map that was itself a further map.'

The umbrella, Self reminds us, is the thing to be forgotten, left behind. See the metal ferule scraping marks in the dirt, names, dates, memories: to be erased in the next shower.

Willesden Junction, mother of railways, welcomes us with giant sheds, car auctions, book distributors. It is comforting to be returning to the western equivalent of Hackney Wick, as it once was, a working place, out on the edge, with road and rail connections. It's good to see rickety stacks of pallet boards that are not art. Kötting eyes a Chinese restaurant, but this is not the moment to pause. It's going to take a healthy push to reef in the Overground line all the way east to Finchley Road & Frognal, in the dark, shadowing burial grounds: Kensal Green Cemetery, Willesden Lane Cemetery, Hampstead Cemetery. He settles for a sticky-choc lump so stiff and fusty it's like licking a crowbar dipped in sugared mud. With a RED BULL chaser.

There's just enough light lemon-squeezed from the bulbs of the sodium orchard by the long station wall to snatch the photograph. GET YOUR ROCK SALT HERE. SUPPORTING THE PROSTATE CANCER CHARITY. Somewhere on the road Andrew has picked up a shocking-pink monkey with green face and cheeky tongue. He tucks it under his arm. And we strike off down Palermo Road. Most of the world, he says, is dark matter. 'You can't see it or touch it or feel it. But you can smell it. Every last inch of the way.' Anxiety. Leaf death. Chip papers. Resurrection.

The Experience of Light

It was too dark at Willesden Junction to appreciate the flood pool of rail tracks; the way that steel tributaries from south and east converge, interconnect, overlap, and stream towards the western horizon in a unified tidal bore. On this stone bridge, in the early 1960s, Leon Kossoff stood, in a state of emotional turbulence, taking measure of the challenge, the panoramic sweep and its painterly potential.

Born on City Road in Islington, and growing up in Shoreditch, Bethnal Green and Hackney, Kossoff became a railway migrant, shifting his studio from Dalston Lane to a builder's shed in Willesden Junction. The railway was his muse and he was its most potent recorder and supplicant. Where Turner and Whistler paid witness to the shifting light of the Chelsea reaches of the Thames that we had passed through earlier that afternoon, Kossoff positioned himself in quiet rooms, in areas of demolition and reconstitution, to record the material force of London's railway system. Which he saw as an organic entity, a living thing.

After our orbital circuit was completed, I had to come back. In yellow twilight, under puddles of artificial light, we tried to align the view from the bridge on Old Oak Lane with Kossoff's monumental charcoal drawings of Willesden Junction from 1962. But the grunge nocturnes of the day's walk with Andrew Kötting were infected by the rogue film-maker's enthusiasm for Tarkovsky's *Stalker* and the Amazonian madness of Werner Herzog. He started doing the voices: the railway was a jungle and the birds and trees screamed with pain. The gantries and signal poles punctuating Kossoff's drawings became black Tyburns, hoists for containers of radioactive cargoes. Andrew's riffs absorbed a post-apocalyptic geometry of unexplained sheds and sidings.

The perimeter fence of the station at Willesden Junction defines the point of transit from road use to a sunken rail-side community. Passengers dissolve on concrete ramps and metal-sided walkways. Recorded announcements, in no recognizable language, are muffled by the acrid smoke of evening. Night cancels time. Whatever discomfort we have experienced from hours of pounding pavements, and hours more stretching ahead of us, is absolved with the loss of detail, the blurring of outline: orange-gold blots of surveillance electricity burn aureoles in natural darkness. We turn back, cross the busy road, and head east, with the sense that, at long last, we are coming home. And we feel good about it. Andrew kisses the monkey.

Old Oak Lane, in late morning, in weak spring sunshine, was a very different beast. I decided to take a day away from writing up my Ginger Line notes, to investigate the geography of those Willesden paintings. I spent some time, up on my toes, trying to convince myself that this was indeed the place where Kossoff perched to make his preliminary drawings. In the aftermath of our orbital walk, it was a necessary period of adjustment; coming back, by way of the Overground, on my own, to take a walk from the site where Kossoff worked with such intent in the 1960s to his present home and studio in Willesden Green. In recent times he has produced a series of more domestic, affectionate paintings of the railway at the bottom of his garden, the gnarled and supported limb of a cherry tree that filters out the insistent presence of the whispering invader.

Kossoff is not a tall man. He wouldn't be able to hold his drawing board in the place where I had my elbows. The

Willesden Junction painting of 1966, with its soaring blues, would have been made in the new studio in Willesden Green. The charcoal drawings of the earlier period are about width and movement, with nothing actually in motion apart from the clouds. And the painter's hand. His nerves. The rapidly retreating perspective of the railway-ladders delivers a history of past and future momentum. A graph of action and reaction. A series of probing muscular spasms digging at the paper. Nothing is referenced by these motifs, this darkness, beyond darkness itself. The Abyss looking right back.

My view from the railway bridge was of resistant bushes, huge yellow hoists, reddish stones, rusty poles and blue-grey mesh fences. If I wanted anything close to the letterbox intensity of Kossoff's Willesden vision, I had to adapt an extreme telephoto mode, so that the overhead gantries are foreshortened, bleeding into a sequence of bridges, while horizontal

diamond patterns of metalwork are countered by the curves of the track.

NO ACCESS TO EUROTERMINAL.

I poke about, trying to orientate myself, and hoping to identify the builder who rented Kossoff a draughty space in which to work. Hippie dope transfers have been plastered to the official sign, confirming its Euro credentials. DINAFEM. ORIGINAL AMNESIA. MOST AWARDED SATIVA FROM HOLLAND. HIGH LIFE CUP WINNER. Elective amnesia of the deadlands. Railside sheds have been made ready for cargoes from everywhere. Of local builders and solitary painters, no trace.

On the map it's no great distance from Willesden Junction to Willesden Green, but Kossoff, as I soon discovered, was achieving a large cultural step: from the rough and tumble of proudly depressed Harlesden to the tranquillity of railway-fringe suburbs nudging Kilburn and aspiring to Finchley & Frognal.

On the corner of Tubbs Road and Station Road, I noticed a fading trade sign still visible in the brickwork, high above a busy road junction. Ghost stencils of this type always remind me of Robert Tressell, the jobbing painter and author of *The Ragged Trousered Philanthropists*. Crafted boards, produced by Tressell for a modest fee, can now be found on display in Hastings Museum. The reputation forged by a righteously angry book saved these casual commissions from oblivion. In certain London districts, and Harlesden is one of them, trade signs are tolerated, unnoticed. In others, rising with the Ginger Line – Shoreditch, Peckham Rye – signs are valued heritage, repainted or pastiched. The elevation of this one proves that it was originally intended to be viewed from the railway. Part of that cinema of transit celebrated by Patrick Keiller and John Berger, advertising artworks exploiting suspended time at a hub station.

CLAUDE BASTABLE, BUILDER. Upper-case lettering like a phantom credit sequence sliding across the carbonized railway bricks between eyebrowed windows gauzed in dead net. A substantial property in mourning for its previous identity. Was this Kossoff's builder? There was plenty of room for a shed around the side on Tubbs Road. Or the potential for a high room in the house, overlooking the railway. Claude Bastable was a good name. Let us award him this act of enlightened patronage. And, if not Claude, one of his now-decamped descendants. Perhaps I was wrong? I read somewhere that it was not a builder's shed but a derelict garage, with the railway bridge close at hand. 'The studio itself,' said Paul Moorhouse, who curated a Kossoff show at the Tate Gallery in 1996, 'offered few comforts.'

Harlesden is different. The Overground walk, made with Andrew Kötting, branching away at this point to narrow dormitory avenues, hugging the railway, and easily blocked by Ocado delivery vans, was concerned about libraries and locality. Quit the orbital circuit and gravity no longer pulls you towards the Finchley Road massif, emigrant cafés, and arts centres with morning coffee-group discussions. Following an outspur of the Overground, depicted in the brochure as an absolutely straight line heading for Watford Junction, was to transfer to another narrative entirely. But the chart was a lie, the Overground has a bias to the west. Leaving me in a limbo between systems. Leaving Harlesden like old Hackney, as an overwhelmed village of nations operating through small brave enterprises, fly-by-night cafés, charity caves, poundstretchers, perpetual roadworks, bus queues. Agent Orange boosterism had not yet arrived with the railway. The dominant element was the North Circular Road to which most of the white-van traffic tended. And the great blue tongue of the M1, a pioneering motorway born a couple of miles to the north. On the map, it seemed to erupt from a tarmac spring associated with the Welsh Harp Reservoir.

This was Brent. Ken Livingstone country. Mired in accusations of cronyism, suspect closeness to builders of high towers, promotion of Westfield and the Olympic circus (as a redevelopment smokescreen), the Thatcher-expelled boss of the Greater London Council took time out as MP for Brent East, before standing successfully for Mayor of London. Willesden Junction was an easy commute down the Bakerloo Line to Charing Cross: change for Waterloo (GLC) or Westminster. Brent, Livingstone's chosen exile, was ripe with allotments, window displays made from tier after tier of fright wigs, nail parlours, cemeteries, dog parks. A terrain of newts and other curious pets, indoor hobbies. Ward politics and nonconforming churches. Barbershops and fast food. Meals consumed at bus stops. Thankfully, there were no Boris bicycles, no blue fences. No high-pumping corporate joggers in charity T-shirts.

I stopped for a late breakfast in a Turkish place that serviced Chapman's Park Industrial Estate. The quantity of food on the big plate would have fed a nuclear family for a week. The chips were excellent, like bundles of dry kindling. They had an oily, oaky aftertaste. The black solar disc of blood pudding sat heavy in me, as I sopped up the juices with soft white blotters of bread. It would have been fatal to rush this road feast. I sucked at a scalding pint of coffee and eavesdropped on the mild flirtation between a van driver and the girl who brought trays to the tables.

'End of the day, you can't top a Harvester.'

Van men from the industrial estate used their delivery runs to the northern fringes of London as reconnaissance for suitable pubs and diners; weekend venues where generic platters could be judged on quantity and the absence of spices and peculiar vegetables, those shiny things that were neither peas nor beans. The driver's wife was a vegetarian, so that worked pretty well. Divide the plate: he took the steak, sausage, pie, curry, grill, and she got the mushrooms and any spare-leaf salad thrown in as bulk.

The waitress, who had a nice way of not contradicting any of the driver's bluntly stated opinions, but also hinting that there were other possibilities, wasn't much bothered, at the end of a long shift, about food. What she required was the view of a lake, a chalet platform on the edge of Epping Forest or a mock riverboat floating on an excavated Essex quarry. To be able to sit outside and enjoy her only cigarette of the evening. And look at insects dancing on water.

Studying my map, while the coffee cooled, I realized that I could take a cut-through at the side of the industrial estate, to find the redbrick school painted by Kossoff in 1982. It was at the corner of Dudden Hill Lane and Cooper Road. And it had been upgraded into the Willesden College of Technology. The photograph of record from my Willesden walk has only the palest relationship to Kossoff's dense seizure, the great molten pink-red crown of a building dominating its pictorial space. Pedestrians drifting through the foreground wear their flesh like liquid brick. The black car looks like a hearse. The road is a gummy and blooded ochre swamp. Everything is charged, seething, volcanic: lava solidifying, cooling after eruption into a field of neurotic slashes, trowellings, dripping threads. Frozen contrails offer an accurate record of the painter's hesitations. A dignified civic agenda is implied, through mass, in this accumulation of bellying towers and narrow windows. Kossoff has recovered something epic from a margin of ground between a bus depot, an industrial estate and a railway.

The walkers have been chosen. They may be members of

his family or regular models. They are not accidental Willesden pedestrians. That was often Kossoff's way, to insert figures important to his private mythology into ticket halls and high streets. When I met him, he talked about the hit of stepping outside; how refreshed he was when he started to move once more through ordinary London places. The redbrick school then became a beacon, a marker for the distance comfortably managed from the painter's home, beyond Willesden Green Station. Technical difficulty, blockage of inspiration, residual gloom, ill health: they fell away as soon as he took that first breath of air. As soon as he registered the light. As soon as he started to walk.

And now? In the little park opposite the school, a good place in which to stand and make a drawing, an Asian group are taking iPhone portraits, arranging and rearranging the combinations around a bench. The twin towers of Kossoff's painting are recognizable; the lineaments of the 1896 school with its decorative motifs have survived. And will add piquancy to the current property development. The educational aspect, of course, is over.

1, 2 AND 3 BEDROOM APARTMENTS AVAILABLE FOR SHARED OWNERSHIP. GENESIS. PART FUNDED BY MAYOR OF LONDON. IMPROVING THE IMAGE OF CONSTRUCTION.

London, 3 April 2014. Improving the image of Leon Kossoff. Improving a great painting with billboards and slogans. Kossoff was always interested in building sites; in the way London renewed herself; in stations, railway bridges, schools, public swimming pools. But he never felt the need for slogans. Construction of paintings, as of sane architecture, requires no image buffering. The act is the act is the thing. It speaks for itself. Promotion, for Kossoff, at the end of a long and honourable career, is a necessary agony.

★

The hinterland was like old Hackney in other ways too. On the day when I was supposed to meet Kossoff at Annely Juda Fine Art in Dering Street, not far from the Bond Street Underground Station, a twenty-year-old man was challenged by cruising police in Christchurch Road, a short walk from the painter's house. Devante Keane, also known as Devon Sawyer, was pulled over as he strolled between the Overground railway and the tennis club, close to Brondesbury Park Station. Devante was stopped and searched on suspicion of being in possession of drugs. The suspicion might have related to his appearance in this quiet suburban place. Photographs posted on the Net show a confident young man in wraparound shades, white T-shirt, slim gold necklace. They show the playful *Scarface* gangsta pose, brandy and cigar, of a football enthusiast, computer-games buff, Amsterdam tourist and keen socializer (according to tribute sites). Devante was down the line, well away from his home turf in Marks Tey, near Colchester. An Essex boy.

Devante ran. He ran into scenes familiar from Dalston to Enfield: helicopter overhead, dog unit, blue-flashing cars. The full paramilitary urban-response squadron. He turned Willesden Green into a parkour demonstration. He hurdled hedges, sprinted through gardens, rolled over fences, swerved through cars in late-afternoon spurts of commuter traffic. In brief surveillance stardom, he was lit from above by searchlight beams, deafened by the clatter of blades, pursued by a chorus of sirens. The manhunt lasted for around forty minutes.

Access to the railway is easy. I can see how slithering through the bushes of the embankment might feel like reaching the Rio Grande, crossing into Mexico in a Sam Peckinpah movie. Witnesses said that their gardens were vulnerable. Runaways could get down to the tracks from the bridge near Willesden Green Station, or over the back of a garden fence in Chatsworth Road.

Devante Keane was pronounced dead at the scene, having been struck, in headlong flight, by a mainline train operated by Chiltern Railways, shortly after 5 p.m. The Police Complaints Commission announced that they would not be carrying out an investigation.

The journey of Leon Kossoff's life and work was duplicated in physical terms by an exhibition of paintings and drawings positioned around the Annely Juda galleries under the title 'London Landscapes'. The show was a double autobiography: of one man's pilgrimage, and of the recorded places informing that personal history. Here was a manifestation of railway consciousness, its grandest justification. Walking around those rooms, in an hour or so, was as absorbing, inspiring, demanding, as walking around the entire circuit of London Overground in a single day.

The heavy doors of the upstairs gallery open on a line of minatory charcoal drawings, linked like coal trucks, and arranged along the floor in a provisional order that will change and be refined before the all-encompassing show opens on 8 May 2013. Tolerated afternoon light insinuates from a west-facing window, to be admitted to a privileged and subtle interior. Pale-grey chambers host a complicated negotiation between high art, patronage and publicity – with the challenge, for all of these, to confront such a raw and overwhelming revelation of the metropolitan soul: the artist's repeated raids, rebuffs, and captures of certain favoured urban motifs. The stations, literally, of a life's chronology: Dalston Junction, King's Cross, Willesden Junction, Willesden Green. The confirmation that it really can be done: sixty years of making drawings on the run, often as preparation for paintings, but always because that is just how it is, a proof of continuity for man and city.

I was thrown off balance by the physical energy of these

marks: the dashes, counterstrokes, overreaching arcs. And how, taken together, and processed down the length of the room, they amounted to something more: a record of struggle and relief in the form of a graphic novel rescued from remembered and reconstituted places. Kossoff is like a man coming back from the other side to make a convulsive map of locations where he can begin to search for himself, to confirm his former existence. There is steady pressure to interrogate the specifics of a valid past, London oases that act like radio beacons: a building site close to St Paul's Cathedral, a pool seething with swimmers in a chlorinated genetic soup, a staircase in the revamped Midland Hotel at St Pancras, vertiginous drops from iron bridges into the propulsive rush of a pre-electrification railway system. The wrestling of mass into free articulation confirms localized fragility. These things will disappear. And the witnesses along with them. The pain in this mortal contract is one of the sources of joy in the physical act of drawing: Blakean joy among dark contraries, soot and clay, gantries and engines.

The artist speaks of the burden of accumulated memories. His earlier life in East London streets was a 'pressure' that fuelled the urgency of his duty to work; the necessity of carrying his drawing board, time and again, to places he acknowledged as sites of unquiet narrative. The act of making a drawing was recognition. When developers swept in, and architects laboured to visualize new towers, the investment silos of the emptying riverside, the painter celebrated this process. He favoured impressionist zones – stations, railway hotels, small public gardens – but his performance was delivered with the expressionist delirium of Ludwig Meidner. The drawings are land*scrapes*: gouged, knifed into a delirious calligraphy of affect. They do not belong within the English tradition of the pastoral. Kossoff's figures do not *own* the ground: they are passing through, wearied by the cobwebs of time. When Kossoff returns to a favourite place or a regular sitter, they are not the same. Light, space, movement: he registers diurnal shifts with a trembling anguish. 'Differences,' he says, 'amount to a sort of pressure.' So begin again, start afresh. New day, new man.

Railways play a large part in the story. Railways as ladders of memory. Railways as metalled rivers sliced by the branches of the cherry tree at the bottom of a Willesden Green garden. An expedition down the length of the gallery begins with a funnelled spillage of tracks, converging on the western horizon, seen from a high bridge close to the builder's shed Kossoff occupied in Willesden Junction. He speaks so affectionately of this period, of wandering through illegitimate places with his young son. The impulse to explore industrial ruins, abandoned allotments, and landscapes shivering between periods of loud exploitation. Unimproved images of entropy. Behind-the-fence secrets. Doodles pinned to the studio door and allowed to take their time. Then the old itch, to be out there, on the move again. A half-conscious scribble becomes a rough sketch, becomes an achieved drawing. Is fixed to the wall (with many others). It becomes a painting. Where did the power come from, the rip of an organizing intelligence? Huge paintings of dynamic complexity would be completed in a couple of hours. Set aside in a back room while the paint dried. There were many failures. But the railway as migration, temporary halt, terminal, was the key metaphor. The managed abyss.

Kossoff's Willesden Junction drawings are triumphs of inhibited spontaneity, elemental forces choked back by the broken ribs of cancelled strokes, weighed down under a curtain of solid smoke. Along the edges of the drawings you will find small puncture marks like sprocket holes on a strip of film. Many of these feverishly worked sheets have been recovered from the studio, where they have been pinned up among post-cards, names, phone numbers and quotations.

The 'London Landscapes' show, for all its generosity, represents only a fraction of the artist's output, his daily practice. There were many days when he was kept inside, waiting for the sitter to arrive from the Underground at Kilburn. And many others, freed from that obligation, riding the railway back east to one of his chosen terminals, railway plazas swamped by the human tide.

Kossoff walked the gallery with me, pausing when I paused, shaking his head; perhaps things were not quite as bad as he anticipated. He made me feel that we were back on Chatsworth Road in Willesden Green, with the railway at the bottom of the garden. The modesty was genuine, but difficult to comprehend against the evidence of extraordinary achievement. We talked about how, when he came to paint the interior of Kilburn Underground, friends and family members appeared like welcome revenants.

Sometimes, when the painter stands waiting for the moment when he will start to draw, there might be a child's voice: 'Here comes the Diesel.' Kossoff's grandson is not seen, but his excited exclamation informs the slices of commuter trains caught in shorthand as they rush past the end of the suburban garden. The circle of the familiar is the support system for the painter's raids on railway London.

When we sit down, after our little tour, Kossoff quotes Blake's *Jerusalem*: 'The Male is a Furnace of beryll; the Female is a golden Loom.' He is a great reader and a great rememberer. 'I behold them, and their rushing fires overwhelm my Soul / In London's darkness, and my tears fall day and night.'

*

The coda to the show comes with the most convincing justification I have seen for those weeks of Olympic hallucination in 2012. When parts of London, away from the flares and trumpets of the action, enjoyed quietness and a stillness that was quite unreal and outside time, Kossoff returned to Arnold Circus in Shoreditch, the Boundary Estate where he grew up. He no longer had the strength to contemplate taking on the rigours of a major painting, but he carried his drawing board, day after day, to make a series of flightier, pinker works. Preliminary sketches shimmer as he traces his own orbit around the bandstand on its man-made hillock. He pauses to look back down Calvert Avenue to the site where his father operated a bakery. The Arnold Circus drawings are the perfect riposte to the unnecessary Cultural Olympiad. To that culture of improving slogans and self-serving commissions. They generate emotion without that compulsion to explain and make loud.

The drawing board could be left overnight at studios that were once the school the 87-year-old Kossoff attended as a young boy. Released from the requirement of acting as prompts for future paintings, the Arnold Circus sketches have a lyricism, a freshness that is delightful. Set alongside the sculptural darkness of *View of Hackney with Dalston Lane*, they float like feathers. The paintings from 1970 to 1975, in the studio that overlooked the East London Line, the German Hospital and Ridley Road Market, come with such a burden of history; facts extrinsic to the act of painting. The railway back then was a ghost line carrying echoes of a terrible freight.

Kossoff spoke of the germination of his railway obsession. He remembered: a young boy in wartime, labelled for transit, boarding at Liverpool Street. He was evacuated, with other pupils from Hackney Downs School, to King's Lynn in Norfolk. Leon would live with a Mr and Mrs Bishop, who gave him encouragement to paint. He remembered: the view from the train window, the sheds, canals, allotments, gas holders. A landscape witnessed in transit is not the same as a walked landscape. 'Railways give you space and light and movement,' he said. Kossoff's friend Andrea Rose, curator of the 'London Landscapes' show, spoke of his 'intense gaze of love'.

That gaze informs our orbital walk. It achieves everything we are stumbling to document. Kossoff's railway paintings are both document and vision. The migration from Dalston to Willesden Green shares with Ballard that sense of contemporary record as prophecy: how a private person, working under laboratory conditions in the London suburbs, strips the veins of the city.

The Kossoff paintings, as they are laid out around the circuit of the gallery, expose the emotional trajectory of the artist's life: the weight of the earlier works and the lightness of touch at the end. Perched above Dalston Lane, unseen, hidden away, Kossoff was torn in two directions, east and west. Then Willesden Junction arrived like a shipwreck, a Crusoe island; the tracks go on for ever like the sea. But he constructs his shed from ruin, he settles. At other times, he circled Mornington Crescent, York Way, the development zone around St Pancras and King's Cross. Before coming, in rosy twilight, as strength for battle fades, to the centripetal revelation of a gentle stroll around Arnold Circus. 'When the animal migrates,' John Berger wrote in *Railtracks*, his own railway meditation, 'the return is part of its journey. One could say an animal migrates for the sake of its return.'

A few years before this meeting at Annely Juda Fine Art, Kossoff suggested a walk from the National Gallery to Embankment Station; another point of transit, another site he had frequently recorded, in charcoal or pastel on paper. I guessed that he combined, after he had travelled in from Willesden Green, a tour of the National Gallery, looking at his favourite Poussins, Titians, Goyas, Rembrandts, with an amble down towards the river, a position of advantage, taking the measure of the crowds milling around the station.

When the day came, Kossoff was too weak for the intended expedition. The walk became a circuit of his drawings, a confrontation with *Christ Church, Spitalfields* from 1999. His spirit shone. A small, bird-like, bright-eyed man in a dark shirt. Wrinkled forehead. Quizzical eyebrows. Oblique, tentative glances. Quick shift of the hands. Where did that power come from? 'I don't remember.' How did he achieve these compositions? 'I don't remember.' He spoke, with a rescued smile, of anger, rage and mess, physical mess, the heaps of drawings, the cans of paint. All that his wife had to endure. 'I don't remember, I don't remember. I don't know.' The awfulness of failure, the gathering up of a life's work. Under persuasion, he yields a little. Perhaps it is not so bad. Perhaps, after all, he touched the edge of it.

And John Berger? He does remember making the same railway journey, when he travelled to his job as a part-time teacher. He wrote about 'the immense marshalling yards of Willesden'. The psychic disturbance at that point of the journey around a loop that ran from river to river, Woolwich North to Richmond. 'I would sit glued to the window.' Berger, like many others, found grandeur in post-war dereliction. He decided to disembark. He started to make drawings of the marshalling yards. 'Lines joining, separating, receding, the colour of stringy ribs of cut sticks of rhubarb, placed side by side, pointing to the horizon, where they stewed.' There was a better future, Berger felt, implied by that horizon. A future he would not live to see. 'A little more justice to the Junction and the world around it.'

I received a letter from Kossoff, regretting his 'heaviness' of the previous day. And telling me about seeing a room of pictures of Arnold Circus made by ten-year-old children from the local school. 'They were better than my drawings,' he said. But, in the teeth of everything, the struggle, the pain, this is what his life had been: the experience of light. 'Maybe, in the end, in spite of myself, it was a joyful activity.'

Willesden Junction to Finchley & Frognal

As ordinary streets extend in parallel with the railway ditch and its riverbank vegetation, we tramp into the night. Kötting squelches. His socks have liquefied and the blister bubbles, growing from other blister bubbles, have burst. Pavements conspire against us. I seem to be kicking through a parade of yawning tombstone lids. It could be that the strength to lift my stride is fading.

Palermo Road, Bathurst Gardens, Clifford Gardens: eastward to Kensal Rise, a series of dormitory dwellings, redbrick with white trim, privet-protected, curving from the north–south stem of College Road like the candelabrum branches of a menorah. The uneasy microclimate of the electrified railway runs me back to 1910, to the kind of house in which I grew up, with late, mass-produced Arts and Crafts elements, colonial porches, diamond details on the pointed gables, half-timber dormers. These are retreats from which we want to retreat, but there is no escape beyond stepping it out, swinging our tired arms. We both grew up in aspirational suburbs, where Arcadian fronts disguised all manner of repression and vernacular weirdness within.

At every roundabout, at every point where a crossroad bridges the tracks, we detour; peer over the railway wall, cut through tangled foliage, to be sure that the blunt yellow-nosed trains are still in service. Unit prices of desirable properties are surely climbing as we move east, but it's more Morlockland than Metroland. A certain residual gloom that goes with the safety of being this far out: *out from where?* Chinese whispers we can't quite hear rumble through the continuous shrouded terrace, as if the miles of bow-fronted conformity made up a single railway mansion.

On my reconnaissance visit it was very different. In the nervous optimism of morning – still alive, still fighting for a crust – these narrow corridors become a rat run; school transport stalled and horn-jabbing against delivery vans summoned by absent nuclear families who have no time to shop. Defiant cyclists, mounting kerbs, extending mortality with sweaty gulps of filthy air, the suicide smog leaking from idling exhaust pipes, strike off across town to their open-plan offices. They mourn, every day, the economic realities that banish them to extended village strips between railways and cemeteries.

This section of London Overground, pioneer metal with a new ginger makeover, has not yet exploded into grass-thatched modernist blocks or factory outlets for Burberry and Aquascutum. The streets are as quiet and regular as the Old Portuguese-Jewish burial ground between Alderney Road and Mile End Road. And the signs are with us, even in the thickening dusk, of a will towards community. LET US RUN OUR LIBRARY!

SAVE KENSAL RISE LIBRARY! This is a zone of concerned post-ers in unpolished windows. Most of them conservationist. One offers: BASEMENT CONVERSIONS. There is no trace as yet of the classic Hackney through-kitchen, the Welsh dressers of Islington, homeworker husbands bent over their light screens.

That modest neighbourhood hub, the Kensal Rise Library, with its locked door, is the battleground. The dignified red-brick building is fronted by shelves of books enclosed in a see-through plastic tent and announced as: THE KENSAL RISE POP UP LIBRARY. Aggrieved clients of the service have taken direct action. All over London, libraries have been decanting surplus stock, flogging off rarities to dealers, landfilling boxes of local history. Tragic Idea Stores – bad idea – try to blend in among branded corporate high streets by looking as gaudy and dysfunctional as the worst of them. The pitch is to be accessible, to offer broadband connections, DVDs of dead TV, hygiene advice, legal advice, budget t'ai chi classes for senior citizens.

The problem with this pop-up library is that it has too many books. Well-wishers are so keen to demonstrate their support for the concept of a library, with its deep-England associations, that they are offloading all the charitable donations they can carry. The nocturnal tent, beside the phone kiosk, has a NOT FOR SALE sign, and a greenhouse aspect that implies a familial relationship with that other threatened railway parasite, the allotment.

The Kensal Rise tent is anti-library: it doesn't let books out, it gathers them in, until protesting shelves are multi-stacked and groaning. This is a shrine to conspicuous altruism. You could build a section of the Berlin Wall with the mounds of unwanted titles. *Daniel Martin* by John Fowles. *The Ebony Tower. He Who Fears the Wolf* by Karin Fossum. *Farewell Horizontal* by K. W. Jetter. Sad orphans are horizontally stacked in alphabetical order. A handwritten note begs patrons: 'please keep book donations at home'.

Advice Andrew Kötting ignores. He digs out the copy of *London Falling* and asks me to write 'something peculiar' on the flyleaf. I can barely see the page, and the presence of all these books in their polytunnel forcing house is no encouragement. I scribble some occulted gibberish that nobody will be able to decipher, then sign and date it as a memorial to our walk. Andrew squeezes yet another unwanted item inside the sweating yurt.

Mark Twain opened Kensal Rise Library in 1900. He felt the same compulsion as current community bibliophiles: he donated five of his own titles and an inscribed photograph. I wonder what became of those? The site was gifted to the railway suburb by All Souls College, Oxford.

Shortly after our visit, the pop-up library with its gazebo was dismantled by agents acting under orders from All Souls (where Salman Rushdie was granted sanctuary in his hour of need, after a fatwa had been issued threatening his life, following the publication of *The Satanic Verses*). The books were left on the pavement in what was described as 'an act of cultural vandalism'. All Souls, it is understood, has a financial endowment of £256 million.

The affair came to the attention of a number of concerned petition signers; some, like Zadie Smith, had direct local connections. Many of the emails supporting the plans to turn the library into private flats were proved to be fraudulent, coming from false addresses. The police, pleading lack of resources, declined to investigate. Under considerable public pressure, the developer, Andrew Gillick of Kensal Properties, after consultation with advisers from All Souls, agreed that space would be allocated for a small community library staffed by unpaid volunteers.

*

Kensal Rise houses got bigger, they stood a little more aloof from their neighbours. The leading on the windows was more pronounced, net curtains protected interiors with real books and flowers and baby grand pianos, weighed down by ranks of coloured family photographs in silver frames. Gables were sharper. Ironwork balconies imitated vines. There were inset panels with wreaths and conches in white relief. The houses were set further back from the pavement.

Kötting's meaty yawns threatened lockjaw. His shoulders slumped. Hunger, I feared, would soon have him rummaging through well-stocked bins. Or kipping down among the laurels. It was the hour of fugue for both of us. The walk became all walks, our own and those whose recorded adventures had inspired us: Werner Herzog making his ice pilgrimage, much improved in the telling, from Munich to Paris. Albert Speer, shaping an epic travel journal/novel from circuits of the prison yard at Spandau, a Berlin suburb. John Ledyard tramping across Russia, heading for the Bering Straits, before being turned back in 1788. Cabeza de Vaca, naked, deranged, roaming the American Southwest, Florida to Mexico, sometimes a slave, sometimes a miracle worker raising the dead. And John Clare. Always John Clare. Labourer, poet, madman.

Clare, on his 'Journey out of Essex', the walk from Epping Forest up the Great North Road to Peterborough and Werrington, describes a period towards the end of the third day when he has been chewing tobacco to stave off hunger. 'Going a length of the road afterwards', shreds of tobacco stuck between his teeth, he remembers nothing; no place names, no details. It's all gone. When he comes to relive it, to write it, to go back into the sensations of the walk, there is a great hole. Pain returns him to himself in Stilton: 'completely foot foundered and broken down'. Ready to drop to the gravel, broken, sleeping where he falls. He hears the voices of two women. The old one thinks he shams. The young one sees that he is done. The collapse is absolute.

We are not there yet. We are moving steadily towards Kilburn High Road and the station Kossoff populated with ghosts. I suggest a break at Ciao-Ciao, a friendly restaurant where I stopped for coffee on a previous circuit, but Andrew is set on identifying the right pub. We talk about reprising the Clare walk, but that is not hard enough for the film-maker. He decides that he must dress as a Straw Bear. Leila McMillan will weave a costume, stitch him into a suit of reeds, and leave him to provide his own mud, internal and external. He'll lurch and prance through the forest, accompanying the troubled poet, who will be played by the actor Toby Jones. Toby, who has done Truman Capote and Alfred Hitchcock, would manage the silence of Clare very well, Andrew reckoned. The pride,

confusion, scorn that always burned and argued beneath the placid surface. Andrew would supply momentum, physical comedy. I wasn't sure how much comedy there was in this episode, but I recognized that we were approaching that state of something close to intoxication, when tiredness is no longer tiredness and roads merge and names are not worth recording or remembering. Even our own.

Kossoff carried his sketching board to the vestibule of Kilburn Underground many times, in a trance of recognition: newspaper kiosk, stairs, ticket machines, checkered floor. Now, when we stop to photograph the revised station, painted ghosts return. Through Kossoff's prescient engagement, they are fixed, even when the building that contains them is altered or abolished. Charcoal preparatory drawings, made on the street outside the station, are unpeopled: railway bridge, lines of force, racing clouds. Kilburn High Road runs north like a funnel of Darwinian psychopathology, energies in crisis.

A number of locations from the necklace of this Overground walk are beginning to fuse: Denmark Hill merges with Hampstead, the Maudsley Hospital with the Royal Free. Now that the BBC had pulled out of White City, as a tactic for exorcizing back channels to Jimmy Savile, in just the way they wiped his gurning obviousness from repeats of *Top of the Pops*, sequences shot within the demolished buildings float back to the surface. When London Overground vanishes underground, to tunnel through the glacial debris, between Finchley Road and Hampstead Heath, memory and topography slip out of synch. We don't have the strength to talk. We free-associate soundbites.

'Wood Lane?'

'Pinter.'

'*Accident*.'

There's a bit in Joseph Losey's 1967 film where the tightly

furled Oxford academic impersonated by Dirk Bogarde, wrestling with briefcase and umbrella, arrives at Television Centre for a conversation about a possible role in a talk show. His contact is not there, he's in hospital. The manically brisk, spectacle-adjusting substitute is Harold Pinter, rattling through his own dialogue. Another BBC arts man, in country suit and squashy hat, perches on the desk to talk straight through Bogarde. This turn is performed by Freddie Jones, Toby's father. Freddie, in his pomp, did John Clare for the serious BBC. It came to us, somewhere between Kilburn High Road and West End Lane, that we should invite Freddie to return to that role; the extinguished poet questioning his identity in the long exile of St Andrew's Hospital in Northampton. While an earlier, brighter self, played by Toby, trudges the road, teased and provoked by hallucinatory glimpses of Andrew Kötting's shambling and shamanic Straw Bear.

As we came under the railway and into Iverson Road, I noticed a black wool glove lying on the pavement. The glove was painted with a set of white finger bones. As if an X-ray had been too forceful and left a permanent print. A polished black car was parked beside the lost glove: CENTRAL PEST CONTROL. MICE – RATS – BEDBUGS & OTHER INSECT PESTS

The creatures Clare honoured in his witness. The quick and secret things of copse and cell.

A sequence I like in Freddie's BBC film of Clare has him picking stones from a field in his time as a guest at Matthew Allen's High Beach Asylum in Epping Forest. London visitors, superior journalists, have come to try him. To poke and prod around the fading lustre of celebrity. First, there is place. The gloomy Millet setting, the nondescript corduroy of the field, so unlike the slurp and ordure and knuckle-breaking grind of the mud farm in Kötting's Zola translation, *Filthy Earth*. The mechanical repetition of the actions performed by the labourers, tamed lunatics watched by their keepers, gives the scene an understated formality. And Freddie as Clare, brought from his fieldwork, his disguise, to take a clay pipe with these alien inter-rogators, catches the balance perfectly. Muzzling his demons, playing the man cured by fresh air and morally improving exer-cise, he nods and smiles. With every answer a tease, spiteful with ambiguity. He knows what lies ahead and is helpless to avoid the first fated step on the road. 'Forget thyself,' Clare would later write, 'and the world will willingly forget thee till thou are nothing but a living-dead man dwelling among shadows and falsehood.'

The Overground walk had achieved its critical state. Kilburn High Road was a manifest border. Kossoff's painted ghosts, his *Hamlet* play of dead fathers in the booking hall, brushed past us with spidery touch. I thought of Chris Petit's novel *The Hard Shoulder*, in which an Irishman returns from the little death of prison to an old life that is no longer there, among Kilburn rooming houses and Irish Republican pubs. Like so many Petit characters, O'Grady is emotionally atrophied. The book's nar-rative is a posthumous dream. The released prisoner is one of the revenants on parade, a face frozen in a train window, glimpsed and smeared by Leon Kossoff in rapid sketches undertaken in his Willesden Green garden, where he waits beside the propped-up cherry tree.

'After West Hampstead,' Petit wrote, 'the train travelled a ridge. Slate sky bled the colour from the view . . . O'Grady felt his stomach contract and thought of riding on, but he got out at Kilburn, pausing to watch the train move away down the long, straight track. He couldn't remember if the carriages had always been silver.'

The dead man stands where we are standing now. 'The Kil-burn High Road had been a ditch when he left, and still was from what he could see.' O'Grady looks for a pub in which to orientate himself while he waits for the sun to go down. 'Now he had grown invisible, which was how he wanted it.'

Kilburn is fed by the railway. Immigrant workers in boots and dirty trainers step from the station with a thirst.

The days when I could get commissions to make films with Petit were over. In some mysterious way, everybody concerned with the commissioning process seemed to be out of commission themselves: incommunicado with pills and pain, post-operative in Germany, convalescent in Deal, dying in a cottage in mid-Wales. The characters who truly understood film, yellow from cheap cigars and years chasing festivals, and sitting all night at tables where you had to shout in three languages to be misunderstood, were old. Crocked. Crippled with integrity. Some of them were almost as old as I was. And the bright folk who took meetings, the intelligent young women, had to be fastidious about accessibility and outcomes. One of them was kind enough to explain to me that I'd have to find a substitute for a tricky word like 'digress'. She suggested 'move'. 'We can't afford to alienate what's left of the audience,' she said. 'Keep literature for books.'

And if the thickening night and the fugue-like weariness referenced our swan-pedalo voyage, it also led me to tempt Andrew with tales from the road, the John Clare walk out of Epping Forest on those blistering summer days. It was the notion of becoming a Straw Bear that really sold it. As we inspected the underwater glaze of the patterned wall of green bricks near West Hampstead Thameslink Station, I could see the physical transformation begin: a slump of the shoulders, a lumbering walk, claws sprouting, matted hair spiking into plaits of straw. Andrew was channelling Herzog's *Grizzly Man*, belly growling, and peering suspiciously at the Hampstead horizon as if he were seeing the Alaskan tundra. His actions cast me in the Timothy Treadwell part; the nutty, bear-watching obsessive who comes to a very sticky end, killed and eaten, off-camera with live sound.

The film of the Clare walk would have to be done, budget or no budget. As we closed in on territory associated with the London exile, and last years of Sigmund Freud, the bear fetish took on flesh, and made itself available for analysis. Anxiety hysteria, in the form of animal possession, sounded very much like a suitable case for treatment.

A few weeks after recovering from our London Overground exertions, we drove to Oxfordshire, to seek out Freddie Jones, the veteran actor who, having played Clare with such bug-eyed conviction, was now the keeper of his spirit. Freddie lived in a converted chapel in a quiet village, not too far from a decommissioned US air base. The abandoned silos and deep bunkers suggested an ideal location in which to record the poems of Clare's madness.

Freddie was alone with his posters, the glory days of performing for Fellini in *And the Ship Sails On*, and an elegant coffee tray set out for him by his absent wife. He was a mime of gracious welcome. He waved us towards the tray with all kinds of amusing business, but he didn't have a clue how coffee was actually prepared. Andrew stepped in. He was in high-register mode too, spilling anecdotes, thrusting books at the unprepared actor, swooping and circling – and beyond all else registering his genuine conviction that Freddie was a great figure and the only possible man for the job.

'Shall we make the coffee a little more interesting?' Freddie said, reaching for the whisky bottle. After two or three cups, the coffee element of the mix was left out.

'I see passages of quiet contemplation,' Andrew bluffed. 'The Straw Bear wandering at the end of his tether, across a busy motorway, in the forecourt of a Happy Eater, stood still in the middle of a ploughed field underneath a wind turbine foregrounded by electricity pylons.'

'Bear? Be-arrrr? What bear? Oh this is delightful.'

In his snowy-white beard, with wisps of hair above pink cheeks, Freddie was the Lear of *Emmerdale*. He had a driver to take him up to Leeds for his appearances in the popular television soap. 'Costs me more than my fee,' he muttered. But the addiction was still there, to steal scenes with his electric disability carriage.

When Freddie slurped and sipped, remembering the earlier Clare, but not where he had left his VHS tape of the performance, and anticipating, with some excitement and necessary doubt, his future engagement with a director as mad and visionary as any from the past, the frown and inward gaze of the poet's lost mind was projected across his private face. And he started to recite, with perfect recall, the song of the road, and all its pains. Clare, in the seizure of inspiration, in his forest incarceration, jumped forward to describe what was still to come.

Life to me a dream that never wakes:
Night finds me on this lengthening road alone.
Love is to me a thought that ever aches,
A frost-bound thought that freezes life to stone.

Maresfield Gardens

There is a young woman in the front garden, her nakedness enhanced by the coarse covering of an old man's winter coat with a fur collar. She is pleasuring a used cigar. Long hair is caught in the lower branches of Sigmund Freud's favourite almond tree. A witness speaks of snot and smoke. Looking out from the study window, where heavy drapes are always drawn, our suppurating ghost is transformed. Unsupported, he walks through looped films that shimmer with faulty light. A 'propatetique' striding forward in eternity.

'Pretend that the others around us are real,' I said, unconvinced by the rasp of my own voice. By Andrew's retreat into his furry carapace. His trundling walk, a bear caught between dances, facing uphill.

Coming now, in the evening of the Overground circuit, to exiled parts of London that are disturbingly familiar, the people on the street begin to look more like themselves. Like characters I think I have known: bookdealers, jobbing translators, migrant Russian women hosting vodka seances to make a scene out of unpromising West Hampstead materials. We are weary enough, after the haul through Brondesbury and Kilburn, to let the fantasies through: self-directed dramas of consolation and reward. In the sodium-gaudy darkness, Andrew's sunglasses have passed beyond eccentricity. Into mimetic blindness. The lecherous grin on the face of his stuffed monkey is justified.

When I snap him against the orange stripe of West Hampstead Station, he holds up a ring of heavy keys. Perhaps he's missing his motorbike? He has the meat solidity of a Sickert portrait, painted wet on dry: thornproof hiking suit, canvas-strap shoulder bag. He yawns. And scratches a few sparks from his two-day beard.

At Finchley Road & Frognal, where the pulse of north-flowing traffic is felt, the Overground becomes an underground, tunnelling into London clay. This notion engages Kötting. Around this point, so he says, our most recent glacier put on the brakes. And the white tongue of the optimistically named 'Last' Ice Age ground to a halt. Viennese cafés nudge against the axial moraine, dispensing elaborate pastries and serious coffee. Motorists in their pods are preparing themselves for the bifurcation of M1 and A1. Small enterprises along this nervous stretch are being replaced by the showy windows of brand leaders.

The unsolved glacial question is carried with us, uphill, into what begins to feel like a condition of perpetual night. Is the Pleistocene a temporal division invented by academic professionals to keep the territory in-house? Or does it, as our discussion implies, invoke something *present* but submerged, an older, fiercer, better part of ourselves? And if I see the Hampstead ridge as a coast, a line of difference with which to contest the memories that drag themselves ashore, Andrew is more direct. How long is the tunnel? When was it built? How much did it cost? Can we find a way to trespass and walk through to Hampstead Heath without frying ourselves?

The tunnel, so I read, is 1,166 yards long. I'm not going to measure it. We will head directly up Arkwright Road, paying our respects to the Camden Arts Centre, and over the hump, putting our ears to the ground, from time to time, to be sure that we are still on the right track.

Contemplation of our failure to burrow under this dune of Eocene sand brought back the morning's challenge at Wapping, when we took the train beneath the Thames, rather than putting in the extra mile that would have allowed us to trudge, choking on fumes, through the Rotherhithe Tunnel.

'My first ride on the Tube,' Andrew said, 'was to Stamford Bridge. Chelsea/West Ham. I was seven. I supported the Hammers because of the World Cup. Peters, Geoff Hurst, Bobby Moore. And the away kit on my Subbuteo team. I had a thing for hoops. Any team with hoops.'

The psychoanalytical bias towards lying on a couch, with some bearded confessor, chin on fist, his chair behind your head, straining to interpret, to catch the halting phrases as they stutter and gush, might be a mistake. Walking releases the lock gates of memory with greater effect. And the process is not so costive, smoke-stained, airless. Walking therapy, side by side, turn and turn about, counters inhibition. Roles are exchanged like hats. No hierarchy. No punishing fee. No guilt. Narratives bleed into the map.

Kötting spoke of his excitement and fear. He was then a wide-eyed innocent going with the bovver boys in their Doc Marten boots, by rattling Underground train, into deepest enemy territory. He polished the symbols as he laid them out. How certain youths handled the black knobs of the cosh-like devices that hung down to steady standing passengers in the swaying viral torpedo. And how the speed-charged lads used the rubbery supports to kick out the window glass, roaring and jeering. Testosterone reek was heady. And carried with the warring tribe deep inside the bowels of the ground.

Andrew Kötting – Straw Bear, biker – fashions his panting-uphill anecdote to integrate material gathered from our walk. 'They came over the wall from Brompton Cemetery.' He made it sound like a Stanley Spencer resurrection. Football-hooligan invaders swinging into the stadium to attack the notorious Shed. While Kötting, the rememberer, being an unimplicated child, is absolved of the violence, the tribalism that has so much appeal.

Of late, he confesses, he has lost that punch. The desire to ram through impossible projects, bounce bureaucracy, is beginning to fade. His frontal lobes have taken one hit too many. He's on his feet, moving as well as ever, but he doesn't always know where he is. Or what he is doing. Pain is constant. His left hand fumbles with necessary straps. 'Stamp on it,' he said, 'and I won't feel a thing.'

We were too late for the Camden Arts Centre, but the venue held memories for both of us. Andrew had exhibited, participated, and checked out shows. I took a refreshment break when I made my preliminary reconnaissance of the Overground route, before I inflicted it on Kötting. Energized now by a sense of familiarity, I dragged my subdued and strategically dumb companion on a minor detour to a major resource, downhill and then up again, to a well-kept house. Although it existed, and glowed a fiery red in our evening reverie, this blue-plaque address – 20 Maresfield Gardens – was as mythical in the psychogeography of London as the rooms associated with Sherlock Holmes at 22b Baker Street. And with my search for Holmesian traces when I should have been in the library of the Courtauld Institute of Art in Portman Square, trying to get my hands on that single copy of some French thesis booked out for weeks ahead.

Sigmund Freud and Sherlock Holmes shared many characteristics. But Andrew was not for halting, and the Freud Museum, the house where the celebrated analyst spent the last years of his life, had closed its doors to paying customers hours before. I kept my dissertation to myself, as we navigated a walled byway known as Shepherd's Path, and on over the crest of the hill. There seemed to be a valid connection between Freud's excavations of the unconscious, impacted layers of repression and fantasy, and the physical tunnelling into the lobes of London, the glacial moraine. The railway interventions in the clay mantle were extreme, a forced lobotomy for Finchley & Frognal.

The Hampstead Junction Railway (later the Broad Street Line, later the North London Line, later London Overground) was an associate of the LNWR. It came into being to link Camden Town (and the NLR) with Willesden (and the NSWJR). An alphabet soup of railway companies and their parasitical developments carving up territory in the teeth of geography; subverting patterns of flow, springs and streams percolating through silt and sand. Hampstead the spa, the retreat, grew up around restorative waters. Quacks in gaudy waistcoats, bottling the chalybeate springs for sale at threepence a flask, declared that Hampstead waters were 'a stimulant diuretic, very beneficial in chronic diseases arising from languor of the circulation, general debility of the system, or laxity of the solids'.

Underground water collected in basins of clay flooded the tunnels. The invaders burrowed, shaping ledges for men and machinery. They burrowed again. Streets were lost, dwellings demolished: much of the present surface, as we pass among neat villas and regimented gardens, is dirt from railway excavations, gaping tunnels covered over with replenished and compacted soil. The metaphors are clumsy, but they won't go away.

Freud, nursing his cancerous jaw, and keeping off flies drawn to the ripe stench of bone rot with acrid cigar smoke, listens to the stories, playing and replaying significant details, teasing out explanations that read like crafted fictions. Like detective stories in yellowback shilling shockers: the Wolf Man, the lurid confessions of Anna O. *Studies in Hysteria*. *A Study in Scarlet*.

The tunnel between Hampstead Heath and Finchley Road

was constructed in 1859, three years after the birth of Sigismund Schlomo Freud in Mähren, Moravia. Financial considerations meant that the bore of this gaping hole, crossing Finchley Road, trepanning Arkwright Road, was narrow. Soil was slippery, unreliable. Records, giving a contemporary account of why this tunnel had to be tighter than others, were not kept. Sealed carriages slid through the dark. Passengers were tense, folded back into themselves, impatient for the return of daylight.

Kötting was unimpressed by my Freudian improvisations, he wanted Gradgrind facts: references, page numbers, dates, measurements. The pedagogic German aspect of the man was becoming clearer as his physical outline vanished in the Hampstead night between puddles of electrified twilight. 'It's all about archive,' he said. 'Archive never fails. An antidote to preciousness. Pure evidence. Live footage from the past rescues me from future depression. Show me any image and I'll subvert it.'

Freud and railways: escape. He travels from Vienna to Paris, a deal brokered with the Nazis after shaming exactions, documents signed, fraudulent claims settled, so that the collection of books and antiquities can be shipped out of Austria to Maresfield Gardens.

June 1938. One of those cinema escapes: last train, misty windows, closed frontiers. France. Sisters left behind. The dog, Lün, a chow, is brought out to perform, after quarantine, in home movies on the Hampstead lawn: the final birthday.

A passenger train transports Freud into London: Victoria Station. Newsreel cameras. Magnesium flares flashing like the assassination in Hitchcock's *Foreign Correspondent*. London welcomed the facsimile of the man, this cultural trophy, like a hieratic Egyptian figurine to be stored in the British Museum. Broadsheets congratulated themselves on their advocacy of the psychoanalytic fad; their liberality in letting such a distinguished alien step ashore, seeing him settled in a suitable quarter of the town. The obvious fragility, the fact that Freud was so close to death, added poignancy to the scene. The swagger of the earlier portraits – watchchain, gambler's drooping bow tie, black cigar – were as much Doc Holliday as Viennese medical man. The repeated and barbaric acts of surgery conducted on Freud's jaw, the cancerous lumps hacked out, the crudely inserted prosthetics, belonged with the kind of dentistry that Holliday might have practised. Freud dosed himself with a couple of aspirins and a fat cigar, and carried on.

'Ne moriare mori,' he said. 'To prevent death by dying.'

Another train. To Manchester. To visit his half-brother Emanuel in 1875. And his sister Rosa in 1884–5. This film of railway England, fields and factories, as witnessed through the smoke, made a deep and lasting impression. Emanuel died on 17 October 1914, after falling out of a train travelling between Manchester and Stockport.

A later Manchester migrant, arriving as a Lektor in the German department of the university, and conscious of the implications of following in the tracks of the philosopher Wittgenstein, was W. G. Sebald. The bricks of Sebald's retreat in Kingston Road, Didsbury, were not as red as Maresfield Gardens: part of a tactful development, not a custom-built Hampstead mansion, with eight bedrooms, three bathrooms, designed in 1920 by Albert Hastilow in the revivalist style, and improved by Freud's architect son, Ernst, who installed a lift to transport the ailing analyst from one floor to the next.

Trains were the weave of Sebald's prose. How many cavernous stations with abandoned waiting rooms? How many station hotels with slits looking out on brick walls and strands of ominous wire? How potent the urge, at the end of all that restless journeying, to lie down on the tracks?

In *Ghost Hunter*, a CBC Radio interview with Eleanor Wachel, Sebald reminds us that there are 'trains all the time' as punctuation between the episodes of Claude Lanzmann's *Shoah* documentary. 'The whole logistics of deportation was based on the logistics of the railway system.' That visibility is so obvious that it doesn't register as a symbol. Holocaust echoes are seeded throughout Sebald's texts: 'the track, certainly, the smoke, and certainly the dust'.

Ghost hunter or ghost detective, Freud appears in London, on the cusp of the Second World War, as a living phantom derived from the speculative fiction of that table-tapper Sir Arthur Conan Doyle. Sherlock Holmes couldn't operate without his *Bradshaw's Railway Guide*. He ventured in the historic period between hansom cabs and primitive aeroplanes, with trains as his favoured theatre. Trains meant timetables, meant the end of clocks set to the whims of local stations: standardization.

Holmes precedes Freud: *A Study in Scarlet*, with the first appearance of the consulting detective, was published in 1887. Freud's *Studies in Hysteria* came into print in 1895. *The Hound of the Baskervilles* stalked the moors and crags in the *Strand Magazine* between August 1901 and April 1902, while Freud's 'Wolf Man', the stern-bowelled Russian aristocrat Sergei Pankejeff, didn't make his way to the Viennese couch until 1910. But the two projections, Holmes and Freud, written into existence, animated by fanatical cultists, had much in common.

Cocaine. And other substance-abuse experiments. Obsessively cluttered London rooms with the blinds drawn. The ability to listen, observe, interpret: to tease out a narrative and to pick it to pieces, practising a form of portraiture by cubism before cubism has been invented.

The supplicant lies prone, or slumps in a chair. The interrogator betrays no special interest, until there is a revealing slip of the tongue, a show that has the entranced listener leaning forward, chin on steepled hands. Psychoanalysis is routine detective work with a higher fee. Clients are always inferiors, whatever their pretensions to wealth and caste. Irene Adler, *the* woman, the only woman for the misogynist Holmes, the American-born beauty with 'the mind of the most resolute of men', is mirrored by Hilda Doolittle, the bisexual poet, H. D., who undergoes analysis with Freud.

'He never spoke of the softer passions . . .' Conan Doyle writes of Holmes in 'A Scandal in Bohemia'. 'They were admirable things for the observer – excellent for drawing the veil from men's motives and actions. But for the trained reasoner to admit such intrusions into his own delicate and finely adjusted temperament was to introduce a distracting factor which might throw a doubt upon all his mental results.'

The Adler case turns on a compromising photograph. When, at the finish, the former opera singer and Bohemian adventuress, marries a man called Norton, and outwits Holmes, after disguising herself as a boy, the consulting detective refuses payment from his royal client and asks instead for a photograph of this woman. Freud decorated his Hampstead study, the retreat of those last fourteen months, with portraits of his own Irene Adlers: the Parisian singer and café-concert performer Yvette Guilbert, and the mysterious woman in furs, Lou Andreas-Salomé, who had lived with Friedrich Nietzsche and whose lovers included the poet Rainer Maria Rilke. The photograph of Guilbert is inscribed and dedicated, and dates from her visit to Maresfield Gardens, when she was in London for a series of recitals at Wigmore Hall. The portrait of Irene Adler that Holmes claims as a fetish, a sentimental trophy, shows her, full figure, in evening dress. It is not inscribed, but comes with a letter. 'Male costume is nothing new to me. I often take advantage of the freedom it gives . . . I leave a photograph which he might care to possess . . .'

Irene's surname, Adler, exposed in the first Holmes story published in the *Strand Magazine* in 1891, anticipates Freud's invitation to Alfred Adler, his colleague and later rival, to join the informal discussion group that germinated the psycho-analytic movement. After a bitter parting of the ways, Adler carried with him, wherever he travelled, the postcard from 1902 with Freud's offer: he wanted proof that he had never been a mere disciple. The hothouse atmosphere in which the Viennese discussion group took place offered as many schisms, rivalries, grudges, psychic assaults as could be found in the bio-sphere of sensational literature cranked out as railway reading in England.

Freud, crossing from Calais to Dover, dreams of wading ashore at Pevensey Bay, making a landfall as significant as that of Duke William of Normandy. With his entourage of per-sonal physicians, lapdogs, wealthy princesses, his strong cigars (the ash of which would tell Holmes so much), the Viennese professor is a Moriarty figure: an intellect as cold and perverse and egotistical as that of his rival, the legendary detective.

A late challenger to Freudian orthodoxy, an infiltrator of the inner circle, Jeffrey Moussaieff Masson, accessed and edited – a detective story in itself – the correspondence between Freud and a colleague from whom he parted on bitter terms, Wil-helm Fliess. An eccentric researcher, Peter Swales, dogged but untenured, picked over the Freud/Fliess letters, and discovered an episode which he proposed as a plot by Freud to murder Fliess by pushing him over a ravine when they were walking together in the mountains. There was a meeting in August 1900 at Achensee, in the Tyrol. A technical argument over who had first articulated the concept of universal sexuality soured the atmosphere.

Fliess, recalling the drama, in a book published in 1906, claimed that it was Freud's intention to lure him into the mountains, in order to nudge him over a precipice and down into the turbulent water below. This strange narrative echoes the famous conclusion of the rivalry between Holmes and Professor Moriarty, author of a treatise on the binomial theorem. Holmes and Watson enjoy a walking tour among 'homely Alpine villages' – until the day arrives for the apparently fatal plunge, when Holmes precipitates Moriarty into the Reichenbach Falls, 'that dreadful cauldron of swirling water and seething foam'.

Each breath nearer the last. We say it aloud but we are not convinced. *The dead die hard, they are trespassers on the beyond.* We echo and quote instead of revealing what we think we mean, or what we mean to mean. The wild surmises of that walk over Hampstead's glacial debris, the skull of the hill with its plaques to Freud and Sir Edward Elgar (HERE HE COMPOSED / THE MUSIC MAKERS / FALSTAFF / THE SPIRIT OF ENGLAND), kept us going, secure within our established roles. I had much more to say, but I would save it for the book. Andrew was calculating: first, the distance to the next bite, and then how he would have to postpone his bike ride back to Hastings and borrow a Hackney bed for the night.

When the circuit of the Overground was done, and it had to be all of a piece, a single day, in order to download its secrets, I would have to come back to Maresfield Gardens. I combined an afternoon visit with a walk from Willesden Junction to Willesden Green, thereby transporting after-images of the paintings of Leon Kossoff into this scrupulously preserved house of memory. Marina Warner, introducing *20 Maresfield Gardens: A Guide to the Freud Museum London*, draws attention to the self-sacrificing piety of Anna Freud's 'act of enshrinement'. Warner reads it as a way of seeing her father 'as an event in history, a new geography of the mind, not only a person'.

And I'm sure she's right: the redbrick villa with its tidy front garden keeping the road at a safe distance, and its generous allocation of windows, like an art school or dance studio, has become a portrait of the dying man. You step inside, at permitted hours, as if offering yourself up as a suitable case for treatment; a role I could never contemplate. 'Mental pain is without end,' says Max Ferber, the Manchester painter in Sebald's 1992 book, *The Emigrants*. But the notion of spilling the mess of memory, rehashing accounts of dreams (as dreary a business as conversations misdescribing the plot of *Breaking Bad*), was far too high a price to pay for normality. For acquiring some hygienic husk of personality as your safety mask in the world.

The first task is to find somebody prepared to sell you a ticket. Rooms beyond rooms, arranged with authentic mementoes, lead to a conservatory designed by Ernst Freud and now stocked with books, cards, customized mugs and novelties such as 'Prof. Sigmund Freud's Fruit & Nut Bar. The Non-Hysteria-Inducing Confection to be taken twice daily'.

The house in the days of Freud's youngest daughter, Anna, in her long residence, was the lair they all wanted to invade. Access was a rare privilege. The cupboard outside Anna's bedroom was crammed with unrecorded letters.

There are two monitor screens impertinently set in the high bourgeois dining room. Home movies flicker like candle flames in a dirty jar. The sunlit garden, once again, hosts a birthday celebration for the man who can barely stand to acknowledge the tributes, the floral gifts. And this happened *here*. Time knots and spirals; place is resolute.

Two gentlemen in formal attire, courtiers from another dispensation, arrive with an enormous ledger, which they invite the professor to sign. He had already signed away, to other authorities, much of his estate. Now, they say, he must pen his full name; the preferred version – *Freud* – won't serve. There is a point at which artists become branded single-name commodities: Picasso, Matisse, Bacon. *Sigmund Freud* is scratched in the register of the Royal Society beneath *Isaac Newton* and *Charles Darwin*. They bring the book to him. He was fit enough, when drawn by powerful bonds of affection, to cross town to visit Lün in quarantine kennels at Ladbroke Grove: the Royal Society, in Burlington House on Piccadilly, was a step too far. All too soon Austrians and Germans in exile, men like Ludwig Meidner and Kurt Schwitters, would be quarantined by internment on the Isle of Man.

Much of the bleached-out garden footage, looped within the twin monitors, lobes of memory, reminds me of my own dreams of a childhood assembled from surviving 16mm home movies. My memories are of the films, not the events behind them: parties, weddings, dead faces laughing. Those who acknowledged the camera and those who learned to ignore its nuisance. My mother before I was born. And my father's father, the medical grandfather I never knew, holding up cake for his dog, the Scottie, to jump. The doctor was not well. He wears a hat. He looks like the established James Joyce, convalescent after the latest eye operation. Like Freud in Maresfield Gardens, he is a border crosser, a bringer of messages from the other side. *The conscious wears away, the unconscious is unchanging.*

Freud disliked cameras, a mechanical system of evaluating the past to rival his own. And he never tolerated rivals. Whenever, as in the secure reservation, the Arcadia of Maresfield Gardens, confrontation became inevitable, a consequence of his fame or notoriety, he submitted, putting on a face as stern as a Greek tragic mask. He refused the Czech-born director Georg Wilhelm Pabst, who requested permission to contrive a film around the person of the Viennese analyst. Freud could have entered our European art-cinema pantheon, alongside Greta Garbo and Louise Brooks. Pabst, by 1930, had evolved a style acclaimed for its psychological prescience. He had what they called an 'X-ray eye' camera style, seeing through flesh and fabric. His London, designed, in *Pandora's Box*, for Louise Brooks as a victim of Jack the Ripper, was a studio set in Berlin. 'Analysis,' Freud told Pabst, 'does not lend itself to any kind of camera.'

The most potent retrieval, the one that transfixed me in front of the monitors in that Maresfield Gardens dining room with the souvenir painting of the Alpine region where Freud loved to walk, showed a young relative, a youth in flannels, blazer, open-necked white shirt, paying his respects to his grandfather. The youth was Lucian Freud. Innocent of the will to challenge the camera as an instrument of record, Lucian walks beside the fading old man, across the lawn to a fishpond. Lucian and Sigmund, side by side for an instant, affect the matter of London. The official story in the guidebook does not record this visit. But letters from young Lucian are on display in a glass case: 'Lieben Pap – we have put up the model railway. Have you already built the skyscraper?'

Painters were the true analysts: Freud, Auerbach, Kossoff. Day after day in their studio-traps worrying at portraiture, persons and places of the city. Scraping off, starting again, setting aside. Like Sigmund Freud, they finesse a narrative, the facsimile of a higher reality. They stay close to railways, using tracks as ladders into past and future, ladders of transience and extinction. Ladders like strips of film. They sketch compulsively, their notebooks are records kept against future portraits.

A different kind of painting, in high-walled mansions of the suburbs, is therapy. It does not belong to those who produce it. It is called 'outsider art'. It requires tactful curation. A vault at the Wellcome Trust. In the now-decommissioned asylum at Netherne-on-the-Hill, the doctors decided to remove all unnecessary internal organs, in case they should be the source of social infection: madness, delirium, vision. They plucked teeth, hacked out tonsils, sliced at the appendix, the worms and tubes of the interior. At mealtimes, nurses came to the table with a great confectioner's jar containing all the sets of teeth, which were handed out and then returned, when the chewing and mangling and dribbling was done.

Climbing the stairs, and not using Freud's lift, if it still exists, brings the paying visitor to the room with the death couch. We have already negotiated the portrait by Salvador Dalí, penned on blotting paper from surreptitious sketches: the Mekon bulb of the consulting analyst's bald cranium and the frown, blind eyes behind the round white disks of the spectacles. The vortex of that great snail's shell grafted on a rictus of cancerous pain spins me back down the route of our Overground walk: Dalí invokes Ballard. As the painting of the wolves in the tree by Sergei Pankejeff conjures thoughts of the remedial art of motorway asylums. And, more significantly, Angela Carter and her stories: 'The Company of Wolves', 'The Werewolf'. 'The wolfsong,' Carter wrote, 'is the sound of the rending you will suffer, itself a murdering.' The beasts painted by Freud's own Wolf Man are soft as white-furred pears. Their song is cloying.

There is a photograph of an Alsatian, together with a poem presented to Freud on his seventieth birthday, hung in Anna Freud's room. The dog belonged to Anna and its name was Wolf. When Hitler took Blondi, his own German shepherd, with him into the Führerbunker of the Reich Chancellery, a puppy was born. He named it Wulf in the mistaken belief that his first name, Adolf, meant 'noble wolf'. There are home movies in existence of the off-duty dictator and his dogs. Subdued familiars. Messengers from Carter's dark forest.

Nobody sits on, or even touches, Freud's leathery death couch. Nearby, old films loop: summer gardens, heavy dresses, bouquets, cake, wine, beribboned dogs. The chow rescued from quarantine would not approach the bed in which the sick man lay. The smell of the gangrenous jaw was too rank. They had to cover what was left of Freud with mosquito netting to keep off the flies.

Downstairs, the study is the heart of the house. The shelved books brought from Vienna. The artefacts. The lithograph, hung above the couch on which patients lay, was *Une leçon clinque à la Salpêtrière* by André Brouillet. The French clinician Jean-Martin Charcot, as showman, presenting a swooning, hysterical woman, in an operatic state of undress, to a room of men in dark clothing.

Now the curtains are always secured against shifts of London light. Another pair of Woolfs, Leonard and Virginia, called on Freud, to discuss the publication by the Hogarth Press of his controversial text *Moses and Monotheism*. Would he consider changing the title? He would not. With a formal gesture of European courtesy, Freud presented Virginia with a flower, a narcissus. Later she recalled: 'a screwed up shrunk very old man . . . inarticulate: but alert'.

Mummy masks, bodhisattvas, amulets: grave goods with which to rehearse a burial. Egyptian cullings and Greek sphinxes, the residue of dealers in Vienna, Berlin, Paris, dominated every inch of the roped-off room in which Freud engaged with his last patients, and in which he wrote. There is barely space on the desk. With so many gods and votive offerings, it must have been like taking simultaneous dictation in a dozen dead languages. The classic and the primitive. Excavated relics snatched from their ritual purpose and made into palliative toys, symbols to invoke the metaphor of analysis as an extension of archaeology.

I think of Freud as that original Hampstead archetype, the homeworker. The writer at his desk. Bedded down ahead of all those who would follow: Elias Canetti, Jack Trevor Story, Aidan Higgins, Margaret Drabble. Laptop labourers glimpsed through unshuttered windows. The artisans of literature who require no railway. A room of one's own. A favoured pub on Devonshire Hill. On Flask Walk. A bookshop. A chess café. A heath on which to walk the dog. A shady pond around which to make new friends.

The fantasy from the start of our tramp up Arkwright Road comes right back: the girl in the garden with her hair tangled in a tree, smoking a black cigar. The Freud Museum has a tradition of encouraging art. From time to time, taboos have been broken. The poet and performance artist Brian Catling, a presence as grave as an escapee from the expressionist asylum of Fritz Lang's *The Testament of Dr Mabuse*, a crazed professor or sane lunatic, approaches Freud's desk with its ranks of twice-sanctified objects. Catling's hair is snowy white. He is stridently besuited. For some reason his jowls flap with ribbons of sticking plaster: a madman who has taken a cutthroat razor to the mirror. He snatches up one of the precious figurines. His other hand is enclosed in a brown paper bag. The audience gasp at the impertinence. Catling/Mabuse gnaws on the phallic god like a starving dog splitting a bone.

Outside, in the front garden, the poet who sings and performs as MacGillivray, and whose voice, unaccompanied, can certainly channel the dead, is woven into Freud's tree. She leaks smoke, naked in a long fur-collared coat. Something of the density of the weave of dreams in that house is undone. And something is confirmed. Her young eyes, never blinking, halt the glaciers.

Hampstead Heath to Kentish Town

Without a visible railway, and cresting the hill, we free-associate. I had the feeling that I never quite qualified for Hampstead: financially, culturally, sartorially. It's hard to get the look just right: Alan Bennett/Jonathan Miller corduroy, V-neck pullover and tie, bicycle Oxbridge, *London Review of Books* kitchen suppers on the lower slopes, the better part of Camden Town – and then Peter Cook, actors and authors, slewed bohemia with dosh, towards the leafy summit.

But that was then, the days of renting rooms in houses where single gentlemen who left the BBC under a bit of a cloud shared a bathroom with bright, shiny, geometric girls from advertising agencies and hirsute Israeli men, maturing in theoretical architecture. On Downshire Hill, becalmed in the Freemasons Arms, that dead Python, Graham Chapman, gestured at the crossword and started mid-morning on lunchtime drinks. The preserved bedroom of John Keats was across the road. When I went to the bar for another heady draught cider – the debauchery! – I tried to see which black Penguin Graham wasn't reading. Hoping it was *The Odyssey*. So that I could mutter under my breath, 'On first looking into Chapman's Homer.'

It would take Muriel Spark in her pomp to do justice to the incipient drama of all this, the social and sexual interactions of the boarding-house group and the ones who are going to snap and do something worthy of a telephone call. Calls were public and not lightly made. Most of the rooms in these quiet hives were composing bits of books; none were published. Piano practice drifted over the reserved crescents like clouds of hay-fever pollen. I walked out to accompany Anna to the Underground station at the top of the hill, picking up newspapers along the way to be chopped into phrases that could be pasted to the page as accidental poetry. Hampstead High Street had a bookshop, a launderette on the corner of Willoughby Road, and a bank where you could walk straight up to the counter and ask them to cash your cheque for two pounds. Nobody was paying in.

I remember being summoned, late on a Sunday evening, to take a call from an elderly Northerner I'd never met, a man with some Hampstead stories of his own. The poet Basil Bunting. I'd approached him, by way of his publisher Stuart Montgomery, about taking part in a film. Very sensibly, he asked about money. There wasn't any. And nobody I hit on, at the BBC or in Germany, showed much interest in the topic.

Fitzjohn's Avenue was where we emerged and where I stopped talking about Freud. I told Andrew that Anna, when I first knew her in Dublin, thought I was making it all up, dreams and sex and *The Psychopathology of Everyday Life*. I must have an ulterior motive, trying to pitch such an unlikely tale. But although she had not at that point come across any of the founding fathers of psychoanalysis, I had to confess that she was far more likely to actually read their books, when the time came, and to absorb what she needed. I dipped in and out, sampled, snacked and stole in my usual magpie fashion.

Kötting wasn't listening. We were a long way from Deptford and a fair step from a bed in Hackney. There were anecdotes on tap about his days ducking and diving in Camden Market, and watching all-night sessions at the Scala, but the silence of these hilltop streets unnerved him. We were exposed, chalk-upland pilgrims whose natural habitat has been invaded by sudden outcrops of sensible housing. Overbred cats who never step outside watched us from behind gleaming windows. I understood the banishment of weeds and windborne infiltrators from these polite gardens. I had worked here, always for Jewish exiles, usually widows, as a jobbing pound-an-hour gardener or heavy-handed grass manicurist, keeping fecund nature in check. On good days I might be asked to get rid of a box of books – or, just once, a folder of erotic Japanese prints. The last vestiges of an unredeemed husband.

We were walking now in our own worlds. I knew there was a direct route, an uplands goat track, that would carry us straight to Hampstead Heath Station and on to the ley-line hub of Gospel Oak, but I wasn't confident, in our present condition, of finding it. Edith Sitwell writes about Rimbaud and Verlaine in their vagabond days wandering through Camden Town. 'They walked in parallel lines, at a dignified distance from each other and unnaturally straight, like two worn-out trams.' Uncanny. And precisely how we came down Lyndhurst Road in a companionable slump.

This was a much older spine, referring back to my first days in London, my intimate association with the Northern Line. I never deviated far from what looked on the Underground map like a straight shot between Kennington (and the film school) and Warren Street, and then out along the north-west diagonal, through Mornington Crescent, with its ghosts of railway-haunting painters, Sickert, Auerbach, Kossoff, to Hampstead. A Dante progress designed by Frank Pick: Camden badlands to shining village on the hill. Submerged rivers ran in the same direction, from Hampstead ponds to the Thames. Striking east is a perversion of the natural order.

Vestiges of Freud's cigars still webbed the almond trees of Belsize. At the peak of his consumption, he got through twenty a day. When his aching jaw was locked and frozen after the latest operation to scrape away the sour fruits of cancer, he propped it open with a clothes peg: an aperture just wide enough to admit a black stogie. Beckett in *Echo's Bones*, that ill-favoured tale of the afterlife, accuses smoke, the residue of crematorium ovens and the final wheeze of stoic philosophers perched on fence posts, of being the medium of exchange between the world of the living and the limbo of the recently dead. Sam had stepped down into enough riverside drinking dens where undispersed blue clouds stood in for the missing man, saturating furniture and fittings, staining portraits of clean-living athletic heroes with nicotine jaundice. 'The dream of the shadow of the smoke of a rotten cigar.'

The Belsize Park hinterland, that triangle between Fitzjohn's Avenue, Adelaide Road and Haverstock Hill, was saturated with anti-psychiatrists, gestalt therapists, kundalinic gymnasts teasing the sex snake from the spinal bow. The shadow of the old man in the garden fell across all of them. Freud's brief London coda, his dying reveries, the smoke, the flies, the packed library, the bonsai forest of votive figures on the desk-top, ice-crawled down the contours. If a social scientist contrived a geological map for class trauma, you would colour this zone as yellow as fine-grained sand.

Visiting R. D. Laing, the mind-guru of the period, in his Belsize Park basement flat in 1967, was confirming the evolution from the grand bourgeois pretensions of Maresfield Gardens to the nakedness of elective bohemia. But still the patients, the troubled ones, made their appointments with their charismatic prophets. Freud and Laing, outsiders in London, agreed to perform, engage with, challenge and interpret, as part of the price for mastering their true calling as writers. Fictions of truth. A cinema of confession and seduction achieved without film. Laing wanted to fill mainstream television screens with a single struck match that would take half an hour to flare. And with the infinitely slow pouring of a glass of water. It was too shocking. Freud's special patient, the poet H. D., was part of an experiment in using film to explore extreme psychic states and their relationship to surface reality. In 1930 she appeared with Paul Robeson in a piece called *Borderline*, funded by her lover, the novelist Bryher. Belsize Park floated on unmade projects, confrontations between psychiatrists, underground documentarists and culture fixers.

I arrived in Laing's flat with a film crew of my own. There were no carpets and not much furniture. A gramophone playing the Beatles' *Rubber Soul* was tended by a young lad, Laing's son. The room where we spread ourselves opened on a wilderness garden. Somebody had cut the outline of a horse from one of the Sunday newspapers and positioned it on the wooden floor.

The youth who accompanied me, recently sent down from Oxford over some standard drug infraction, and soon to become a Laing client, asked a question about tactics and confrontation. With the arrogance of the privileged half-born, he told the anti-psychiatrist that he was guilty of trying to induce a flash of consciousness, with no idea of how it was going to happen.

They were, both of them, cross-legged, red-eyed and comprehensively stoned.

'You either shoot them or you turn them on,' Laing said. 'And there is no violent, coercive, authoritarian mode of persuasion or seduction that will turn people on – except to be turned on oneself, as far as one can allow oneself to go. And that seems to me to be all that you are saying.'

My own – and only – engagement with place was through mapping. And walking. No sooner was I settled in my Hampstead room in 1966, and travelling to a part-time job force-feeding general studies to motor mechanics in Walthamstow, than

I plotted an excursion as a method of linking figures who struck me as binding the territory together, contributing to that underlying and still-unexposed London mythology. Tim Powers, in his 1983 novel *The Anubis Gates*, managed the trick without leaving California: there is a portal, a time gate, accessible on Hampstead Heath, leading to a subterranea of Egyptian magic (Freud's figures come to life), chthonic monsters and archaic poetry.

I roped in a couple of companions, floaters from Dublin, and led them to Golders Green Crematorium, where we paid our respects to Freud's ashes. All that heat and smoke reduced to an ornamental urn. Between mourners, we processed the paved walkways, the Italianate colonnades, failing to acknowledge the traces of other London figures cremated here. All those already recorded, installed on commemorative tablets. Or those still to come, slots reserved for a future date. Anna Freud and Doris Lessing from Finchley and West Hampstead. The architect Erno Goldfinger with his brutalist towers, twin spectres of Westway and Blackwall Tunnel approach. Concrete obelisks for a city that never happened. And Joe Orton: butchered in Islington. Bram Stoker banishing Count Dracula to Purfleet. But our biggest miss of all was Percy Wyndham Lewis whose trilogy – *The Childermass*, *Monstre Gai*, *Malign Fiesta* – was the most accurate topographic chart I knew of the soul's attempt to penetrate the labyrinth of the radiant city. 'Some homing solitary shadow is continually arriving in the restless dust of the turnpike,' Lewis wrote. Prefiguring past and future pilgrims, from John Bunyan to John Clare. The almost-living in pursuit of the not-quite-dead.

From Freud to Karl Marx, by way of the Llandin, as Parliament Hill was known to antiquarians. We touched the stone of assembly, a recent intervention proving the site of the Gorsedd of the Druids, a sacred elevation. And moved on to the massive head of Marx in Highgate Cemetery. Here was the materialist antidote to arcane speculations constructing an essentially conservative version of the city involving hierarchies of power, privileged access to the gods, and lines of terrestrial force that squabbled for precedence like our current energy suppliers, the frackers and reckless spendthrifts of fossil resources.

Karl's glowering, leonine head was an iron chess piece honoured, on the day of that first London *dérive*, by small parties of excited Chinese men in long coats and Mao caps. There was no strict pattern to this walk: Freud, Marx, and a vague attempt to identify the room where Rimbaud stayed with Verlaine in Royal College Street. The notion of these provocative exiles taking up residence in London gave that other metropolis, the city within the city, the city of our imagination, a certain lustre.

Drifting through the graves and memorials of St Pancras Old Church, we found ourselves on the disputed towpath of the Regent's Canal. The narrative of our pinball zigzag between persons of interest evaporated. We were liberated by the absence of memory. We infiltrated a terrain suspended between eras of economic adventurism; the working barges had gone and the barriers and mesh fences of the energy companies had not yet arrived.

Railway cathedrals on the horizon. Gas holders. Allotments. Warehouses. We carried on, making a detour around the tunnel under Islington, and pushing east until we arrived at Victoria Park – which reminded one of our party, a Francophile, of Louis Aragon's surrealist excursion with André Breton to the Buttes-Chaumont. The Parisian park was a 'shared mirage'. It destroyed boredom. The meandering paths and shaded avenues suggested 'a great revelation that might transform life and destiny'. We emerged into the streets of somewhere shabby, self-contained, and utterly mysterious: a place called Hackney.

The cinema has disappeared from Pond Street. The Royal Free Hospital, an intimidating, multi-balconied hulk, links us to Denmark Hill, to the Maudsley and King's College Hospital. A TV woman, her prompt notes kept out of shot, is delivering a snappy piece about healthy meal initiatives for patients, along-side a KFC monster burger bus stop dressed with the slogan: FILL YOUR TANK. Listening to Andrew's creaking joints and squelching boots, I can't decide if we should check him in to outpatients or find a pub.

With the reappearance of the Overground at Hampstead Heath, our steps quickened. We were returned to the actual, the facts of the street. An architect called Robert Dearman had gussied up his narrow grey strips of window with a set of five bright-coloured Olympic rings. They struck a redundant note on a street with more impatient cars than people, so far from the Stratford development zone. The misted glass pan-els, I realized, were a design conceit, intended to reference a top-down view of swimming lanes or a section of the run-ning track.

I let Gospel Oak pass without comment. We were too tight against the railway that loomed above us to go back to my old source book, *Prehistoric London: Its Mounds and Circles* by E. O. Gordon. 'At the foot of Parliament Hill is Gospel Oak Station,' Gordon wrote. 'A name which connects the Druidic with the Christian religion, and links British and Saxon cus-toms.' I swallowed the story and recorded Andrew smiling behind his dark glasses, belly rumbling.

Kentish Town West to Camden Road was suspension of disbe-lief, a necessary sliding away and letting go. There were too many railways. Too many carpet shops. Too many Hackney migrants from the communal era of the 1960s had settled on these welcoming slopes. A beggar started his pitch, looked at

231

our ruin, and thought better of it. He gestured towards Kötting with a generous can.

Marina Warner, inheritor of Angela Carter's role as fabulist,
recaster of fairy stories, wise woman of the west, lives here
in a book-filled house threatened by the vibrations of passing
trains. Marina investigated the way that local public houses
were associated with the myth of old women as witches, predators, baby boilers, cannibals. The loss of the names of hostelries
for travellers and traders, Old Mother Red Cap, Jorene Celeste,
was felt as much as the loss of the buildings themselves, their
inevitable conversion into more commercial enterprises. 'Does
any of this matter?' Warner asked. 'On the scale of things, with
all the other problems near and far, hardly. But there are reasons for minding, apart from the general loss of memories and
stories that connect people and places.'

Marina regrets the dissolution of spaces in which unsponsored yarn-spinners, drunks, derelicts, ragged passerines, can
tell their tales. Oral histories must have legitimacy beyond the
remit of respectful academic recorders. Writers with the peculiar ability to process this free-floating material, hard-working
soaks like Julian Maclaren-Ross and Robin Cook, have been
unhoused. It was breathtaking to watch how Cook could,
over a heavy session, after a reading in Compendium Books,
take a story involving characters he'd never met, or even heard
of, and make it completely his own. An improvement on the
original.

Andrew wasn't buying it. 'People drift and leave their marks,'
he said. 'Dogs' droppings on the end of the shoe.'

When I recorded him outside the station at Kentish Town
West, he gestured derisively towards the Overground map. It was
that time of night, the hour of slippage. A young man coming up from the platform had the rat-chewed hair of runaway
Rimbaud. He was prematurely grey. Fever-flushed: burned by

booze and pills, not suntanned. He was chewing his nails to the quick. A yawning turnip head secured with the relic of a tartan scarf. Rimbaud was fascinated by the Underground. He wrote about railways emerging on all levels from stations like grand hotels.

The pub we chose was the Abbey Tavern on Kentish Town Road. I don't know what Marina Warner makes of that name, but it worked for me: ecclesiastical pit stop with a dash of W. B. Yeats and Dublin. The foundation stone was set on the 3rd of December 1891 by Mr A. T. T. Cowling. The door instructed patrons to DRINK EAT GARDEN.

Refuelling was a requirement, but sitting down would carry the risk of our not being able to rise again. Pints were delivered, swilled back, replenished, before a bowl of steaming fish pie made it from microwave to table. The pub interior was high-ceilinged and roomy, but intimate enough to allow the lurching approach of a person in a black satin bowling jacket who introduced himself as Tony Martin. He looked like trouble in Christmas wrappings. Kötting had taken off his boots and placed the hideous objects on the table, where he could keep an eye on them as he hobbled towards the bar, hoping to secure a stronger fork, and a linen napkin on which to pop his blisters.

He was close to done, but the food and drink, and a couple of hours in the Abbey Tavern, should stiffen his resolve for the final haul. This was not the moment to tell him that we'd be detouring by way of Royal College Street.

'I don't like the way you keep kicking the kerbstones,' he said, as he set down my pint. 'You've been struggling, son, since Kensal Rise. That library on the pavement took the wind from your sails.'

Tony Martin, whose hair was black as cuttlefish ink, and

whose remaining teeth were yellow as candlewax, offered to sell Kötting a pair of slip-on dancing pumps. His own. For a tenner in the hand. Or another pint of Bacardi and coke. He'd take the old boots in part exchange, for use in the garden, as plant pots for olive trees. Andrew snatched them back. They slopped with blood and worse.

Our new friend's name rang a carillon of alarm bells. Could this be Tony Martin the Norfolk farmer convicted of blowing away a burglar from the Travelling community with a pump-action shotgun? Unlikely. It was worse than that: an unemployed impersonator of the well-known San Francisco crooner, once married to Cyd Charisse. Tony was about to launch into his interpretation of 'Lover Come Back to Me'. It was time to make our excuses and get back on the road.

A few days later I took the Overground to Camden Town. I wanted to check out the Oxfam bookshop a few yards up the road from the Abbey Tavern. It had been shut when we limped past, but I had an instinct that something in there was waiting for me. Sure enough, after a thorough scan of the usual necrophile stock and overpriced nonentities in the locked glass case, I excavated a copy of Knut Hamsun's *Chapter the Last* in a nice 1929 blue-cloth US edition. I parted with £4.99. 'Truly we are vagabonds in the earth,' it began. 'We wander by roads and trackless wastes, at times we crawl, at times we walk upright and trample one another down.'

Camden Town to Haggerston

It was that point, around the mid-watch of the night, when walking becomes dreaming. Legs could not remember a time when they weren't keeping my weight off the pavements. Those grey Camden flagstones were another sky. Tarmac was treacle. My soft cartilage was so worn down that I could hear the grinding of bone on bone. I was a xylophone of improperly attached skeletal parts. Kötting was thick meat, sploshing and squelching, as blister-pods popped and burst in an obscene harvest.

'On islands,' he said. 'On small islands, elephants get smaller. And rats get bigger. Until they meet, somewhere in the middle. Imagine a rat the size of a baby elephant.'

He was losing it fast. A late Overground train, windows illuminated by an uncanny storm-light glow, ferried a party of circling warlocks across the Camden Road bridge: a Jules Verne submarine out of its element.

The house to which I'd brought Andrew, while letting him believe we were on the most direct route for Hackney, was set with a plain tablet, very much like a gravestone: as if a double coffin had been slid straight into the white wall. THE FRENCH POETS / PAUL VERLAINE / AND / ARTHUR RIMBAUD / LIVED HERE / MAY–JULY 1873.

It was enough for now to have it confirmed, that this was indeed the location from which the poets, with their few words of English, set out in combative and temporary alliance on long walks across the city that symbolized the *moderne*. From this window – *which window?* – Rimbaud registered the secular cathedrals of the stations, King's Cross and St Pancras. 'Je vois des spectres nouveaux roulant à travers l'épaisse et éternelle fumée de charbon.'

Odd couples. Coal smoke. Intertwined smoke serpents from the engravings Gustave Doré made to illustrate Blanchard Jerrold's *London: A Pilgrimage*. The two men, the English journalist and the French artist, were yet another pair of questing urban wanderers, tramping in the footsteps of Dickens and Henry Mayhew, in the expectation of forcing the uncatalogued sprawl to give up its secrets.

London: A Pilgrimage was published in 1872, when Rimbaud and Verlaine visited London for the first time, taking lodgings at 34–5 Howland Street, off Tottenham Court Road. Overground railways and cavernous arches were part of the nightmare dreamscape of the modern city, the new Babylon. Rimbaud, in the period of his runaway vagabondage in Paris, slept under the arches. Edith Sitwell tells us that the hands of the young poet 'were covered with chilblains, no matter what the weather was like, since they never recovered from the icy nights he spent huddled under the railway arches of Paris'. Doré's final engraving for Jerrold's attempt at a microcosm of London is called *Under the Arches*. It depicts rough sleepers huddled under a bridge alongside a *bateau ivre*, a drunken boat freighted with the dead. Smoke-shrouded trains, wherever they are found, crawling on ladders above the dark chasms of the imperial city, are ferrying the damned across the Styx.

Ludgate Hill – A Block in the Street is the best known of Doré's railway visions: a steam locomotive, frozen mid-bridge, as we look towards the melon dome of St Paul's, down the stalled highway of Fleet Street, with its omnibuses, carts, hearses, hawkers, idlers and workers in their multitudes. With obelisks, spires, chimneys, trade signs.

Jerrold the nightwalker records the first stirrings of outlying districts: 'The sometime silent City is filling at a prodigious rate. The trim omnibuses from Clapham and Fulham, from Hackney and Hampstead, make a valiant opposition to the suburban lines of railway. The bridges are choked with vehicles.'

Doré depicts *The Workmen's Train* as an arched subterranean vault illuminated by hanging globes, while the first glimmers of daylight are projected through a line of apertures. Labourers with their bundles crowd into third-class trucks. From the start, railways asserted hierarchy, each in his place. The slave classes setting out before dawn. Clerks next, breakfasted in Hackney and Holloway. And then, first class, the merchants and bankers, in time to make a show before taking a leisurely luncheon at the club. Rimbaud called the regiments of London's poor 'poverty's cattle'.

The Doré illustration that returns me to our walk is titled *Over London by Rail*. The arch of a bridge becomes the frame of the engraving; the tight terrace curves away to the next bridge, on which, inevitably, a train is making its black-smoke transit. We are invited to stare down into a nest of backyards, laid out like pens, making this segment of London into a factory or factory farm.

One of the few English words Rimbaud brought with him to London in September 1872 was 'railway'. V. P. Underwood in an essay dealing with 'English influences in Rimbaud's work', published by *Adam International Review* in 1954, describes a period when Rimbaud stayed with his mother and sister at 12 Argyle Square, near King's Cross. 'Crowded trains hurry in all directions, and they stop to watch the new Metropolitan line, partly underground, its trains dashing in and out of tunnels. Is it not this that makes Rimbaud imagine, long before Fritz Lang, his vast Palais-Promontoire which *leurs railways flanquent, creusent, surplombent*? Most of his visionary *Villes* of modernity or futurity seem to have *points de départ* in London landscapes.'

That early refuge at 34–5 Howland Street was once commemorated by a plaque for Verlaine, with no mention of his youthful partner in crime. Underwood, in a footnote to his essay, tells us that he was walking down Howland Street 'on the precise day in 1938 when the house was being demolished to make way for a telephone exchange'. He rescued the Verlaine plaque that had been unveiled in 1922 by Paul Valéry. At the time of writing, he still had it.

It's a nice notion, as Patrick Keiller points out in his film *London*, that the lover-poets are now honoured, not by a modest plaque, but by the priapic absurdity of the Post Office Tower. A sculpture of unsatisfied male desire. 'L'acropole officielle outre les conceptions de la barbarie moderne les plus colossales,' Rimbaud wrote in 'Villes', one of his *Illuminations*.

Allen Ginsberg would have been excited by the connection. When I interviewed him on Primrose Hill in 1967, he made constant reference to the 'thorn tower' and its magnificent thrust, bristling with paranoid listening devices. For the Beat poet, this was the ultimate symbol of the City. When a young boy, dodging school, sat on the grass for a smoke, Ginsberg interrogated him.

'Hey, you know that big tower up there, what is it?'

'It's the GPO Tower.'

'No. The tower tower tower tower. The round thorn tower. Is that a hotel?'

'General Post Office Tower. They send all the television relays out.'

'They got radar on the top. In case a war starts.'

We come through a tight passageway, one of those urban secrets allowed to survive between eras: a crack, a cranny, old bricks brushing our shoulders. It's an effort of will to reconnect with the Overground and not to drift on to St Pancras Old

Church, the railway terminals, redeveloped warehouses, Euro shopping zones, canal veins ghosting towards the Islington tunnel. The whole area is up for grabs.

We plodded back to the point where the railway crosses Camden Road. I remembered a Day of the Dead window I wanted to photograph: flowered skulls and tombstone teeth rioting in psychedelic frenzy. In our present condition, a little woozy, a lot weary, those brilliant, sharp-edged skulls were enamel badges to be pinned straight to our white eyeballs. We were well prepared for our future engagement with John Clare and his 'paraphrenic delusions', as Geoffrey Grigson called them. Clare as a night-wanderer in London was super-sensitive to emanations associated with the cracks and fissures between buildings, the slippage between centuries: 'Thin, death-like shadows and goblins with saucer eyes were continually shaping on the darkness from my haunted imagination.'

I was sympathetic to the description of his condition on the form filled out for his induction into Northampton General Asylum. A mental collapse brought on 'after years addicted to Poetical prosing'. Soon Clare would believe that his eyes had no pupils. Soon we would believe that the end was in sight and a second circuit was not required.

Andrew was cowled in silence. We were on parallel tram-lines, locked into our separate derangements. Whenever he came up alongside me, he seemed to be muttering the same phrases on a loop, as a form of neurotic penance or bizarre humour.

'Almost mathematical,' he whispered. 'Make up your own rules. Own rules, own rules. Make it up. Flesh radios. Start at the end. Reverse engineer meaning.'

Sanity was preserved by the bones of the railway, dragging us towards Caledonian Road & Barnsbury, the residential squares and visible aspirations of Islington. The sort of territory from which the Blairs could move on to oligarchic wealth and global infamy.

Agar Grove shadowed the Overground with not much between road and railway. In 1966 Leon Kossoff, coming west down the old line from his perch on Dalston Lane to the builder's shed at Willesden Junction, paused on York Way. There is a promising railway bridge that it would be churlish to resist. Cross-town workaday traffic is a modest intrusion on the landscape, while economically significant intercity services gush out of King's Cross. Here you will find the random accumulations, fragments of wall and shed, that passengers, settling back, if they have managed to secure a seat, register as symbolizing the essence of the city they have paid so much to leave behind.

Kossoff sketched York Way Railway Bridge, and from those sketches made a number of large drawings, charcoal and pastel on paper. Again he seems to be registering, in landscape format, the seminar of floating huts, shredded sky, stumps of towers along the curve of the horizon. All this energized space is seen in bright, sunless illumination, like the afterflash of an explosion at night. The method of choosing a number of privileged viewpoints, and returning to them, time after time, had its advantages over the steady plod around the entire circuit; a technique fated to decline into more poetical prosings. A queasy flicker-show of snapshots and echoes. Misremembered dialogue and overloaded prose. Painters have the purity of gesture: thought as act as meaning.

Impossible to tramp down Brewery Road without recalling Beckett's *Murphy*. I knew and honoured the hawk-faced Dubliner as a great and perhaps undervalued London walker: there was much ground to be covered between the early decades in Foxrock and Paris. Biographers call these 'The Bad Years'.

London was mental anguish, frustration, psychotherapy; visits as a close observer to the Bethlem Royal Hospital in Bromley; the suburban version of the original Bedlam. The hospital was useful research for the novel that became *Murphy*. Beckett, in his disaffection with work, place, life, stamped many miles across the metropolitan area. He has spoken about how, on one occasion, out of nowhere, he found that he had stopped moving. There was no valid reason to take another step. He sought help from psychoanalysis, in the person of W. R. Bion. Psychoanalysis was not available in Dublin, though the town was well supplied with madhouses.

Like his leading character, Beckett lived in World's End, West Brompton, while he wrestled with the novel. Presumably he was attracted by that name: World's End. I was fascinated by the way the geography of *Murphy* predicated our Overground circuit: from dealings with Lots Road, Cremorne Road and Stadium Street, 'the smell of the reach', the proximity of the burial ground with its specialized cruisers, to our present map reference on the approach to the old Caledonian Cattle Market.

Murphy relocates to a room in Brewery Road: 'between Pentonville Prison and the Metropolitan Cattle Market'. He likes to take the sun on a bench where he can enjoy the perfume of 'disinfectants from Milton House immediately to the south and the stench of stalled cattle from the corral immediately to the west'.

I mention these things to Kötting, whose feet are now advancing in a mechanical Cartesian fashion, very true to the spirit of Beckett. Push out. Test the surface, as if the toes were fingers. If the pain is acceptable, draw the leg back and repeat the prescription. As a proselytizer for Sam, Andrew looked more to the plays than the novels.

'The unfathomability,' he said. 'The placelessness that is *his* writing.'

I found nothing but place, place transformed. Andrew is more the poet. He talks of 'contemplation as a means of navigation'. I'm a clay-footed literalist. I saw in the deserted street Murphy's long climb home. 'And while Brewery Road was by no means a Boulevard de Clichy nor even des Batignolles, still it was better at the end of the hill than either of them, as asylum (after a point) is better than exile.'

Putting on time, the element that is never truly put on, Murphy makes repeated pedestrian circuits around Pentonville Prison – where so many, including numbers of his countrymen, met their ends. Sir Roger Casement, the Irish republican and author of the notorious *Black Diaries*, was hanged within these walls. Oscar Wilde, whose sad wraith, in transit between Wandsworth and Reading, we encountered on the platform at Clapham Common, was lodged here. Murphy walked as Beckett had walked in other cities around silent cathedrals after they had sold their last tickets for the day.

There is a circulation, of prisoners in privatized vans, cattled between the holding pens of remand and facilities adequately furnished as places of execution. A circulation of footballers, rising and falling, injured and ageing, between railway-accessed stadia. A circulation of poets and political exiles moving between rooming houses. A circulation of figures trapped in the limbo of novels specific to certain districts of London. A circulation of images of circulation: the terrible clockwise procession of silent men in Doré's engraving *Newgate – Exercise Yard*. They shuffle under brick walls that cancel any prospect of the sky. The motif is reprised by another London visitor, Vincent Van Gogh, in *Prisoners Exercising (After Doré)*, which he completed in the asylum at Saint-Rémy-de-Provence in February 1890. The painful circularity of asylums and motorways and railways for commuters.

Murphy waits for the sound of the bell from the prison

tower of Pentonville. He remembers a bench of refuge in a small public garden south of the Royal Free Hospital that now 'lay buried under one of those malignant proliferations of urban tissue known as service flats'.

The ineradicable circularity of reference is undoing us. We are so much taken with figures projected out of fiction, with poets worrying at expeditions in quest of serviceable images of the quickening city, that we are quite incapable of knowing where, at any given moment, we are. The shadow-lines on Kötting's face are the acid bite of cross-hatched engravings. If we pause for a moment on the heights of Caledonian Road, somewhere between Holloway Prison and Pentonville Prison, female and male, force-fed suffragettes and waxwork murderers, Neville Heath and John Reginald Halliday Christie waiting for the rope, we don't appreciate stragglers heading for home, exhausted nightworkers: we are too busy flipping the carousel of quotations. Ill-assorted couples embarked on their voyages of derangement.

The Two Pilgrims at Highgate. Doré's London expeditions begin with a vision of the twinned conspirators, writer and painter, at the start of their journey; silhouettes seen from behind, under the sails of the trees, paused, looking down on the rumour of a city. 'We are Pilgrims,' Jerrold wrote, 'wanderers, gipsy-loiterers in the great world of London . . . We are wanderers; not, I repeat, historians.'

Wanderers are amateurs of geography, literature, statistics; scavenging researchers, provokers of exploitable accidents. They behave like suspended detectives with no proper brief, going through the motions. They stalk other stalkers. Georges Simenon manages this alienation very neatly in his slim Maigret novel from 1931, *A Crime in Holland.* A monoglot French detective investigates a crime in a sombre Dutch town, where the rivermen and farmers have no other language. Walking is the only tool of interrogation. 'Maigret, by dint of walking in step with the other man, could literally sense his state of mind.'

Brewery Road was a boulevard of unexplained warehouses and distribution centres, but the new digital industries, the solicitors of commissions, were in evidence. One former storage space was now dressed with crimson carpet, apologetically thin furniture, and a large glass door with a slogan spelled out in red dots: THIS IS NOT A DOOR.

Pentonville Prison has not yet been rebranded as a boutique hotel; the sour bricks resist it. Churchy windows offer a view of the Overground tracks that no prisoners, locked in their hutches, lights out, will enjoy. The voodoo of capital, budget balancing, outsourcing, has found some bright navy paint to hint at blue-sky thinking. Pinned to the slatted panel is a sheet that mimics a notional window, behind which a skeleton rattles the bars of his cell. HMP PENTONVILLE WAR ON DRUGS. WILL POWER IS REAL POWER. When there are no solutions to a problem, invite the ad men to come up with a punchy image. That's the trick: sell the problem, not the answer.

Climbing up Offord Road, back on familiar territory, and reacquainted with the Overground, I know that it's almost done. We can hear the never-satisfied pre-climactic sigh of the trains. Highbury & Islington Station is a short step. Then it should be less than thirty minutes to our beds. The effect Simenon mentions, reading another person's mind by falling into step with him, or tracking behind and regulating your pace, has not kicked in. Andrew is at sea. There is a peak of exhaustion, chill creeping through leaky wetsuit, he associates with swimming for more than an hour on a turning tide. Achieving that state on land, he converts ground to mud, then brine. Mouth agape, he struggles to take an honest breath. He is making agonizingly slow, steady strides over waves of tarmac, hair stiffening to thatch in anticipation of his future role as a Straw Bear in the film of John Clare's escape from the High Beach Asylum. And as he becomes more sculptural, more of an English scarecrow, I speed up, in the neurotic urgency to tell the tale, get all the connections in before we arrive in a Dalston that must have changed out of all recognition in the hours we've been away.

Andrew does not need this. But I can't stop; he has to know about what it was like to get inside the house on Royal College Street. The poet Anthony Rudolf offered me the chance to join a select group of Rimbaud enthusiasts on a visit arranged with the current owner of the property, Michael Corby.

I met Rudolf – lean, professorial, engaged – as I stepped down from the Overground at Camden Road. Waiting on the doorstep of 8 Royal College Street was James Campbell, Francophile author and Beat Generation promoter. The big debate between the two scholars concerned the particular window from which Rimbaud watched Verlaine returning from the market with an undernourished herring for his tea: top floor or first floor? Rimbaud, the mannerless hoodlum poet, sniggered at the absurdity: the older man, in his silly pudding of a hat, carrying a fish in one hand and a bottle of oil in the other. Like a pantomime advertisement for their soured physical relationship. The tempers of narrow London beds in close, low-ceilinged rooms, oppressed them both. And the little ritual Rimbaud habitually indulged, of playing with a clasp-knife before engaging in obligatory acts of congress. More a poetic duty than a sexual imperative.

Verlaine plodded up the stairs. 'Do you know how ridiculous you look?' Retaliation came with a slap of wet fish across Rimbaud's cheek. The brief London interlude of wandering and drinking and consorting with socialists and warming themselves in the Reading Room at the British Museum was over.

Campbell thought that the poets, who drank at the Hibernia

tavern in Old Compton Street, *might* have come across Karl
Marx. Who might also have crossed aisles with Rimbaud in the
British Museum. Late speculations provoked walks, as walks
provoked essays. Like Patrick Keiller, Campbell relished the
romance of disappearance, of seeking out the heat traces of
poets and artists who passed through London suburbs, lodged
in obscurity, leaving their marks in secret notebooks, posthumous *Illuminations*. 'Their heads lolling on the slopes of strange
parks . . . their railways cut alongside.'

As sketched by Félix Régamey, as they argue through the
streets, the French poets are a fugitive couple, so studied in
bohemianism that they look like undercover agents. Behind
the firmly inked outline of Verlaine with his papers, walking
stick, cigar, and the vagrant farm boy, Rimbaud, with his clay
pipe, is the ghost of a caped and helmeted London bobby. Verlaine's cultivated paranoia was an accurate prophecy of the
modern city as a labyrinth of eyes, a surveillance state. Spies
were tracking him. Divorce agents. Political police. Graham
Robb in his biography *Rimbaud* says that the Paris Préfecture
was 'receiving high-grade intelligence' from London. A city so
eager to launder the world's money, the fruits of colonial plunder, is ripe for the double-dealing of Joseph Conrad's *The Secret
Agent*. In every discussion group of malcontents, there is at
least one informer. And, as with Mr Verloc's grubby shop,
pornography is the convenient medium of exchange. Poetry
was a vice to be exposed and eliminated.

Detouring around an electrified disability carriage of Stephen
Hawking proportions, we were admitted to the hallway of the
Royal College Street boarding house. And confronted by a vast
portrait of Lady Thatcher on her throne, hair burnished, toy-
ing with a bundle of state papers. The impact was like that slap
of wet fish. Thatcher, taking pride of place, was accompanied
by more modest renderings of Winston Churchill and Alec

Douglas-Home. Michael Crosby, a man with theatrical affilia-tions, and the ambition to present his property as a haunted set, caught my eye.

'Don't worry, I'm not a Tory,' he said. 'I'm Ukip.'

Facing Thatcher, on the opposite wall, was a poster for a play by Crosby, *Dracula's Dream*.

We took off our shoes to make the ascent to rooms compet-ing to supply the window from which Rimbaud watched his partner return from market. Crosby, in canary-yellow shirt, untucked, with large cuffs, sprawled in a bedroom chair, in a close cabin that was all bed and oval mirror. Rudolf's hawkish profile played nicely against a gilt-framed portrait of some fierce Scottish bird of prey. We peered down into a token gar-den arranged with obelisks and a cherub.

The house had history and Rudolf was just the persistent kind of poet-researcher to tease it out. He recalled a period when these rooms were squatted by ketamine-snacking veter-inary students. The Rimbaud legend was then entrusted to local visionaries like Aidan Andrew Dun, whose poem *Vale Royal* namechecks the French visitors as elements in a new mapping of a mythology of place. Bob Dylan paid a visit. And Patti Smith put in an offer to purchase this chunk of counter-cultural heritage.

Crosby points out that Royal College Street was where the taxidermist had his premises in Hitchcock's *The Man Who Knew Too Much*. He didn't say which version.

After Highbury, we levitated. The railway was an old rib. It seemed to work best to stay off Ball's Pond Road. And to come down the handsomely proportioned Mildmay Grove with the tracks always alongside, singing us into harbour.

There were more dead Christmas trees lying on the pave-ment. Andrew, gripped by some primitive reflex, rolled himself over a low wall, to piss at prodigious length in the bushes of a block of flats.

When we came to the bridge over the railway, I decided to detour down Kingsbury Road, to identify the house where my early books, and the Albion Village Press publications by Brian Catling, Chris Torrance and J. H. Prynne, had been printed. *Back Garden Poems*, from 1970, featured a map of the locality on the fixed endpapers, a register of persons and landmarks drawn by Renchi Bicknell. Many of the named presences were now decamped, others were dead. Buildings had been demolished, public houses converted into flats. Ted's radio-repair shop on Kingsland Road was a distant memory.

The print shop is indicated with a directional arrow. But, curiously enough, there is no railway. Or bridge over Middleton Road. Or so I thought, until I got out a magnifying glass for a closer inspection. And then I realized that what I took for a decorative flourish down the spine of the book was in fact shorthand for the line running down towards the City. The railway was the armature supporting all the words and images. New flats were going up on Holly Street. 'Anna was cheered by these signs of human habitation,' I noted at that time. 'But I am uneasy: the height, the isolation, some of the windows already broken.'

Why hadn't I investigated this burial ground before? Between the narrow house where the books were printed and the railway was a small, enclosed Jewish cemetery. I had been told by a rabbi with literary ambitions that the ground in which a Jew is buried belongs to that person until the end of days. Through the bars of the gate, it was possible to make out ranks of railway-facing slabs, obelisks like stone trees dwarfed by London planes and draped in ivy.

The buzz of youth on Kingsland Road, the nocturnal energies of nail bars, pubs, Turkish grocers, knew nothing of the contemplative silence of the Jewish burial ground. Electrification made the street into a carnival of loud talk, laughter, and tablets tweeting and spitting universal gossip. Smokers in overexcited pavement knots. 'Like like like,' they shrill. The world is a simile; nothing is fixed and solid. The laughter of whippets: rains of shiny grey nitrous oxide cylinders. Inspiration for Gilbert & George as they march towards their chosen Hackney restaurant.

Returned to the ginger glow of the Overground at Haggerston, the station that was our end as well as our beginning, I took the obligatory photograph. Andrew flexed his muscles. Rubbish was black-bagged around the bin. EXPECT DELAYS said the latest sign.

Blood on the Tracks

I was amused by the names they imposed on the latest reefs of development in ground-zero Haggerston, the tired public housing that had to be swept away to create post-architectural performances worthy of the orbital railway: sleep-shelves sold on the promise of the time it takes to get to Liverpool Street ('18 minutes'), a better class of station. Those old brown blocks, like a congress of mechanics in nicotine overalls, were given mysteriously elegant calling cards derived from Samuel Richardson, father of the English novel: Clarissa Street, Pamela Street, Richardson Close, Samuel House, Harlowe House and the rest. The first wave of regeneration, between substantial, community-orientated blocks and the elevated railway, featured modest units, bits of garden, an imported urban-suburban estate. When they looked for a suitably inspirational name for a canalside 'Close', they picked Mary Seacole. Of Scottish and Creole descent, Seacole provided for wounded soldiers from the battlefields of Crimea. She managed a recovery station behind the lines and achieved great popularity through her reputation for generosity with allowances of alcohol. She returned to England, funds exhausted. She had no connection with Hackney. And never lived in the borough.

What struck me when I set out, the Overground walk completed, to see what had happened while I'd been away, was how unreal everything was. A single day's tramp had smoothed my eyes to porcelain eggs: like those of John Clare, in his distress, when he believed that he had lost his pupils. Stones had been set in his head. Rays of invading light brought no fresh intelligence. Identity had dissolved. The long walk from High Beach in Epping Forest to 'rescue' by farm cart in Werrington left Clare 'homeless at home'. He had completed a futile circuit, from village to London, obscurity to exposure, with a delusional trudge back to a memory-place that was no longer there, a muse who was already dead. Patty, his earthly wife, tried him for a few months and found him wanting. The written account of the walk was a letter to Matthew Allen, his keeper. And a letter to Mary Joyce, his imaginary childhood love, chiding her for dying. He is done with living women. 'The worst is the road to ruin and the best is nothing like a good Cow.'

At a time when careers are scuppered over private emails (which are never private), and when councils are appointing guardians, salaries reflecting the dignity of their status, to prosecute ill-judged language in public office, it was something of a surprise to find the gleaming avenue through the latest railway flats being named after a notorious rapist. LOVELACE STREET (PRIVATE ROAD). Richardson's Robert Lovelace keeps the virtuous Clarissa Harlowe for many months in a brothel. Assisted by the madame and the other whores, Lovelace drugs and rapes Clarissa. The madame is called Mrs Sinclair. But nobody has named a passageway, cul-de-sac, or excrescence of designer flats, after her. Not yet. Railway satellites are going up so fast, and selling off-plan before completion, so there is still a chance. The potential for exposure in the *Hackney Citizen* is very much alive. It's like dedicating a crèche to Jimmy Savile.

How those namers give themselves away! The Haggerston Baths swimming pool, opened in 1903, and once a much-loved local resource, has been boarded up for years, blind-windowed, allowed to decay, so that funds could be siphoned into more glamorous projects. Imagine the tightness of my smile, when I discovered on this ramble of reorientation, that the path alongside the pool has now been declared a protected right of way: SWIMMERS LANE (PRIVATE ROAD). No apostrophe. No irony. The boast is not heritage, it's outrage. Private Road! The public footpath to a public facility, swimming pool, slipper bath, laundry, is doubly stolen. Along with all established rights of passage through the flats. Not for nothing is the glass block at the end of Lovelace Street (which is no street) called Spinner House.

Negotiating the canyon between the Overground and the parasitical bicycle-rack flats is to drift, sometimes on original cobbles, sometimes on an interim carpet, through a gallery of toxic Me-ism: the constantly revised doodles of spray-stencil egotists with their crews and bag-carriers. Along one hidden stretch, just off Whiston Road, where a single sprayist had assembled a series of oblique satiric panels, some joker trumped him by composing art-speak critiques and sticking them up like those explanatory cards from Tate Modern. The illegitimate show lasted a couple of days, before wrecking balls, improving the image of destruction, took them out.

Another graffito – IF YOU CYCLE, RING TWICE FOR BORIS – was gone in an hour. A neat white rectangle of civic redaction. Which local taggers instantly defaced with script that looked like knitting with barbed wire.

My rather melancholy tour of reintegration with locality, after the turbo-thrust of a day hiking with Kötting, was broken by a coffee stop at the flat of a film-maker with whom I had collaborated in the past. Managed gloom was this man's métier: days could be productively disposed of in calculating the precise degree of stubble required for an appearance before a dedicated handful of enthusiasts, at some post-educational bunker in the Elephant & Castle, where he would slump, cosh-microphone in hand, raincoat collar up, pronouncing, like a radio voice letting us know the bomb has dropped, on the death of cinema. Nothing was being commissioned. His respected producer was laid up in Germany after a back operation. There had been a fantastical forty minutes on the phone with Christopher Walken, coming to the realization that this was it. *The call was the film*. The status of being unfunded was the world as it was always going to be. Films without film. Novels that degrade into research files: names, numbers. Everything is archive; nothing is live. Committed activists are out there making collections of abandoned shopping lists. And photographing plastic bags caught on security fences.

And then, out of nowhere, a mirage, a solar bounce of fool's gold: Boris Johnson in the flesh at Old Street, barking like a seal, shaking the straw of his signature fringe from cold eyes. He is in full cry, stuttering with mangled emphasis, saluting the economic boosterism of Silicon Roundabout. London's celebrity mayor lumbered and swayed, finding his land legs after leaping down from the bike, before marching with intent towards a knot of summoned journalists. Boris is a canny hick, a street-smart bumpkin. The on-message symbol of the sacred bicycle, the chosen steed that will save our city, is creatively framed by tame camera crews, to keep out the caravan of back-up taxis, black-windowed people carriers required to service tonight's newsclip.

Dull pavement chaff, such as myself, along with fast-food dribblers and snackers from Whitecross Street, are suckered in towards the pool of boosted light. Johnson, a stocky figure in a tight Sunday-grey chapel suit, deploys his yellow cycle helmet like the Plexiglas shield of a TSG policeman on kettling duty. He is childishly greedy for credit, loud in his approval of the viral pace of transformation of an ugly junction into a thriving nest of Internet hornets. The crowd love him, love the way he is just what he appears to be on television: a turn, a force of nature. You could bottle his sweat and sell it to a mid-morning mob frantic for selfies. 'It's really him,' a woman phone-shrieks to her partner, who is running down the road from Hawksmoor's obelisk at St Luke's, to catch this precious moment.

Remounting, photo-op concluded, chosen entrepreneurs dismissed, Boris wobbles into the maelstrom of the Old Street roundabout, trouser cuffs flapping, naked ankles exposed, helmet wedged tight enough on golden thatch to obscure vision, while HGV drivers honk and motorists jeer, some swerving as they feint to bag this headline trophy. The mayor is immune, without shame, protected by a combination of innocence and feral cunning. I don't know if he pauses, once he's out of range of the cameras, to be picked up by one of the petrol-guzzling taxis, but my instinct is that he stays on the bike. That he takes it all the way back to the river.

'He's dead, but he's still breathing.' A quotation I have used from time to time, and scribbled across a set of photographs of Andrew Kötting perched in a thorn tree, became one of the phrases the film-maker looped and tested, soundlessly, as he swam up out of the sump hole, the fathomless abyss at the base of consciousness.

He wasn't dead on the Old Kent Road, but it was a close thing. He left half his body's ration of blood sprayed across cockney blacktop. When I was plodding out, assembling material to discover what the oracle of the Overground walk had told me about the present condition of London, Andrew simply scrubbed off the experience and deflated his blisters with salty wallows in the winter sea, and delirious motorbike swoops across the mist-shrouded Romney Marsh to his professional job at Canterbury. He raided London, beating on reluctant funders, shaking coins from the stitched pockets of arts bureaucrats, bear-hugging friends, doing funny voices for

Bangladeshi waiters, visiting the sick, performing at the Purcell Rooms on the South Bank. After a session with his favoured sound designer and audio engineer, the monkishly bearded Phillipe Ciompi, Andrew leathered up and fought to man-handle his bike through the evening traffic towards Old Kent Road and his usual pilgrim route back home to St Leonards.

The hit came at 9 p.m., at the junction with Rotherhithe New Road. 'The route which I would normally have taken back to the Pepys Estate.' Andrew was snaking down the inside lane and then – *crunch* – he *was* light: thunderflashes, starbursts, neon ants spelling out idiot equations. The metallic ring of detached phrases spat against white tiles: 'Get up, you maggot.' 'He's dead!' 'It's a crime reconstruction in a different place.'

The left elbow was mangled, facing the wrong way. The heavy machine came down on top of him. The silver spear of the wing mirror pierced his thigh. He fountained, he leaked. He was already out of it, lifted from London. He was fortunate in his choice of an accident spot: Old Kent Road was lively with traditional bother, yowling with squad cars. A competent Polish policewoman got to him very quickly and did all the right things.

He might have rewound the tape of our Overground march by taking a red helicopter to the Royal London Hospital in Whitechapel. There wasn't time. They wanted, if they could, to save the leg. And everything that went with it. Andrew thinks he remembers some of the sentences they spoke as they drove him, sirens on, lights flashing, to Denmark Hill: King's College Hospital, right on the railway tracks. The place he swam to – beyond pain, beyond medication – was the park he had walked across a few weeks before the collision. Jeremy Harding, in his introduction to a new Penguin selection of Rimbaud's poetry, stressed the role that epic hikes play in the shaping of poetry. The walks 'only stopped with the onset of a terrible pain in his right leg that presaged his death'.

Leila McMillan kept friends informed of the victim's progress. 'I haven't attached a picture this time as the last ones I took had his scary wound visible and that might just make you go weak at the knees!' It was a spectacular gouge, a sinkhole. The man had no modesty in his physical traumas. He wanted an articulate gash, a puncture that screamed. A bloody mouth in his thigh. He enjoyed the cocktail of morphine derivatives and approved highs dripping into the acoustic mash-up of memories, Herzog film fragments, and drunken English folk songs that kept him floating over Ruskin's lost Arcadia in Denmark Hill. But a few days was enough. The replays of our orbital circuit, sometimes on foot, sometimes mounted on a plastic swan, tightened the ligature that kept what was left of his blood in the scratched carapace of his biker's uniform. When they asked if he could wiggle his toes, he flopped from the bed and reeled away to the bathroom. 'Not a pretty sight,' Leila said. 'He has one of those bum-revealing gowns on.'

Andrew decided, as soon as he crept back to something like functioning consciousness, to come off the morphine and ketamine and the painkillers. Braced on the arm, his left leg stitched like one of the less attractive victims of *The Texas Chainsaw Massacre*, he paid his respects to the doctors and nurses by freeing up a bed and being driven to the seaside. 'The NHS is the saviour of all things civilized,' he emailed. 'My flashbacks are black rectangles.' He arranged for the collection of bloodstained and shredded clothes that might prove the excuse for a gallery installation.

Mr Kötting, the future Straw Bear, was returned to his basement kitchen by the seaside, high on pain, not analgesics, and plotting the next moves. 'I dabble with the vertical,' he reported, 'but invariably remain horizontal.' One of his daughter Eden's helpers, brisking downstairs, came unsuspecting on the wound, the ankle-to-underpants flesh trough in all its pulsing red-blue exposure. She made it to the back door, to fresh air, just in time.

Cargo cult offerings in the form of books, saucepans of chicken broth, DVDs, chocolates, flowers, cheeses, piled up at the door, in anticipation of a voodoo sacrifice. By the time I paid a visit, a week or so after he had discharged himself from the hospital, Andrew was on his foot. The spare leg looked like the debris of a shark attack, stapled to his swimming shorts as a token rudder. His left arm, fetishized in black straps and pads, was robotic, prosthetic. Who would have thought the young man had so much tarmac in him? His head, the blunt bone helmet of it, had done considerable damage to the kerb. He doesn't really know what happened and witnesses at that time of night on the Old Kent Road are not famous for coming forward with statements.

Four days of the mind map had vanished and there was no recovering them. He went somewhere else. The film of the ambulance ride, the surgery, the trauma ward, muttering doctors, alarmed family, was not of his making. The chosen location for the collision alarmed me, provoking memories of the morning of the Overground walk, when we paused, at the point where the railway crosses the A2, and looked down Old Kent Road to the place where the accident would happen; before moving on to Peckham Rye, Denmark Hill and King's College Hospital. And I couldn't help dredging, beyond that, fuzzy recollections of nights reeling home to Hackney after dining too well and drinking too much at the home of Brian Catling, on the other side of this road. A couple of hundred yards from the blood-soaked junction. There was a notebook poem from that time called 'A Handshake on the Telephone'. It began with a quote from Genesis P-Orridge, about dreams being descriptions of how things really are. 'They are accurate. As real as a car smashing a cat in the road.' I associated this Camberwell territory with shifting focus, inebriation, rucks, roadkill. 'Consciousness extinguished on a wheel,' I wrote.

'You do not / die of it or lose one single life. And where the beams cross / an accident awaits the supplicant.'

Andrew spurned leg coverings, to show off the wound, describing it, to strangers on the street, as the aftermath of a battle with a marine predator. When forced to wear trousers for some lecture or assault on a commissioning editor, he dropped them like a red-nose clown.

Now he hobbled to the stove to make me a cup of coffee. And explained how he intended, at the end of the week, to drag himself into a Hastings cave, in hospital gown, to project images from Pyrenean caverns – bison, aurochs, antlered shamen – on the damp walls.

I photographed the over-shiny, razored leg. There were puncture holes on either side of a central track of thread, angler's twine, with which they had stitched up the evidence of their fishing for veins. Sculpted, in ridges of angry flesh, was the perfect symbol of our walk, a railway map in meat. A fly, miming the action of a furious washing of hands, licked and sampled. Before setting off on an epic journey down the film-maker's mutilated thigh.

Acknowledgements

The day's tramp around the London Overground circuit wouldn't have happened, or not in this way, without the presence and witness of Andrew Kötting. For better or worse, he made the labour of documentation and debate into a mind-film. He resurrected never-forgotten Deptford days and Camberwell nights. And like the unfortunate lady tapped so frequently for dropsy, and now resting in a stone tank in Bunhill Fields, he never repined at his case.

I am grateful to Anonymous Bosch, pinhole wizard, for returning with me to a number of significant locations, to make a record of things that should have happened. He is an unrivalled tapper of ghosts and spectral traces.

Thanks also, for advice, company, connections, books, to: James Campbell, B. Catling, Michael Corby, Gareth Evans, Stephen Gill, Antony Gormley, Leon Kossoff, Leila McMillan, MacGillivray, Bill Parry-Davies, Anthony Rudolf, Anna Sinclair, Marina Warner. And, for permission to quote from works of inspiration and information, my thanks to: Allen Fisher, Patrick Keiller, Chris Petit and Will Self.

Angela Carter, J. G. Ballard and Bill Griffiths provide the dominant sonar echoes of certain territories we passed through on our circuit. They are the true figures of place.

As ever, I'd like to thank my editors, Simon Prosser and Anna Kelly, my copy-editor, Sarah Coward, and my agent, Laura Longrigg.

IAIN SINCLAIR

HACKNEY, THAT ROSE-RED EMPIRE

Hackney, That Rose-Red Empire is Iain Sinclair's personal record of the area of north-east London where he has lived for forty years.

In this 'documentary fiction', Sinclair meets a cast of the dispossessed, including writers, photographers, bomb-makers and market traders. Legends of tunnels, Hollow Earth theories and the notorious Mole Man are unearthed. He uncovers traces of those who passed through Hackney: Lenin and Stalin, novelists Joseph Conrad and Samuel Richardson, film-makers Orson Welles and Jean-Luc Godard, Tony Blair beginning his political career, even a Baader-Meinhof urban guerrilla on the run. And he tells his own story: of forty years in one house in Hackney, of marriage, children, strange encounters and deaths.

'An explosion of literary fireworks' **Peter Ackroyd**, *The Times*

'Gloriously sprawling, wonderfully congested, one of the finest books about London in recent decades' *Daily Telegraph*

'Iain Sinclair's twisty love-letter to Hackney . . . the book London's most unusual borough deserves' *GQ*

'Remarkable, compelling, bristles with unexpected, frequently lurid life. On Sinclair's territory there's nobody to touch him . . . a gonzo Samuel Pepys' *Sunday Times*

IAIN SINCLAIR

DOWNRIVER

WINNER OF THE ENCORE AWARD AND THE JAMES TAIT BLACK MEMORIAL PRIZE

The Thames runs through *Downriver* like an open wound, draining the pain and filth of London and its mercurial inhabitants. Commissioned to document the shifting embankments of industry and rampant property speculation, a film crew of magpie scavengers, high-rent lowlife, broken criminals and reborn lunatics picks over the rivers detritus. They examine the wound, hoping to expose the cause of the city's affliction . . .

'Remarkable: part apocalyptic documentary, part moth-eaten ghost story, part detective story. Inventive and stylish, Sinclair is one of the most interesting of contemporary novelists' *Sunday Times*

'One of those idiosyncratic literary texts that revivify the language, so darn quotable as to be the reader's delight and the reviewer's nightmare' *Guardian*

'Crazy, dangerous, prophetic' **Angela Carter**

IAIN SINCLAIR

LONDON ORBITAL

Encircling London like a noose, the M25 is a road to nowhere, but when Iain Sinclair sets out to walk this asphalt loop – keeping within the 'acoustic footprints' – he is determined to find out where the journey will lead him. Stumbling upon converted asylums, industrial and retail parks, ring-fenced government institutions and lost villages, Sinclair discovers a Britain of the fringes, a landscape consumed by developers. *London Orbital* charts this extraordinary trek and round trip of the soul, revealing the country as you've never seen it before.

'Erudite, ingenious, exhilarating, involving, unpredictable, enchanting … as a Hobson-Jobson to the quirks of a hidden England you feared had vanished it's unbeatable' *Spectator*

'Lucid, accessible, inventive, witty' *Independent*

'A journey into the heart of darkness and a fascinating snapshot of who we are, lit by Sinclair's vivid prose. I'm sure it will be read fifty years from now' *Observer*